Tales and Teachings of the Buddha

Tales and Teachings of the Buddha

The Jātaka Stories in relation to the Pāli Canon

by

JOHN GARRETT JONES

London
GEORGE ALLEN & UNWIN
Boston   Sydney

First published in 1979

GEORGE ALLEN & UNWIN LTD
40 Museum Street, London WC1A 1LU

© George Allen & Unwin (Publishers) Ltd, 1979

British Library Cataloguing in Publication Data

Garrett-Jones, John
   Tales and teachings of the Buddha.
   1. Buddhist doctrines
   I. Title
   294.3′4′2   BQ4132   79-40377

   ISBN 0-04-294104-0

Typeset in 11 on 12 point Baskerville by Bedford Typesetters Ltd
and printed in Great Britain
by Billing & Sons Ltd, Guildford, London and Worcester

Acknowledgements

The author is heavily indebted to those self-effacing scholars who have, over the years, made available to us the Pāli texts in English translation. He would also like to thank the Rev Y. Dhammapala of the University of Sri Lanka (Peradeniya) for helpful conversation and access to his draft thesis, Dr Marrison, Curator of Oriental Books at the British Library, for his helpfulness, Miss I. B. Horner, President of the Pāli Text Society, for her encouragement at the inception of this work, much help during its writing and a very generous Foreword on its completion, Dr Robin Bond, a colleague at the University of Canterbury, for assistance with translation, Mr John Hardy, the publisher's editor, for his great care and patience in steering a difficult manuscript through the press whilst its author was on the other side of the globe. He is also indebted to the Council of the University of Canterbury for granting the study leave which made the final research for this work and its actual writing possible.

The author also wishes to thank Schocken Books Inc. for permission to quote from *An Understanding of the Buddha* by Oscar Shaftel. Copyright 1974, Schocken Books Inc. E. J. Brill, Leiden for permission to quote from *The Paccekabuddha* by Ria Kloppenborg. Copyright 1974 E. J. Brill, Leiden, and The University of Hawaii Press for permission to quote from *Causality: The Central Philosophy of Buddhism* by D. J. Kalupahana. Copyright University Press of Hawaii, 1975.

Foreword

by I. B. HORNER, *President of the Pāli Text Society*

It gives me much pleasure to present to the English speaking and English reading world both a new book in the field of Pāli Buddhist studies and a new author who obviously is in perfect command of his subject. He writes in a fluent and relaxed style, eschews all padding, and is never pretentious, tedious, confused or confusing. All is plain sailing for the reader.

The 547 Jātaka Stories form "the oldest, most complete and most important collection of folk-lore extant", as T. W. Rhys Davids has said. Vast in extent, with the verses regarded as canonical and the narratives connected with them as commentarial, they have aroused the attention, often the enthusiasm, of listeners and learners down the centuries. Mr Jones compares the doctrinal and ethical content of these stories with that of the Four Nikāyas – the principal doctrinal source for canonical Pāli Buddhism, but he also makes occasional reference to the Vinaya, or book of monastic discipline.

In this book, *The Tales and Teaching of the Buddha*, very interesting and balanced comparisons, principally between the standpoint taken by the Pāli Jātaka Stories and the Four Nikāyas on the aspects of Buddhist teaching of most relevance and concern to the layman, are here made for the first time. Mr Jones is well-versed in both Jātaka and Canon, and is thus able to draw on both not only with apparent ease but also with aptness and accuracy and dependable documentation.

The results of Mr Jones's findings on the discrepant attitudes that may be taken by the Jātaka and the Nikāyas are always revealing and sometimes surprising. For example, the difference between the canonical teaching and the Jātaka view regarding an enduring *attā*, or "self", and its rebirth is here fully examined for the first time and squarely faced with no difficulties shirked. This alone is a most valuable and original contribution.

Or again, though the disparaging sentiments to be found in some of the Jātakas on "the wickedness of women" are fairly common knowledge, this wickedness has never been pin-pointed before, any more than there has been collected the complete number of examples of it contained in the Jātakas. Here each is investigated and assessed on its own merits with astringency or compassion as the case may be.

Mr Jones has found new facets to present both of the ancient Jātaka tales where, in his former births, Gotama was still the Bodhisatta striving for his final enlightenment, and also of the ancient Pāli Nikāyas. I much hope that this book will find the place it deserves in contemporary Jātaka literature where it should act as a stimulus, an adornment and a delight.

Contents

Introduction

A great deal of interest has, in recent years, centred upon various attempts[1a] to investigate the actual practice of Theravāda Buddhists in relation to their theoretical beliefs. The Theravāda attracts particular attention because its theory is so uncompromisingly otherworldly. Inevitably the question arises, "how is it possible for people to adopt views so inhospitable to ordinary worldly standards, yet continue to live so comfortably in the world?" The question obviously has more force when applied to the lay Buddhist than when applied to the monk, since the latter has explicitly renounced at least the more obvious worldly pleasures.

What the present work attempts is similar in that it too is concerned to investigate the relationship between the stricter minority and the laxer majority within the Theravāda community. It does this, however, not by comparing scriptural precept with customary lay practice, but by comparing the core of scriptural teaching, contained in the Four *Nikāyas* of the *Sutta Piṭaka*, with the teaching implied or expounded in the most popular religious literature known to the average lay Buddhist, the *Jātaka* stories.

There are many reasons for attempting this. The most pressing is the need to gain a more realistic perspective on the Theravāda world. Too often it has been assumed that a careful study of the Pāli Canon will give an accurate indication of the beliefs, values and aims of the average Southern Buddhist. This overlooks the fact that the average lay Buddhist has only the sketchiest and most fragmentary acquaintance with the scriptures of his faith. He may have received some instruction at home or school or during occasional visits to the monastery and this may, in part at least, have been based on passages from scripture. The chances are, however, that he will never, at any time of his life, have held any part of the canonical scriptures in his hand; he will only have encountered them through an intermediary. The reason for this may simply be that he is illiterate. Even if he can read, it is not easy for him to obtain more than brief anthologies of the scriptures since the Canon in its entirety would span upwards of forty volumes, many of them inaccessible. The scriptures, therefore, although they are treated with utmost veneration, encapsulating, according to widespread belief, the very words of the Lord Buddha himself, and therefore constituting the treasury of true *Dhamma* (teaching), are virtually unknown to the layman at first hand. Though treated with awe, they are regarded as hard to grasp and beyond the reach of the average person. Only the monk can normally be expected to have attained the refinement of mind and the long hours of leisure needed to grapple with them.

For the layman, it is the Jātaka stories which provide the main source of Buddhist guidance and instruction. These stories are close enough to the Canon in their historical pedigree to enjoy something of its awe and veneration, but sufficiently different from the Canon in style and content to enjoy enormous popularity. With this kind of material, illiteracy is no bar. It is not necessary to ponder the written texts of the Jātaka in order to be able to fathom their meaning or even commit them to memory. These are stories which can live in a people's imagination. They can be told to small children as bed-time stories and provide much-loved texts for early ventures in reading at the village school; they can be enacted by travelling troupes of players, enchanting peasant audiences into the early hours of the morning; incidents from the stories can furnish an ever-fertile source of allusion for secular writers and dramatists and have, for centuries, been depicted in beautiful paintings and carvings. In the ordinary day-to-day life of the village, these stories serve as constant reminders of the penalties remorselessly pursuing those who succumb to greed or passion and of the rewards which inevitably crown the efforts of the virtuous. Certainly, the Jātaka tales are not the layman's sole source of Buddhist nutriment. There are other incidents from early Pāli sources, some of them canonical, and especially those relating to the early career and to the last days of Gotama himself, which are equally popular and which enjoy an equal place in the imagination and the affections of the simple villager. Nevertheless, there is no disputing the fact that, throughout the Theravāda world, there is no part of the Pāli Buddhist tradition which can, as a whole, approach the Jātaka in its appeal to, and in its firmly entrenched position within, the popular culture.

This being the case, it must seem strange that, whilst there has been a steady stream of literature emanating both from Western scholars and from Asian scholar-monks describing the life and teaching of Gotama, there is very little literature which gives more than a few passing references to the Jātaka stories. There are a number of reasons for this. One is the phenomenon of what

Winston King has called "export Buddhism".[1b] Asian Buddhists writing for English-speaking readers have been anxious to emphasise the cool rationality and the intellectual candour of their founder; they have not wanted to draw attention to such popular legends and superstitions as proliferate in the Jātaka. Western scholars have been similarly selective. Their prime interest has usually been to track Buddhism down to its source and to get as close as scholarly method can to the actual man, Gotama, and his teaching. The Jātaka stories, whilst many of them probably antedate Buddhism in their origins, are, in their present form, a much later accretion, throwing very little light on the origins of Buddhism. They have thus been largely ignored. It should also be noted that, although the Jātaka stories are currently available in English translation, they are contained in three bulky volumes. Each of these contains two volumes of the original six-volume edition and, since the pages have been reduced in size, the print is very small. The whole collection runs to well over a million words and presents a formidable aspect to one who is already inclined to regard it as of minor or peripheral interest. The *Nidāna-Kathā*, which constitutes the very popular introduction to the Jātaka, was translated, together with a fascinating preliminary essay, by T. W. Rhys Davids under the title, *Buddhist Birth Stories*, in 1880. This can now be obtained only from the enterprising Indian publisher[2] who recently re-issued it.

The time has come for this situation to be rectified. The aim of the present book is to look closely and analytically at the Jātaka stories, noting especially the ethical and doctrinal message they convey. As we shall see, the majority of the stories are simply folk tales, owing no specific debt to Buddhism. Nevertheless, they have been adapted – very successfully – to the task of purveying Buddhist teaching to the ordinary lay Buddhist. It is this Buddhist adaptation which is of particular interest for our present purpose. After two preliminary chapters in which our two main sources, the Jātakas themselves and the Four Nikāyas of the *Sutta Piṭaka*, have been explored, we shall turn our attention to the specifically Buddhist content of the Jātakas as it relates to various ethical, social and religious aspects of the teaching. This material will, in each chapter, be checked against the relevant teaching of the Four Nikāyas. A final chapter will examine the mythological content of the two sources.

It is hoped that this study will be of interest to the general reader as well as to the specialist. No attempt is made to go yet again over ground which has already been well worked, yet prior knowledge is not assumed and guidance to the best available published sources of further information is provided, at relevant points, in the footnotes. Whilst the latter simply indicate the author and date of publication of the book cited, the bibliography provides detailed information relating to all books or articles referred to either in the text or in the footnotes.

This book will, hopefully, enable its readers to come to a much fuller and more comprehensive knowledge of the Jātaka stories than would have been possible before and, in so doing, to form a more accurate impression of the type of Buddhism which has infiltrated most deeply into the lives of ordinary Theravādins. At the same time, the reader will be able to gauge the extent to which this popular form of Buddhist teaching faithfully reflects or subtly distorts the teaching of those Nikāyas which constitute the heart of the Pāli Canon.

All references to the Pāli Canon are to the English translations published by the Pāli Text Society (see "Abbreviations" for the appropriate codes) unless there has been some special reason for referring to the Pāli text itself, in which case it is again the P.T.S. edition in romanized Pāli to which reference is made. Similarly, all references to the Jātaka Stories are to the English translations published by P.T.S. unless there has been some specific reason for referring to the Pāli. Preference has been given to the English versions because this book is intended to be of service to the reader who knows only English. It would have been very cumbersome to have referred both to the Pāli and to the translation. If references had been given (as they often are) only to the Pāli sources, the reader who might otherwise have felt impelled to consult the Nikāyas and the Jātakas themselves would have been prevented from doing so. This would have defeated one of the major objects of this book, which is to encourage its readers to go from reading about these texts to reading the texts themselves; that is precisely why so many references are given in this book. The Pāli scholar, on the other hand, will have not the slightest difficulty in finding his way to the Pāli texts from the references to the English translations.

Abbreviations

Primary Sources are referred to by the following code:

A   Aṅguttara Nikāya (5 vols) (Pāli; for ET see GS)
D   Dīgha Nikāya (3 vols) (Pāli; for ET see DB)
DB   Dialogues of the Buddha (3 vols) (ET of D)
ET   English Translation
GS   Gradual Sayings (5 vols) (ET of A)
J   Jātaka (6 vols & Index) (Pāli; for ET see JS(S))
JS(S)   Jātaka Stories (6 vols) (ET of J)
KS   Kindred Sayings (5 vols) (ET of S)
M   Majjhima Nikāya (3 vols & Index) (Pāli; for ET see MLS)
MLS   Middle Length Sayings (3 vols) (ET of M)
S   Saṃyutta Nikāya (5 vols & Index) (Pāli; for ET see KS)

Full details of the editions of these sources used in this book are given in the table entitled PRIMARY TEXTS.

Primary Texts Used in this Book

THE PĀLI TEXT:

ITS ENGLISH TRANSLATION:

(a) *The Four Nikāyas:*
(1) *Dīgha Nikāya* (D)
    ed. T. W. Rhys Davids &
    J. Estlin Carpenter
    3 vols 1890–1911 London

Dialogues of the Buddha (DB)
tr. T. W. & C. A. F. Rhys Davids
3 vols 1899–1921 London

(2) *Majjhima Nikāya* (M)
    ed. V. Trenckner &
    R. Chalmers
    3 vols 1888–1899 London
    Index: C. A. F. Rhys Davids
    1925

Middle Length Sayings (MLS)
tr. I. B. Horner
3 vols 1954–1959 London

(3) *Saṃyutta Nikāya* (S)
    ed. M. Leon Feer
    5 vols 1884–1898 London
    Index: C. A. F. Rhys Davids
    1904

Kindred Sayings (KS)
ed. C. A. F. Rhys Davids, Suriya
Sumangala Thera & F. L.
Woodward
5 vols 1917–1930 London

(4) *Aṅguttara Nikāya* (A)
ed. R. Morris & E. Hardy
5 vols 1885–1900 London

Gradual Sayings (or More-numbered
Suttas) (GS)
tr. F. L. Woodward & E. M. Hare
5 vols 1932–1936 London

(b) *The Jātaka*
The Jātaka together with its
Commentary being tales of the
anterior lives of Gotama
Buddha. (J)
Edited in the original Pāli by
V. Fausbøll
6 vols 1877–1896 London
Index: D. Andersen 1897

*The Jātaka or Stories of the
Buddha's former births* (JS)
Translated from the Pāli under
the editorship of E. B. Cowell
vol 1 tr. R. Chalmers   1895
vol 2 tr. W. H. D. Rouse   1895
vol 3 tr. H. T. Francis &
        R. A. Neil   1897
vol 4 tr. W. H. D. Rouse   1901
vol 5 tr. H. T. Francis   1905
vol 6 tr. E. B. Cowell &
        W. H. D. Rouse   1907
(all volumes were republished in
London in 1969)
N.B. The Introduction to the
Jātaka (*Nidānakathā*) though
included in vol 1 of Pāli Text is not
in E.T. It was separately translated
by T. W. Rhys Davids (see
bibliography).

Part I: THE SOURCES

I   *The Jātaka Stories*

There are many uncertainties about the origin of the Jātaka
stories. The verses which accompany the stories proper were
eventually admitted into the Canon as the tenth of the fifteen
"minor" discourses which constitute the *Khuddaka-Nikāya*. The
latter is the fifth and final Nikāya of the *Sutta Piṭaka* ("Sermon"
or "Dialogue" collection). It is generally agreed to be a later and
less reliable compilation than the preceding four Nikāyas, which
form the subject of the next chapter.

Although the *Khuddaka-Nikāya* is generally regarded as later and
is more disjointed and more open to later influences than the other
four, it is nevertheless acknowledged that parts of it, particularly
parts of the *Sutta Nipāta*, seem to be very early. It is only the composite form of the works as we now have them that is unquestionably later.

The canonical book of the Jātaka verses remains so far unpublished.[3] Part of the reason for this is the uncertainty as to where
the verses begin and end in some cases, complicated by the fact
that, in at least one case, that of the *Kuṇāla Jātaka* (JS 536) –
though W. B. Bollée, in his 1970 edition of it, believed this Jātaka
to be unique in this respect – the main frame-story is also regarded
as canonical. At a number of points in the *Aṅguttara-Nikāya*, the
Jātaka is specified as one of the nine *aṅgas* (divisions) of the
Buddha's teachings.[4] These references are of limited value since (a)
there is every possibility of their being later in date than much of
the other canonical material, reflecting a period when the sacred
texts were beginning to be collected and classified, and (b) there
is no certainty as to the scope and contents of the "Jātaka"
referred to in these passages.

What does seem to have been firmly established is that many of
the Jātaka stories were well known by the third century B.C. since
they play a major part in the bas-reliefs at Sānchī, Amarāvatī and
Bharhut, which have been authoritatively dated in that period.[5]
When Fa Hsien visited Ceylon in the fifth century A.D., he saw the
tooth relic being carried from Anurādhapura to Mahintale, both

sides of the road being decorated with pictures depicting the five
hundred different births of the Buddha. They were painted in
different colours, and "executed with such care as to make them
appear living."[6] From this period onward, the Jātaka collection,
more or less as we know it, has been a dominant influence in
Ceylonese art and literature, an influence which was further
deepened when the Pāli stories were translated into a much-loved
Singhalese version in the fourteenth century A.D.[7] A similar
pattern of influence can be traced in the development of other
Theravāda countries.[8]

We shall never know how the Jātaka stories emerged in the
form in which we now have them. Did they, or at least some of
them, originate with the Buddha himself? The pious Buddhist,
bred on these stories, will want to answer in the affirmative –
though even he "will admit that the present collection contains
some fables, fairy-tales, 'Joe Millers', and records of everyday
experiences, such as are in no way peculiar to Buddhism, but are
the common property of the world, floating down the ages."[9]

In favour of an affirmative answer is the fact that, in addition
to the recognised Jātaka stories which occur also in the Four
Nikāyas,[10] there are other passages in the Four Nikāyas which,
whilst clearly having the form of Jātakas, are not represented in the
official Jātaka collection.[11] If these canonical Jātaka stories,
whether or not they form part of the traditional Jātaka collection,
are held to stem from Gotama himself, then of course there can be
no doubt that some at least of the Jātakas must be regarded as
originating with the Buddha. Yet this is still a big "if". As we shall
have occasion to note in the next chapter, the Four Nikāyas have
themselves had a long and chequered history before arriving at
the fixed, written form in which we now have them. No critical
reader would ascribe all this material to the same early point of
origin. So far as the Jātakas occurring in the Four Nikāyas are
concerned, the reader must ask himself: is it likely, from the over-
all impression the Canon enables us to form of the character, aims
and teaching of Gotama (bearing in mind that this impression is
necessarily subjective, however carefully and patiently formed),
that he would have resorted to stories purporting to recall his
previous births, often in circumstances which strike us as improbable and far-fetched,[12] in order to reinforce his teaching?

A negative answer to this question is clearly possible and has,
in fact, sometimes been given.[13] Those who take this view regard

the whole Jātaka corpus as a later, popular accretion, owing nothing to the genius of Gotama himself. The Jātaka is seen as a special case of a general tendency to heighten the supernormal attributes of Gotama and to give to his teaching the sanction of information and insights not accessible to the ordinary run of humanity. Another example of this tendency, which would be regarded as equally spurious though equally firmly embedded in the Canon, is the tradition that Gotama's body was endowed with the thirty-two marks of the Buddhas, including such things as the imprint of a thousand-spoked wheel on the soles of his feet, a sheath-encased penis and a set of forty teeth.[14]

The position adopted by Professor K. N. Jayatilleke was more flexible. He argued strongly for the rationality of the Buddha, noting that, in his determination not to be misled by linguistic forms and conventions, he anticipated modern linguistic and analytical philosophers,

> . . . but there was one difference. For perception, according to Buddhism, included extra-sensory forms as well, such as telepathy and clairvoyance. Science cannot ignore such phenomena and today there are Soviet as well as Western scientists, who have admitted the validity of extra-sensory perception in the light of experimental evidence."[15]

Clearly, if the Buddha laid claim to extra-sensory forms of perception and regarded such forms as valid empirical evidence, then it is certainly possible that he claimed the ability to recall experiences from previous births and did in fact sometimes recall and narrate such experiences in order to reinforce his teaching.

Considerable difficulties attach to this position however. In the first place, even if Gotama did have the power to recall previous births, how likely is it, in view of his frequently expressed aversion to the display of supernormal powers,[16] that he would have used such recalled experiences for didactic purposes? Secondly, there is the considerable objection that, when Jayatilleke argues for the admission of extra-sensory experiences as empirical evidence, he overlooks the basic philosophical criterion for the acceptance of empirical evidence, namely that of public accessibility. Thirdly, there are all the problems associated with the claim to be able to recall previous births within a framework of thought which specifically denies the possibility of there being any psychic centre to survive the break-up of the *khandhas*, the five ever-changing components of personality which are held in a measure of unity during the lifetime of the individual but which utterly disintegrate at the moment of death.

There is thus good ground for the view that the Jātakas gain entry to Buddhist canonical literature during a period later than that of Gotama himself, but, in view of the archaeological evidence, not much more than a century later, at least in the case of some of the stories. Geiger is of the opinion that the *Jātakaṭṭhavaṇṇā* (the commentary on the Jātaka verses, i.e. the prose stories, etc., as we now know them) was compiled by a Ceylonese priest and, if not by Buddhaghosa himself, by somebody close to him in time. This was very much a compilation rather than a composition, however, since the stories had already enjoyed a long oral history. Geiger believes that the stories were associated with the verses from the outset since most of the verses "give no sense at all" without the stories. Yet whilst the verses were regarded as fixed and unalterable, a good deal of latitude was allowed in the telling of the story so that the latter sometimes came to contradict, or grow independent of, the associated verses.[17] Malalasekera enters into a much fuller discussion of the method of transmission but agrees with Geiger in attributing the work of compilation to a Ceylon monk, not Buddhaghosa himself, but possibly a lesser namesake who lived soon afterwards.[18] If these judgements are accepted, and if the tradition that Buddhaghosa flourished in the early fifth century A.D. is also accepted, we can date the standard Ceylonese Jātaka collection in around the latter half of the fifth century A.D.[19]

One thing is quite certain. The prose stories of the Jātaka collection belong to the commentarial period in the history of Theravāda Buddhism. Whilst there are passages in the canonical scriptures which exhibit the same traits as this commentarial literature (the canonical Jātaka-stories and the passages describing the thirty-two marks of the Buddha, already alluded to, would serve as examples), these passages are rare and untypical. The traits which characterise the Jātaka stories, on the other hand, are entirely typical of the commentarial literature as a whole and indeed form the main focus of attention at this period. Indeed, in the commentary on *Pettavatthu*, (another of the fifteen books constituting the *Khuddaka Nikāya*), no fewer than three Jātaka stories are reproduced within a few pages, though none of them seems particularly relevant.[20] The dominant interest at this period is quite clearly the emphasis on the law of karma, relentlessly at work, causing the rewards and punishments of a being's previous deeds to mature as he or she proceeds from birth to birth, the doctrine of *anattā* (no soul) being strictly disregarded.

(ii) FORM

Yet the Jātakas evolved a form which is quite distinctively their own. We shall now look at the various elements which go to make this distinctive form.

(a) *Number*

Each story is assigned a number according to the number of the verses associated with that particular story, as indicated by the following table:

Book	Jātaka numbers	Number of verses	Pāli Nipāta ("section")
1	1–150	1	Eka
2	151–250	2	Duka
3	251–300	3	Tika
4	301–350	4	Catukka
5	351–375	5	Pañca
6	376–395	6	Cha
7	396–416	7	Satta
8	417–426	8	Aṭṭha
9	427–438	9	Nava
10	439–454	10	Dasa
11	455–463	11	Ekādasa
12	464–473	12	Dvādasa
13	474–483	13	Terasa
14	484–496	15	Pakiṇṇaka
15	497–510	20	Vīsati
16	511–520	30	Tiṁsa
17	521–525	40	Cattālīsa
18	526–528	50	Paṇṇāsa
19	529–530	60	Saṭṭhi
20	531–532	70	Sattati
21	533–537	80	Asīti
22	538–547	"great"	Mahā

We thus get a collection of five hundred and forty seven stories arranged in twenty-two books in an order determined by the number of verses associated with each story. In actuality, the situation is a good deal more complex than this. Apart from the fact that the same, or very nearly the same, story may recur a number of times, there are also a number of places where the editor of the Pāli collection has omitted a story altogether, simply recording that the story in question is narrated at another place. Such instances are:

(1) JS 8, where it is noted that the Introduction and Jātaka are the same as JS 462, although "the stanzas are different". Only the stanza is given and an ending.

(2) JS 52, where we are told that "all the incidents that are to be related here, will be given in the Mahā-janaka-Jātaka". The Mahā-janaka is number 539 (though it had not been edited at the time of Chalmers' translation). Only the stanza is given here.

(3) M. L. Feer, in his invaluable pioneering study of the Jātakas, notes that numbers 82, 104, 362 and 439 are "only four versions or variants of the same text".[21] There is a mistake or a misprint here; number 362 should read number 369. The Pāli editor notes at JS 82 (Mittavinda J) that the "incidents of this birth . . . will be related in the . . . Mahā-Mittavindaka J." The translator's footnote identifies this as number 439 but also notes, "see No. 41" – a Jataka not in the Feer group. At JS 104, again entitled "Mittavinda J.", the Pāli editor notes that "the incidents are the same as those in the previous story of Mittavindaka" and the translator's footnote again refers us to number 41. At JS 369 (yet another "Mittavinda J."), the Pāli editor says that "the incident that led to the story will be found in the Mahāmittavinda Birth" (No. 439 according to the translator's footnote at JS 82, but here JS 439 is not mentioned; the footnote here refers to nos. 41, 82 and 104). When we come to JS 439, we find that it is not entitled "Mahā-Mittavindaka" after all; it is called the "Catu-Dvāra J." A translator's footnote refers to nos. 82, 104 and 369 (no mention of no. 41 this time).

This rather muddled situation has clearly been brought about by the recurrence of Mittavinda(ka) in the titles of JSS 82, 104, 369 and in the name of the leading character in JSS 41 and 439 (which are entitled Losaka J. and Catu Dvāra J. respectively). Only the latter two give a complete story; the earlier three simply record their stanzas and a very brief prose comment, referring us elsewhere for the story in full. The most specific reference is at JS 82, where the Pāli editor tells us that the story "will be related in the Tenth Book in the Mahā-Mittavindaka Jātaka". There is no Jātaka in the Tenth Book with that title, but JS 439 opens the tenth book and is clearly the story intended. A further complication is that story 439, in its introduction, states that "the circumstances have been already set forth in the first Birth of the Ninth Book", i.e. in JS 427, one that is not included in the Mittavinda(ka) cluster but one which, as the translator observes, bears a very close resemblance to yet another story, JS 381.

Comparing stories 41 and 439, both share one very striking incident in which the main character, Mittavindaka, Jonah-like, brings bad luck to his fellow sailors when the ship in which he is a hired hand (41), or which he owns (439), is becalmed. In both stories, the sailors cast lots to discover the cause of their misfortune. The lot falls seven times (41) or three times (439) on Mittavindaka, who is promptly put overboard on a raft whilst the parent ship as promptly begins to move again.[22] In both stories, Mittavindaka comes to an island where, in a crystal palace, four goddesses dwell. The castaway enjoys life with these four for seven days but, as both accounts tell us, these particular goddesses alternate between seven days of bliss and seven days of woe. Mittavindaka moves on to where eight goddesses dwell in a silver palace, then to the jewel palace of sixteen and then to the golden abode of thirty-two goddesses.

Apart from the remarkable similarity between the two stories in this their common kernel, they are otherwise quite dissimilar. In JS 41, Mittavindaka has been a monk in a previous birth but has been guilty of cheating another monk of food which was offered to him. For this sin, he goes to hell to be tormented for hundreds of thousands of years. This is followed by five hundred successive births as a constantly hungry ogre, followed by five hundred as a hungry dog, then his birth as Mittavindaka, in the home of a village beggar. He brings such bad luck to his already unlucky family that he is driven from home and finally joins the pupils of a world famous teacher, the bodhisatta (i.e. the Buddha-to-be in one of his previous births). Having caused great trouble to his teacher, he runs away, marries and has two children. Ill luck continues to dog him; demons kill and eat his family. It is at this point that he decides to go to sea. After shipwreck and the meeting with the thirty-two goddesses, he goes to a city of ogres. He catches a goat by the leg, hoping to make a meal of it, but the goat turns out to be an ogress in disguise and hurls him all the way back to

Benares in her anger. In Benares he again seizes a goat, thinking that he might thus get hurled back to his delectable goddesses; instead he is arrested by goatherds as a thief. He is rescued by his erstwhile teacher (the bodhisatta), who chances on him as he is being dragged off to the king. He becomes the teacher's slave and is told that all his sufferings spring from "not hearkening to those who wished him well".

In JS 439, Mittavindaka is the son of pious, wealthy parents, though he himself is wicked and unbelieving. His mother's attempts to improve him are in vain. He becomes very wealthy and decides to go to sea as a trader. When his mother protests that this is too dangerous and unnecessary, he strikes her and goes to sea just the same. After he has been shipwrecked and has encountered the goddesses, he comes to a city with four gates (Pāli, *catu-dvāra* – hence the title) which is, in reality, the Ussada Hell. He thinks he sees a man with a lotus on his head and is determined to have it for his own head – only to discover that the "lotus" is really a razor-sharp wheel, which instantly reduces him to gory anguish – his retribution for having struck his mother. Whilst he is in this pitiful state, the bodhisatta (who is, in this story, the king of the gods) happens to be "making a round through the Ussada Hell" and is thus able, in ten stanzas forming a dialogue between himself and Mittavindaka, to explain the workings of karma to its unfortunate victim.

In the light of all this, we may conclude that all three of the storyless Jātakas in this cluster are alluding to JS 439 and not to JS 41. This is because all three make reference to torment in hell, a theme which is quite absent (except in Mittavindaka's previous lives) in JS 41. Feer thus seems to be right in not including JS 41 in this group.

(4) JS 88 (Sārambha J.), where it is noted that "the introductory story and the story of the past are the same as in the Nandvisāla" (JS 28). The only difference, apart from the verses, is that, whereas JS 28 depicts the bodhisatta as a bull, JS 88 has him as an ox.

(5) JS 101 (Parosata J.), where it is noted that "this story is in all respects analogous to the Parosahassa" (JS 99). Even the verses are almost identical.

(6) JSS 110, 111, 112; not even the verses are given for these three Jātakas. It is simply noted that the relevant material will be found in the Ummagga J., which had not been edited at the time when these three were translated, though it is in fact JS 546. Later, we

discover that JSS 170, 350, 364, 452, 471, 500, 508, 517 all refer forward to the same Jātaka and again, in each case, we are simply given a title and the forward reference but no verses. This makes the Mahā-Umagga J. (JS 546) not only the longest in the collection (90pp. in the ET; the next longest, JS 547, has 59pp.) but also the one to which the largest number of other Jātakas, no fewer than eleven in fact, refer.

(7) JS 132 is a unique case since here the story is taken up from the point at which a previous story left off. The Pāli editor refers to the "Takkasilā" J. but the translator's footnote points out that there is confusion of title here. It is the Telapatta J. (JS 96) that is intended.

(8) JS 341 (Kaṇḍari J.) gives no verse but simply refers forward to the Kuṇāla J. (JS 536 in the Fausbøll edition, not 523 as the translator's footnote states).

(9) JS 363, where the Pāli editor notes that "both the introductory story and the story of the past are related in full in the concluding Birth of the ninth division of the first book". The division referred to is the *vagga* (comprising ten stories each) into which the larger *nipātas* were sub-divided. The last story of the ninth *vagga* of the first book will thus be JS 90. Just enough prose is added to introduce and cap the different verses given here.

(10) JS 441 (Catu-Posathika J.), where no verses are given, simply the information that "this birth will be described in the Punnaka Birth". There is no story in the collection with this title, but since *catu-posathika* means "the four who kept the fast (or observed *uposatha*)" and since JS 545 tells of four friends who independently decide to keep the fast on the same day,[23] and since this story features a Yakkha named Punnaka, there is no doubt that JS 441 is referring to JS 545 (Vidhavapaṇḍita J.).[24]

(11) JS 464 (Culla-Kuṇāla J.), where no verses are given but there is a forward reference to the Kuṇāla Birth (JS 536).

(12) JS 470 (Kosiya J.), where again no verses are given but there is a forward reference to the Sudhābhojana Birth (JS 535).

(13) JS 224 (Kumbhila J.) is unique in that, apart from the two verses given here, there is no story and no reference to any other story. It is simply noted that "this story the Master told at the Bamboo Grove, about Devadatta".

We may summarise our findings regarding the numbering of the stories by noting that, of the 547 stories numbered in Fausbøll's edition, there are twenty four (JSS 8, 52, 82, 88, 101, 104, 110,

111, 112, 170, 224, 341, 350, 363, 364, 369, 441, 452, 464, 470, 471, 500, 508, 517) which actually have no story of their own. Of these, there are fifteen (JSS 110, 111, 112, 170, 341, 350, 364, 441, 452, 464, 470, 471, 500, 508, 517) which do not even record verses. Thus, of the original 547 stories, only 523 actually tell a story and only 532 record verses. In addition, there is one story, told in two instalments (JSS 96, 132), relating to the same birth. The number of separate stories, on grounds of numbering alone, is thus reduced to 522.

(b)   *Title*

It will already be clear that this was the cause of considerable confusion because no consistent principle was observed in naming a story. As Feer noted,[25] the title could indicate the subject of the tale or the name of one of its characters or one of its first words. A Jātaka could have, and frequently did have, a number of different titles, whereas a number of different Jātakas could be given the same title.

(c)   *Quotation*

Probably because of the unsatisfactoriness of the titles and the confusion consequent upon this, this third formal characteristic was introduced. This was the brief quotation immediately after the title of the opening words of the first stanza associated with the story in question. It was probably found to be more reliable than the title as a means of identification. Whilst all 547 stories have a number and a title, there are eleven which have no opening quotation (JSS 1, 101, 170, 341, 350, 364, 441, 470, 471, 508, 517). Apart from JS 1, these are all Jātakas which give neither verses nor story, but simply refer the reader to another Jātaka.[26] There are a very few cases where the words quoted do not correspond with the first words of the first stanza. In most cases, this is because the first stanza(s) occurs in the Introduction rather than the story proper (see JSS 4, 25, 40, 67, 70, 78, 132, 269, 296, 321, 400, 408, 466, 512, 533). There are a few cases where, even of the stanzas in the story, the quotation is not from the first. In the following references, I have indicated in brackets after the number of the story the number of the stanza from which the quotation is taken: JSS 31(2), 35(3), 211(3), 259(2), 276(2), 482(2), 483(3), 545(11), 547(3).

Even the quotation is not an infallible means of identifying a particular story since there are small clusters of stories in which the first line(s) of the stanza quoted is (or are) identical. Such clusters are JSS 41, 42, 43; JSS 44, 45; JSS 46, 47; JSS 51, 52; JSS 57, 58. It will be noticed that all these instances occur in the first book and that, in each case, the Pāli editor has grouped the stories concerned together.

In JS 536, the quotation is not from the first of the eighty stanzas, but from the beginning of the prose story. As Dr. Bollée has observed, this particular story, the Kuṇāla, is unique in a number of ways.[27]

(d) *Introduction*

The most important function of this is to place the story which follows in its supposed context in the life of the Buddha. The usual procedure is to say where the Buddha was at the time and to mention briefly the circumstances under which the story was first told by him. These circumstances are then elaborated in the main part of the introduction, "the tale of the present" (*paccuppannavatthu*). The introduction may be quite brief or it may, on rare occasions, grow to such proportions that it quite overshadows the story which follows.

There is a number of instances where the Jātaka story, or at least a substantial part of it, follows the introductory story so closely that only a summary is given, with a note to the effect that all happens much as, or even exactly as, in the introductory episode. Such instances are found at JSS 45, 47, 53, 67, 77, 78, 79, 83, 86, 87, 90, 102, 166, 171, 200, 256, 271, 280, 314, 332, 343, 409, 417, 426, 453, 493.

Apart from the above instances, in each of which the actual birth story makes direct reference to the introductory story, there is also a number of stories in which, although no reference is overtly made to the introduction, the birth story, or a substantial part of it, does in fact repeat the introductory story, sometimes with minor variations, sometimes almost word for word. Such instances are JSS 49, 64, 76, 84, 103, 109, 167, 195, 205, 217, 225, 232, 235, 245, 246, 268, 278, 287, 293, 312, 320, 324, 333, 344, 413, 473.

Four of the above stories deserve special mention:

(1) In JS 109, although the Jātaka story closely parallels the introductory story, there is an interesting variation at the point in the Jātaka where a poor man, having worshipped the castor-oil

tree by offering his husk-cakes, is told by the tree-sprite (the bodhisatta) that he will find pots of treasure buried round the tree. In the introductory story, the poor man offers his husk cake directly to the Buddha, who treats it with special honour, bringing the donor such fame that he himself receives lavish offerings on condition that he gives the merit he has earned to the donors. Gotama instructs him to "take what they offer and impute your righteousness to all living creatures".

This is noteworthy, not merely because the Introduction avoids the mythological elements (the tree-sprite and the buried pots of treasure) of the birth story, but also because it provides dominical sanction for the practice of merit-sharing, a practice which can hardly be described as canonical.

(2) In JS 217, not only does the story closely parallel the intro-duction, but the introduction itself only gives a summary, noting that "the circumstances have been already given in the First Book". The reference is to JS 102; it will be found that the Jātaka of 217 is almost identical in content to the introductory story (as also to the Jātaka) of JS 102.

(3) There is a similar backward reference in JS 333. The reference, though the Pāli editor does not say so, is to JS 320, though JS 223 is also substantially the same story.

(4) JS 268, the well-known story of the monkey-gardeners who pulled up the roots of the trees they were watering so that they could match the amount of water they gave to the length of the roots,[28] is almost identical, both in its introduction (allowing for a changed location) and in its birth story, to JS 46, though this is not noticed by the Pāli editor.

It has been said that "not even the most critical scholar will deny . . . that some of the narratives of the *Paccuppannavatthu* con-tain genuine fragments of the life of the Buddha",[29] but one may perhaps be forgiven for being sceptical about this. It should not be forgotten that the introductions, just as much as the prose of the birth stories, are commentarial, not canonical. The birth stories had to be given a respectable pedigree by being placed in the context of Gotama's life and teaching, but most of the corres-pondences between introduction and birth story referred to above illustrate very aptly the extreme artificiality of this process. Even when, as noted in (1) above with reference to JS 109, the introduc-tion seems deliberately to reduce the mythological content of the birth story in the interests of historical verisimilitude (and this is by no means always the case; a glance at chapter eight will confirm that there is much mythological material in the introductions themselves), it often incorporates other elements (like the dominical sanction given to merit-sharing in the present instance) which render it historically unacceptable.[30]

The typical introductory story ends with some conversation among the monks which the Buddha happens to overhear and enquire about or, alternatively, with some monks going directly to the Buddha to ask him about an incident. Either way, the Buddha replies to the effect that it is not the first time that it has happened thus but that it has happened just like this in former times, when . . . – and the scene is set for the Jātaka proper.

(e) *Jātaka proper*

The "story of the present" (*paccuppannavatthu*) paves the way for the "story of the past" (*atītavatthu*), which tells of an incident in one of the Buddha's previous births. These stories belong to the time when he is not yet fully enlightened and is thus designated the bodhisatta, i.e. the one who has the character of enlightenment because, aeons ago, in the time of the Buddha Dīpankara, he formed the resolution to become the Buddha[31] and, throughout his long succession of subsequent lives, manifested the determination and the perseverance in virtue to ensure his eventual attainment of the supreme enlightenment which characterises Buddhahood.

The tales are always told by the Buddha and he, as bodhisatta, always features in the tales, usually as a main participant in the action, but sometimes merely as a witness, the latter being a very convenient device for transforming a non-Buddhist folk tale into a Buddhist birth story with a minimum of effort.[32]

The table which follows shows the various roles played by the bodhisatta during the course of the Jātaka tales. I have grouped these for convenience and have noted the total number of appearances in a given form in each case:

Form of Birth	Number of appearances in this form	Jātaka references
King – Ascetic	8	9 (52) 406 459 525 529 539 541
King Brahmadatta – Ascetic	2	511 519
Prince – King Brahmadatta – Ascetic	1	378

Form of Birth	Number of appearances in this form	Jātaka references
Prince – Ascetic	7	181 460 472 505 507 510 538
King's Chaplain – Ascetic	5	86 290 330 362 423
King's Chaplain's Son – Ascetic	5	310 411 509 522 530
Brahmin – Ascetic	4	10 77 453 477
Teacher – Ascetic	1	41
Rich Man – Ascetic	10	43 66 390 425 431 440 444 480 488 532
Gardener – Ascetic	1	70
Householder – Ascetic	2	328 348
Ascetic	62	17 63 81 87 99 (101) 106 117 124 134 135 144 154 161 165 166 167 169 173 180 197 203 207 234 235 244 246 250 251 253 271 273 284 293 299 301 312 313 314 319 323 334 337 (341) 346 376 380 392 403 414 418 426 433 435 436 443 467 496 523 526 528 285
Naked Ascetic	1	94
Ascetic's Son	1	540
Outcast – Ascetic – Deer – Osprey – Ascetic	1	498
King	18	95 160 229 230 233 240 260 276 302 303 343 351 424 428 456 494 504 547
Rāma	1	461
King Brahmadatta	4	14 67 225 248
Prince – King	9	193 257 258 454 468 499 527 531 542
Prince – King Brahmadatta	20	6 7 50 51 55 62 100 126 151 191 262 269 282 289 327 347 349 355 416 420
Householder – King	4	194 309 415 421
King's Adviser – King	1	247
(Yakkha) – Courtier – King	1	432
Brahmin Ascetic – King	1	73

Form of Birth	Number of appearances in this form	Jātaka references
Tree Spirit – King	1	445
Prince	11	31 96 132 156· (192) 263 358 371 446 513 537
Prince – King – Sakka	1	458
Merchant – Sakka	2	291 450
Sakka	21	(82) (104) 202 228 264 300 344 (369) 372 374 386 391 393 410 417 439 469 (470) 489 512 535
A Divine Being	3	326 449 457
Brahma Nārada	1	544
King's Chaplain	10	34 120 163 216 241 377 413 422 479 487
King's Chaplain's Brother	1	515
Chaplain – Judge	1	220
Lord Justice	2	218 332
King's Minister/Adviser	30	25 26 27 92 149 158 176 183 184 186 195 214 215 223 226 306 320 331 333 336 345 396 401 402 409 441 462 473 495 545
Courtier	3	8 107 108
Treasurer	10	4 40 45 47 53 83 84 125 127 131
Valuer	1	5
Brahmin – King's Favourite	1	211
Chief Forester	1	265
Trader/Merchant	31	1 2 3 44 54 79 85 89 90 93 98 103 155 171 232 238 242 249 254 256 261 288 315 317 324 340 (363) 365 366 382 493
Brahmin	11 (3010)	61 68 76 80 162 174 (237) 259 367 368 442
Wise Man	5	46 49 268 281 490
Teacher (often Brahmin)	18	64 65 71 97 119 123 130 150 175 185 200 213 245 252 287 338 353 373
Brahmin's Pupil	7	48 305 356 405 447 478 481

Form of Birth	Number of appearances in this form	Jātaka references
Squire	1	39
Householder	2	199 280
Brahmin Field Labourer	2	354 389
Landowner's Son	1	352
Musician	1	243
Wonder Man	12	(110) (111) (112) (170) (350) (364) (452) (471) (500) (508) (517) 546
Acrobat	2	116 212
Farmer	2	56 189
Drummer	1	59
Conch-blower	1	60
Doctor	1	69
Treasurer's Barber	1	78
Gambler	1	91
Stone-cutter	1	137
Elephant Trainer	2	182 231
Potter	2	178 408
Mariner	1	463
Carpenter	1	466
Smith	1	387
Poor Man	2	201 398
Low-caste Man	3	179 474 497
Robber Chief	1	279
Robber	1	318
Tree Fairy	29	18 19 38 74 102 105 109 113 139 187 205 209 (217) 227 272 283 294 295 298 307 311 361 400 412 437 465 475 492 520
Kusa-grass Sprite	1	121
Fairy	2	13 485
Air Sprite	2	147 297
Sea Sprite	3	146 190 296
Mountain Deity	1	419
Garuda King	2	360 518
Golden Goose	5	270 370 379 434 502
Goose	4	451 476 533 534
Singila Bird	1	321
Golden Mallard	1	32

Form of Birth	Number of appearances in this form	Jātaka references
Brahmin – Mallard	1	136
Quail	5	33 35 118 168 394
Pigeon	6	42 274 (275) 277 375 395
Partridge	2	37 438
Peacock	3	159 339 491
Parrot	9	145 198 255 329 429 430 484 503 521
Crow	3	140 204 292
Vulture	4	164 381 399 427
Woodpecker	2	210 308
Cock	1	383
Fowl	1	448
Bird	6	36 115 133 384 (464) 536
Winged Horse	1	196
Stag	5	11 16 359 483 501
Deer	4	12 15 385 482
Antelope	2	21 206
Bull	3	28 29 (88)
Ox	2	30 286
Buffalo	1	278
Lion	10	143 152 153 157 172 188 322 335 397 486
Elephant	7	72 122 221 267 357 455 514
Monkey	11	20 57 58 177 208 219 222 342 404 407 516
Horse	3	23 24 266
Dog	1	22
Jackal	2	142 148
Hare	1	316
Pig	1	388
Rat	2	128 129
Iguana	1	141
Lizard	2	138 325
Nāga	3	304 506 543
Prince – Ascetic – Nāga King	1	524
Frog	1	239
Fish	3	75 114 236

NOTE: A Jātaka reference in brackets indicates that the story is only referred to, not narrated, under this number.

The above list accounts for all 547 Jataka stories with the sole exception of JS 224, for which, as already noted, we have only the verses, which provide no clue as to the Birth involved.

It would be highly misleading, however, to imagine that we are supplied with stories about 546 preceding lives of the Buddha. Apart from the fact that all the stories referred to in brackets are simply alluding to stories narrated elsewhere, there is the fact that, whilst in a few stories the bodhisatta goes through more than one incarnation in one story (e.g. 498), it can occasionally happen that the same incarnation is divided between two stories (e.g. JSS 367, 368).

Furthermore, there is one story (JS 68) which tells of no fewer than three thousand births in the space of one or two lines.

Perusal of the list of births tabled above yields some important information, which may be summarised as follows:

(1) The most striking single fact is that, in spite of the tremendous diversity of forms which the bodhisatta assumes, he never once appears as a woman or even as a female animal. Even when he appears as a tree-spirit or fairy, he is always masculine. That this is no accident becomes clear when one scrutinises the animal births. Animals held to be especially sacred in Hindu literature, like the elephant and the monkey, are well represented – seven and eleven manifestations respectively. The most sacred animal of all, however, is conspicuous by its absence. The bodhisatta appears three times as a bull, twice as an ox, once as a buffalo, but not once as a cow. As we shall see in chapter five, this is consistent with the general attitude of the Jātakas towards women.

(2) In view of Gotama's own biography, we might have expected the theme of royal renunciation to figure more prominently than it does. Of the 100 stories in which the bodhisatta becomes an ascetic, only in 18 has he previously been a king or a prince. This is balanced, however, by the consideration that, of these 18, no fewer than 13 come amongst the longer and more popular stories occurring in Book Ten or later.

(3) There are eight stories in which the bodhisatta makes the opposite progression, from commoner to king. Three of these are especially interesting since they show how virtue can reverse the pressures of an entrenched social order. Though born as a pariah (JS 309), or into a poor family (JSS 415, 421), he yet becomes a king. In the case of the last two stories, virtuous living only leads to the throne when, after dying and being reborn within the course

of the stories, the bodhisatta attains birth as a prince. In JS 309, however, the jump is made within the one lifespan though, because of his pariah birth, the bodhisatta can reign only by night; the reigning monarch retains the throne during the daytime, having said to the bodhisatta, "had you been of a high caste family, I would have made you sole king". The interesting thing about these stories is that they adopt a typically Buddhist attitude toward caste, seeing it as something trivial and external which can be rendered irrelevant by a character strong enough to surmount it. On the other hand, they are reluctant to break with the idea that the caste one is born into indicates the kind of karma one has acquired previously; it would therefore be impossible to graduate from a very lowly birth, however great one's virtue, to the rank of king, at least by daylight, within one lifespan.

(4) Does a group of stories which depicts the bodhisatta in the same type of incarnation show signs of being derived from a common source? This is too big a question for a detailed answer to be attempted here. What can be said is that there are instances where the answer to this question would be an unequivocal "yes". The group of five stories describing the bodhisatta in the role of a king's chaplain who becomes an ascetic (JSS 86, 290, 330, 362, 423) affords a good example. Though no two stories occur in the same Book, there is absolutely no doubt that the first four of these stories are simply variations on a theme – that of the chaplain who, wishing to satisfy himself that he is valued for his virtue and not for his high office, and resorting to a little mock-thieving by way of a test, goes off to be an ascetic when he has satisfied himself as to the supremacy of virtue. Even the verses are related. Three of them (in JSS 86, 290, 330) refer to the fact that, in spite of its evil form, men call the cobra a "good snake". There are many other groups displaying a strong family resemblance which we shall encounter in later chapters.

On the other hand, there are groups where the family link is much less pronounced or non-existent. In the vulture group (JSS 164, 381, 399, 427), for instance, only two of the stories (JSS 381, 427) are similar. In the quail group (JSS 33, 35, 118, 168, 394), not even two of the stories seem to resemble each other.

(5) The various forms of the bodhisatta are distributed between the various planes of existence as follows: 357 as human, 66 times as god and 123 times as animal. This is if we regard JS 68 as relating to a single birth rather than the 3,000 it strictly does refer

to and, in cases where there is more than one birth within one story, if we only count the final birth. The bodhisatta never appears in any of the hells,[33] nor does he appear as a "hungry ghost" (*peta*) nor as an *asura*.[34] The tendency of the Four Nikāyas is to speak of only five bourns: (1) hell (2) animal life (3) *peta* realm (4) human life and (5) heaven – see MLS I 98; GS IV 301f; DB III 225.

There is one story (JS 432) where a *yakkha* gives birth to the bodhisatta. In a previous birth, the mother had protested her innocence with the oath, "if I have sinned . . . I shall become a female Yakkha with a face like a horse". She had sinned and in her next birth she was indeed a horse-faced Yakkha, with an insatiable appetite for human flesh. Having carried off a brahmin who had strayed into her allotted territory, she became infatuated with him and, instead of devouring him, she had the bodhisatta by him. When the latter has grown to childhood, he asks his father why he does not have the same kind of mouth as his wife's. The brahmin replies, "your mother is a Yakkha and lives on man's flesh, but you and I are men." It seems that the law of karma is quite indifferent to the laws of heredity and the bodhisatta is quite uncontaminated by his mother's yakkha-nature.[35]

Appearances in the "tree-fairy", "sea-sprite", etc., group do not fit into the canonical "five bourns". They clearly represent animistic nature-spirits rather than the canonical gods. The latter are thought of as enjoying heavenly bliss as a reward for accumulated merit, rather than as inhabiting trees, etc. In the context of the Jātakas, the fairy-type of incarnation is, more often than not, merely an excuse for introducing the bodhisatta as a witness to an incident in which he has not been actively involved.

Regarding the human and animal births, whilst there is a noticeable preference for more exalted forms (as king or ascetic or as lion or monkey), the narrator has dared on occasion to sink to the level of the despised and rejected (the outcast and robber, the rat and the pig). The singular exception, as already noted, is the whole dimension of femininity.

(6) It is noteworthy that, in one of his incarnations, the bodhisatta appears as Rāma (JS 461) in a story which is clearly a very much abbreviated and somewhat altered version of the Rāmāyana story. When Vaishnavite Hindus later depicted Gotama along with Rāma as one of the many *avatāras* (incarnations) of Vishnu, they would have this story to appeal to, though they were in fact

reversing the intention of the Jātaka story; instead of a leading Hindu figure being absorbed into a Buddhist framework, the Buddha himself is now absorbed into one of the main streams of Hinduism.

Passing now to the setting of the Jātakas, it is remarkable that no fewer than 395 of the stories are set in the time "when Brahmadatta was reigning in Benares". In 24 stories, the bodhisatta himself becomes Brahmadatta. Even granted that there was a long line of kings in ancient Benares with the dynastic name of Brahmadatta, it is quite clear, when one looks at most of the stories in this group – fables in which animals are often the only spokesmen – that they have no historical setting at all. In such cases, the Brahmadatta formula performs the same function as "once upon a time" in European folklore. There are incidents in certain stories (JSS 77, 336, 462, 468, 489 for instance) which may have some basis in history as popularly remembered.[36]

(f) *Verses*

We have already observed that it is the *gāthā* (verses) alone which are regarded as canonical and that the arrangement of the Pāli Jātaka collection into twenty-two Books is based entirely on the number of verses associated with a given story. In actuality, more than half the stories contain three verses or less. This is because the early books, containing the stories with the fewest stanzas, are the books which contain the largest number of stories.

When there is only one verse, it normally comes towards the end of the "story of the past" and is spoken by the bodhisatta. As the number of verses proliferates, there is an increasing tendency for the verses to be spread throughout the "story of the past" and for them eventually to take on the dimensions of epic poetry, a large part of which will consist of dialogues between the bodhisatta and his protagonists. As this happens, the prose tends to get relegated to the role of a connecting link between, or a commentarial explanation of, the verses. It should be stressed, however, that this only applies to a minority of tales at the end of the collection. Many of the early verses are entirely moralistic and aphoristic in tone and give no hint of the stories with which they came to be associated.

It is hard to account for the number of verses in some of the stories since they have more verses than the Book in which the story has been placed would indicate. It is sometimes difficult to

be sure precisely how many stanzas a given story does contain
because of uncertainty as to how blocks of verse should be sub-
divided. With the exception of the stories noted earlier which are
only alluded to and which, at the number in question, include
neither story nor verse, there is not a single case of a Jātaka having
fewer than the expected number of verses.

(g)   *Identification*

The final formal characteristic of the Jātaka is the brief note at the
end identifying the main characters in the birth story. This post-
script to the tale, termed the *samodhāna* in Pāli, was always spoken
by the Buddha. It was a kind of rounding off and capping of the
introduction.

The indispensable part of the *samodhāna* is the identification of
the bodhisatta. This is always done, with complete disregard for
the doctrine of *anattā*, with the formula "*aham eva ahosi*" ("and I
myself was . . .").

Quite often, the bodhisatta is the only individual to be specifically identified. The other characters in the story may be unidentified or identified with somebody who has been anonymous in the
introductory story and who remains anonymous in the *samodhāna*,
e.g. "The self-willed Brother was the Vedabbha-brahmin of those
days" (JS 48). Sometimes a group of characters in the story will
be vaguely identified as being now the "followers" or the "disciples" of the Buddha (e.g. JSS 50, 54).

An interesting feature of the Jātaka stories, however, is that, not
infrequently, individuals who play distinctive roles in the Four
Nikāyas, are identified, in their previous births, as characters who
had dealings with the bodhisatta in former times as well. In such
cases, they often display the very traits which distinguish them in
the canonical accounts.

Devadatta, depicted in the canon as a would-be schismatic
(KS II 162ff; GS III 96f) as a lover of "gain, favour and flattery"
(GS II 83, IV 109, cf IV 271), as a man declared by the Buddha
himself to be unpardonable and destined for hell (GS III 286ff),
frequently appears in the Jātaka tales and always manifests the
same disposition. In JS 11, after being depicted as schismatic in
the introduction, he is the ambitious son of the bodhisatta (here
a stag) who, unlike his brother (identified as Sāriputta, one of the
most revered of Gotama's disciples), proves totally inept when his
will to lead is put to the test. His ambition and ineptness are again

stressed in JSS 143, 160, 231, 241, 243, 278, 329, 335, 367, 404, 466, whilst in JS 294, his fondness for flattery is lampooned. In JS 12, it is the selfishness (a quality which re-emerges in JS 139) rather than the ineptness of his leadership that is stressed, whereas in JS 457 the wrongness of his teaching is paramount. In JS 221, Devadatta has become an utter charlatan, donning the robes and posing as paccekabuddha in order to hunt elephants – the bodhisatta being their king in this story – in order to make his fortune by trading in their tusks (cf JSS 277, 326, 438, 505). In JS 20 he is a water-ogre seeking to devour the king of the monkeys (the bodhisatta) and his followers, a theme which recurs in JSS 57, 208, 342, 357, 448. In JS 51 he is found guilty of lechery (cf JS 194) and treachery, and in JS 58 (this time as the monkey-king himself) he is so jealous of power that he gelds his male progeny with his teeth, the bodhisatta being his only son to escape. This story is unique in that this time the bodhisatta is actually Devadatta's son. Another interesting feature is that when, later in the story, Devadatta tries to get the bodhisatta devoured by a water ogre he is resorting to the same type of monster as he himself was in JS 20. The theme of murderous jealousy returns in JSS 122, 220, 313, 358, 407, and is introduced into the introductory story of JSS 533, 542.

In JS 72, though Devadatta owes his life to the white elephant (the bodhisatta), he nevertheless returns to hunt him for his tusks (cf JS 221) – and is swallowed up by the flames of hell in consequence of his monstrous ingratitude (cf JSS 73, 131, 174, 308, 482, 516). As King Upacara, he goes to hell for a quite different reason in JS 422. Living in the "first age", he has invented the lie and stubbornly persisted in it in spite of being warned that "a lie is a grievous destruction of good qualities" and "causes rebirth in the four evil states" (cf JSS 445, 474, 518). In other stories, Devadatta is just a generally unpleasant or crafty character – the jackal in JS 113, the mutilated criminal in JS 193, the cruel hunter in JSS 222, 514, the wicked king in JS 240 and the snake charmer in JS 506. In JS 117, he is simply the leader of garrulous fools.

In the introduction to JSS 150, 530, it is Devadatta who incites Prince Ajātasattu to murder his father, King Bimbisāra, but Ajātasattu is filled with panic when he hears that Devadatta has been swallowed up by a huge chasm in the earth. In JS 353, Devadatta is depicted as a priest who leads a cruel king – cruel in spite of his former teacher (the bodhisatta)'s efforts to change him – to new depths of wickedness (cf JSS 542, 546).

The message of these stories is the rather sombre one that evil tendencies are deeply ingrained and will recur in life after life. Even when Devadatta and the bodhisatta are born of the same womb – as they are, as parrots, in JS 503 – their identical parentage is offset by the fact that a wind blows one bird to a hermitage and the other to a robber village. Each bird acquires the characteristics of its new environment with the result that one becomes the paragon of virtue, the other the epitome of vice.

A happier theme is the friendship between Ānanda and Gotama, a friendship which has characterised their lives in innumerable former births. This is a theme which will be explored in detail in chapter five.

Of the other canonical characters identified in some of the stories, the two most in evidence are Sāriputta and Moggallāna. The latter is, in the Nikāyas, the great master of *iddhi* (supernormal powers) (MLS I 306ff, 395ff; KS V 261–8, 287f, 319; GS III 233, IV 140ff). In the Jātakas, he displays the same powers. In the introduction to JS 78 (a gloriously funny satire at the expense of a miserly Treasurer), Moggallāna sits and paces in mid-air, belches out smoke and enables the Treasurer and his wife to travel 45 leagues to see the Buddha simply by walking downstairs; the head of the staircase remains where it is whilst the bottom step is miraculously transported to Jetavana. Again, in the introduction of JS 168, Moggallāna is explicitly characterised by the Buddha as the disciple who "has been shown to possess supernatural power"; in the same passage, Upāli is singled out for his knowledge of the sacred law, and Sāriputta for his high wisdom. In the stories themselves, these disciples are identified with characters who are closely associated with the bodhisatta rather than with characters who exhibit their own traits (e.g. JSS 316, 326).

The scriptures constituting the Theravāda canon are voluminous. They fall into three groups (*tipiṭaka*), of which one (the *Abhidhamma*, or "supplement to the dhamma") is generally regarded as of later origin than the other two and another (the *Vinaya*, the "discipline") is mainly concerned with the monastic rules of the order of monks. This leaves the *Sutta Piṭaka* (Collection of Discourses), which is the "chief source of our knowledge of the dhamma. It is therefore often directly called *dhamma* as opposed to *vinaya*."[37]

Although the Sutta Piṭaka is made up of five *nikāyas* (collections), the first four of these have always been given the position of pre-eminence. This is partly because the fifth, *khuddaka* (short, minor), *nikāya* is fragmentary, comprising no fewer than fifteen separate works, only a small part of which claim to convey actual words of the Buddha. Another factor is that "among the Buddhists of Ceylon, Burma and Siam there is no complete agreement as to the pieces belonging to it."[38] It is to this fifth *nikāya* that the verses of the Jātaka tales belong.

The compilation of the canon is traditionally ascribed to the council of Rājagaha which followed immediately upon the death of the Buddha about 483 B.C. There is every reason to suppose that the process of compilation did in fact begin at this early period. The canon is supposed to have been brought to completion at the third council convened by King Asoka in the second half of the third century B.C. (i.e. well over two hundred years after the Buddha's death), though, according to the Ceylon chronicles, it was fixed in writing only under King Veṭṭagāmani, in the last few decades B.C.[39]

For nearly four centuries, therefore, the canon existed only in oral form. It was probably handed down from monk to monk in groups which were each responsible for a particular section of the collection. A monk was expected to commit his section very carefully to memory and to preface his recital of it by the formula, "thus have I heard" (*evaṃ me sutaṃ*). It was the responsibility of larger gatherings of monks, especially at the Councils, to hear and sift and, in satisfactory cases, to give their corporate approval to

these recitals. Even so, some of those accepted were manifestly at
odds with others, and some bore all the signs of being of later
origin than the time of Gotama's ministry. As is usual with oral
traditions, a good part of what was remembered came to have a
liturgical, formulaic or catechetical ring. This ensured that those
elements which were considered to be of central importance would
easily become embedded in the memory of all the monks and nuns
and also of pious laymen and laywomen.

Because of the way in which it came to be compiled and
written, the Canon presents critical problems which Geiger
believes may "never be solved satisfactorily".[40] The Four Nikāyas,
though enjoying such exalted status, are themselves of very un-
equal date and value, ranging from "the actual reminiscences of
the last days of the Master" to what seems to be "purely monastic
fiction".[41]

The Four Nikāyas (also termed the Four *Āgamas*) are written
mainly in prose, whilst the fifth is mainly in verse. They comprise:

(1)   *The Dīgha Nikāya (The Long Collection)*
This, as its name suggests, is made up of discourses which are
mostly of substantial length, especially if repeated material is
included *in extenso* and not just in summary (as it usually is in the
English versions). There are thirty four *suttas* in all, divided into
three parts: the *Sīlakkhandavagga* (1–13), *Mahāvagga* (14–23) and
the *Pātikavagga* (24–34).

(2)   *The Majjhima Nikāya (The Middle Collection)*
A collection of suttas considered to be of moderate length and,
therefore, more numerous than those in the first nikāya. There are
a hundred and fifty two *suttas* in this collection arranged in three
groups: *Mūlapaṇṇāsa* (1–50), *Majjhimapaṇṇāsa* (51–100) and
Uparipaṇṇāsa (101–152).

(3)   *The Samyutta Nikāya (Grouped Collection)*
Geiger considers that "the third and fourth Nikāyas are more
pronouncedly later and supplementary collections",[42] but this
seems to be a rather hazardous generalisation. Granted that the
method of arrangement in these Nikāyas is obviously more
artificial and studied than is the case with the larger discourses,
this does not necessarily reflect on the authenticity of many of the
fragments so arranged. There is every reason to suppose that many

shorter fragments, as authentic as anything in the longer discourses, found their way into these Nikāyas. In this third nikāya, suttas are grouped according to their contents. There are fifty six of these groupings, comprising 2,889 *suttas* arranged in five parts.

(4) *The Aṅguttara Nikāya ("One-limb-more" Collection)*
This section admirably manifests the monks' delight in ordering the teaching into numbered lists. Occasionally these lists are chains, with each link dependent upon, and providing the support for, its neighbouring links, but more often they are simply lists of attributes of, or requisites for, a given phenomenon. There are "at least 2,308"[43] *suttas* arranged in groups of ten or more (very rarely less). The lists go in ascending order from those of just one item to those of eleven items, though the latter are often highly contrived, being simply combinations of previous shorter lists (e.g. 6 plus 5 or 3 plus 3 plus 3 plus 2, to give a composite list of 11).

Part II: THEMES

3 *Karma and Rebirth*

(a) THE FOUR NIKĀYAS

In treating of individual themes, karma and rebirth seem to be the obvious starting point since these twin concepts constitute the general theory underlying the very idea of a Jātaka story. Without belief in rebirth, there can obviously be no tales of this type.

Yet there is something extremely puzzling about the canonical teaching regarding previous births. The Hindu belief in a transmigrating soul (*ātman*) has been firmly rejected in favour of a doctrine of "self" as a ceaselessly changing complex formed, for the duration of an individual's life, of the five aggregates – form (*rūpa*), feeling (*vedanā*), perception (*saññā*), volitions/habits (*saṅkhārā*) and consciousness (*viññāṇa*).[44] There is no continuing ego.

In spite of this, it seems to be maintained that there is a one-to-one correlation between a given "I", living now, and a whole series of "I"s (though not necessarily human) in past time and a projected series of "I"s stretching indefinitely into future time. Though there is no metaphysical ground for this "I", it being a merely conventional construct, useful for describing a complex web of rapidly changing but highly integrated and continuous causes and effects, it nevertheless does seem to have the remarkable capacity to survive the death of the body and the consequent dissolution of the *khandhas* (aggregates) by somehow leaping over into some other form of life. No Buddhist has ever, to my knowledge, satisfactorily explained what it is that makes this leap.

The late Professor Jayatilleke refers to a passage in M III 19, which he translates as follows: "a certain monk entertained the thought that since body, feelings, ideas, dispositions and consciousness is without self, what self, can deeds not done by a self, affect." His comment is that, although this monk is faithfully rehearsing the Buddha's teaching of *anattā* (no soul), he is also going beyond the teaching of the Buddha in the consequences he wishes to draw from it. The Buddha, says Jayatilleke, expressed joy, after his enlightenment, that he had been saved from rebirth, belief in which "is therefore an integral part of Early Buddhist belief and much of Buddhism would be unintelligible without it."[45]

Whilst one may readily agree that the Buddha believed in re-birth and that this belief is crucial for an understanding of his teaching, it is not clear – and Jayatilleke makes it no clearer – what it is precisely that is reborn. On another occasion, the same author wrote:

> The belief that the Buddhist doctrine of anattā implies a denial of any kind of survival after death rests on a misunderstanding of this doctrine. The doctrine denies a permanent entity or soul which runs through different existences without change of identity but does not deny the continuity of an evolving con-sciousness.[46]

This is extraordinarily puzzling. Again, one may readily agree that the Buddha does seem to have taught both a radical doctrine of metaphysical selflessness and also an apparently contradictory doctrine of rebirth, but surely nothing is done to resolve the con-tradiction by introducing such concepts as "the continuity of an evolving consciousness". Consciousness (*viññāṇa*) is one of the five *khandhas* which are dissolved at death. Deprived of its physical basis, or, if we prefer it, its physical correlate, how could it possibly survive death? In MLS I 313, 320f, Gotama does in fact vigorously refute the "heresy" of a persisting consciousness. If it is argued that Gotama is here referring only to the crude egocentric con-sciousness and that there is another, subtler, ego-free consciousness which can survive, we should have to ask two questions: (1) what is the basis for this idea of an ego-less consciousness in the doctrine of the *khandhas*, which plays such an important part in the Nikāyas? (2) if it is argued that there is such a basis, how could this be consistent with the doctrine of *anattā*? How could one defend this "subtle consciousness" from the charge that it is really only an *ātman* in disguise? In addition to these two questions, there is the even weighter objection that, in order to maintain a plausible doctrine of a continuously evolving consciousness, one would be compelled to engage in precisely the kind of metaphysical theorizing which Gotama seemed so determined to avoid.[47]

The truth of the matter seems to be that, whilst Gotama did, with ruthless analytical rigour, debunk the idea of there being some mysterious, metaphysical "ghost in the machine" – and this debunking recurs so often and is so inhospitable to popular beliefs that it would seem impossible to doubt its authenticity – he also seems to have rejected what seem to be the logical consequences of his radical analysis. There is one passage[48] where the possibility of there being "no world beyond" is seriously entertained. In this passage, it is argued that, even if there is "no fruit and ripening of deeds done well or ill" in future lives, at least virtuous living ensures freedom from enmity, oppression and sorrow here and now.

This passage is untypical, however. What is more typical is the fact that, whenever the Buddha was faced with the proposition that, since there is no abiding soul, ethics are deprived of any sanction save that of present expediency and that, therefore, so far as an individual's destiny is concerned, it matters little how one behaves, he recoiled from this proposition.[49] He never offered any theoretical justification for his recoil as this would have infringed his self-imposed veto on speculative theorizing and endangered his doctrine of *anattā*. What it amounts to is that he clung to a metaphysical belief on intuitive grounds, appealing no doubt to the "intuitive wisdom" (*paññā*) arising from his enlightenment, but disdained to offer a metaphysical theory in support of it. It is true that the theory of karmic causality can, insofar as *it* can avoid metaphysical contamination, furnish a measure of support for the idea of rebirth. Jayatilleke himself attempts such an empirical appeal to karmic causality when he says, "Man is conditioned by his psychological past, going back into prior lives, by heredity and by the impact of his environment."[50]

There is a sense in which it would seem to be eminently reasonable, even scientific, to suppose that the kind of lives we lead, the kind of dispositions we acquire, will have unforeseen consequences for other lives, not merely in the immediate future, but possibly countless generations hence. We might like to refer to these consequences as "karmic", but, if so, we have to be very careful. Granted that "I" am in large measure conditioned by genes I inherit through my parents, in what sense can I describe this genetic inheritance as my "psychological past, going back into prior lives"? This type of description is neither rational nor scientific; it is metaphysical. Not only so, it entirely fails to account for my conditioning if, as on Buddhist premises might well have been the case, "I" was, in "my" previous birth, not a human being at all – much less a blood ancestor – but, say, a dog.

It is at these points that any Buddhist attempt to appeal to a strictly empirical, non-metaphysical theory of karmic causality as a justification for belief in rebirth *must* break down. Such attempts can never tell us (a) how this present "I" can be in some kind of ethical continuum with other "I"s nor (b) how a dog's "I" can transfer itself, at the moment of death, to a human's "I".

Oscar Shaftel would seem to be right when he says of the Buddha, "Some assumptions of the day he too assumed, such as karma and rebirth, presumably because they bespoke a system of active personal responsibility."[51] Certainly the assumption was not blindly accepted. Gotama was very well aware of other possibilities. He lived through a period of vigorous, and often creative, religious and ethical thinking and debate. If he opted in favour of the doctrines of karma and rebirth it was not for want of alternatives but because he had his reasons. Shaftel seems to be right when he implies that these reasons were ethical rather than rational in the narrow sense; Gotama was opting for "a system of active personal responsibility." He seems to have been convinced that, however much the rational, analytical part of his teaching – especially the doctrine of *anattā* – might seem to deny it, the laws governing sentient life on this planet and beyond are not amoral. He himself displayed a resolute will to be good and was utterly unwilling to believe that this will to goodness was optional or inconsequential. He regarded it as the only foundation upon which the two other planks of his teaching, meditation (*samādhi*) and wisdom (*paññā*), could be laid.[52] He could claim that this conviction was empirically based insofar as it had withstood the test of experience – his own and that of his disciples. He could not claim that this conviction had a sound basis in the rational, analytical part of his teaching; indeed, it would seem to me not too strong to say that there is a hopelessly irreconcilable contradiction between the two.

How does the law of karma work? There is not much speculation about this in the canon. The idea most often conveyed is of an impersonal, natural law which operates quite impartially and inexorably according to a strict causal necessity. Just as, if one puts one's finger in the fire one will surely get it burned, so everything one does will have its consequences. What strains credulity is the belief that the consequences may be very far removed in time from their causes and that they always manifest a strictly moral character. It is not possible for good causes to have evil consequences, and vice versa. There would seem to be no necessity for this to be the case unless this happens to be a moral universe obeying moral laws. If it is such a universe, this fact would seem to demand some explanation. The morality of karmic consequences seems to call in question the strictly impersonal nature of karmic processes since, if these are moral processes, the only type of morality for which we have empirical evidence is that associated with personality. There is thus a tension between the impersonal and the moral attributes of karma.

Within the Four Nikāyas, this tension sometimes comes to the surface. Although the general tendency of the canon is to associate the working of karma with the theory of causality known as the theory of "dependent co-origination" (*paṭicca-samuppāda*),[53] there are passages, which may well be later in origin, which picture the karmic process as being presided over, impartially but *personally*, by Yama, the Hindu god of death. In these passages, which are in the minority, the tension between impersonality and morality has been resolved by yielding the ascendancy to the latter and admitting a measure of personal intervention into the system. Such passages are found in MLS III 224ff; GS I 122, 125.

For the Buddha, as for many Hindu sages before and since, acceptance of the doctrine of karma and rebirth was only of qualified religious value. It was better that life be governed by moral laws than not, but these moral laws were more of a threat than a promise. Whilst the accumulation of great merit could ensure a blissful existence for a very long time in one of many heavens, it could not prevent the law of karma operating after that. When one's merit was exhausted, one would have to return to the weary round of lower existences. It was maintained that more ex-devas were reborn in purgatory than as men or as gods again (GS I 33), so that the long-term prospect, even for a god, was gloomy. A curious exception was the "never-returner". He was the disciple who had graduated from being a "stream-winner", i.e. one who was assured of a good rebirth, and who had passed through the second stage, that of the "once-returner", i.e. one who was assured of only one more rebirth before attaining the final stage of *arahantship* (which we shall be treating in detail in chapter seven), and who was now in the penultimate stage of "never-returner", i.e. one who knew that, although he had not quite attained the supreme goal in this life, he was so close to it that he would have just one more rebirth in the highest heaven, and from there he would never return. At the end of his allotted period in heaven, he would attain *nibbāna*.[54]

Even stranger is the passage which states that, whereas an "ordinary man", going to the "devas of the Brahma-group", is there for a kalpa, and then is reborn in purgatory or in the animal or *peta* (hungry ghost) realm, a Buddhist disciple, after his period of bliss. "finally passes away in that same state"; but the heaven to which he goes is higher and the length of his stay there longer according to the level of *jhāna* (meditative trance) to which he has attained (GS II 130ff). The idea that greater attainment leads to a longer stay in heaven prior to final release seems to be at odds with the idea that the supreme goal is *immediate* final release. It would seem that those who, at death, are closest to, but not actually at, attainment will have to wait longer before they attain final *nibbāna* than those who are less advanced – which seems to be a good reason for suspecting that this gradation of discipleship into four stages is a later and rather muddled invention.

Generally speaking, the true disciple is the one who has "cast out both wickedness and (all the work of piling) merit..." (KS I 231). The translator's footnote to this verse adds that "making merit and reaping its reward was mere layman's creed... not that of a genuine bhikkhu, who by entering on the Path had renounced heavenly goals". This is not to say that this "layman's creed" does not figure quite prominently in the Nikāyas. It does. At MLS III 302f, we learn that there are fourteen grades of offering, in descending order, depending on the worth and merit of the recipient, with corresponding rewards, a hundred-fold being the least one can expect. The next passage (pp. 303f) lists seven grades of offering to the Order, which are no less fruitful than the fourteen previously mentioned. Even the poorest man who wholeheartedly embraces Buddhism, will go to the "heaven of the thirty-three",[55] outshining many who had thought themselves his superiors (KS I 296). On the other hand, a fool who has "gone to the Downfall" has less chance of becoming a man again than has a blind turtle of putting its head through a yoke with only one hole in it, a hundred years lapsing between each attempt. This is because, in this dire state, there is no holy life or righteous living and therefore no good deeds and working of merit, "just cannibalism and preying on weaker creatures" (KS V 383f). A number of passages[56] expatiate on the miseries of purgatory.

The general impression one gets from the Four Nikāyas is that, whilst rebirth is synonymous with suffering and non-rebirth with the cessation of suffering,[57] it is yet true that virtuous living can improve one's lot within the woeful wheel of *saṃsāra* (the cycle of rebirths embracing all planes of existence), whilst wickedness will assuredly bring dreadful consequences. It is rarely questioned that one's present state is the effect for which one's own actions, either in this life or in a previous life, constitute the cause.

There is one remarkable exception, however. The Buddha is reported as saying, on one occasion, that it goes "beyond experience and what is generally acknowledged by the world to say, as some do, that 'whatsoever pleasure or pain or mental state a human being experiences, all that is due to a previous act'." He then goes on to list eight causes of our present condition (including such things as bile, phlegm and wind), only one of which is "the ripening of karma". (KS IV 155f). This seems extremely odd. If one is plagued by phlegm or wind, there seems to be no reason why this, as much as any other aspect of one's present state, should not be attributed to karma. Again, one may suspect that this passage is later and spurious. Belief in karma, insofar as it implies causes which antedate our present existence, could never be based on experience, unless it be extra-sensory experience. If the latter, it could hardly be described as "what is generally acknowledged by the world". The whole objection seems too arbitrary and too untypical to be regarded as an accurately remembered statement of Gotama's, but it does indicate a certain amount of scepticism regarding the explanatory function of karma amongst some of the early bhikkhus.

(b) THE JĀTAKA

For the compilers of the birth-stories, a simple solution is found to the teasing problems posed by the canonical doctrine of karma and rebirth. When two propositions conflict, the simplest possible solution is to ignore one of them – which is precisely what the Jātaka does. There is no contradiction in the Jātaka between the doctrine of *anattā* (no soul) and the doctrine of a series of lives of the same individual because the doctrine of *anattā* is simply ignored.

As we saw in the first chapter, the typical way in which the Buddha identifies himself in one of his bodhisatta incarnations in the *samodhāna* at the end of each story, is by the formula, "at that time, I myself was . . .". This formula is unlikely to furrow the brow of a simple listener because it never suggests that, from a Buddhist point of view, serious problems attach to the expression "I myself". Since it is unlikely that the listener himself will find these words problematical, he simply assumes that the person who speaks these words is remembering a life which he himself lived at another time, in another place and in a different body. As we have seen, the complexity of the canonical teaching puts out of bounds so simple a transmigratory view of rebirth. On this issue, the Jātaka is seriously at variance with the Four Nikāyas.

In other respects, however, the teaching about rebirth conveyed by the Jātaka stories is consistent with what is taught in the Canon, at least in its "layman's creed". It is simply made more graphic and circumstantial.

At its most basic and, one suspects, for unsophisticated believers, its most pertinent level, the doctrine of karma and rebirth is a doctrine of reward and punishment. Thus, when the daughters of the gods tell Guttila the Musician (the bodhisatta) what acts of virtue brought them to heaven (JS 243) and when King Sādhīna (again the bodhisatta) is, as a result of his virtue in almsgiving and keeping of the fast-day vows, transported in Mātali's chariot to heaven, where he is allowed to dwell in bliss for seven hundred years, accompanied by twenty five million nymphs (JS 494), and, again, when the bodhisatta, this time as one born into a poor family, sees the glory of the Serpent King and becomes covetous of it, "having given alms and lived a virtuous life", is reborn as the serpent king himself seven days after the death of his predecessor (JS 506) and, finally, when the bodhisatta is tormented with lust for his commander-in-chief's wife, a girl who has been born intoxicatingly beautiful in fulfilment of a request made at the time when, as a poor girl in a previous life, she donated her precious scarlet robe to a passing monk (JS 527) – all are furnishing examples of virtue in one life being rewarded by bliss in another.

Yet in three of these four examples, there are little nuances which suggest that working for karmic reward is a less satisfying vocation than might appear. King Sādhīna, nearing the end of his seven hundred years of bliss, found that, when "his merit was exhausted", "dissatisfaction arose in him". When Sakka, king of the gods, offers to allow him to outstay his merit, the Great Being replies:

I care not blessings to receive given by another's hand,
My goods are mine and mine alone when on my deeds I stand.

Grace is rejected, it seems, because it threatens independence and rights of ownership. The bodhisatta spends seven days distributing alms accumulated during the seven hundred years he has been away and acquires enough merit to ensure that, when he dies on the seventh day, he returns immediately to the heaven of the thirty-three (JS 494).

Here, the cautionary note is very restrained; just a reminder that even a bodhisatta's merit does not last for ever and that, when more is needed, there is no help like self-help. In JS 506, however, the cautionary note is more pronounced. As a man, the bodhisatta has coveted the Serpent King; when, having lived virtuously, he attains the coveted goal, he is filled with consternation: " 'As a consequence of my good deeds', quoth he, 'I have power laid up in the six chief worlds of sense, as corn is laid up in a granary. But see, here am I born in this reptile shape; what care I for life!' And so he had thoughts of putting an end to himself."[58] Virtue may cause one's wish to be fulfilled, but a wish fulfilled may be more frustrating than a wish unfulfilled – or more dangerous to others: JS 527 tells of a girl whose virtue in a previous life had caused her to be born so beautiful that she became a serious threat to the virtue of the bodhisatta himself!

So much for reward; punishment is just as much a reality. We read of a queen who advises her son to blockade a city for seven days; her punishment is that, when she becomes pregnant in a future life, she has to carry her child for seven years and then endure labour pains for seven days (her child being the former prince who had blockaded the city) (JS 100). Similarly, when an ascetic is impaled by the king on a charge of robbery – a crime of which he happens to be quite innocent – "there arose in him the knowledge of former existences." As he surveyed his past lives, he realised that he was being punished now for having impaled a fly with an ebony splinter in a former life. The circumstances of his own punishment are made, in a rather far-fetched manner, to imitate his earlier treatment of the fly (JS 444).

In the Introduction of JS 41, we encounter a monk, Losaka Tissa, who, though he seems to be hounded relentlessly by ill-luck, yet attains to Arahantship. When the Buddha is asked by the brethren to account for this puzzling inconsistency in his fortune, it emerges that, in a former life, he had, as a monk, been moved by jealousy and selfishness to cheat another monk of his food-offering. For this sin, he suffered in hell and then as a dog for countless years and then he was born as Mittavindaka, a beggar's son.[59] But, according to the introduction, after all his sufferings, "it was by his meditating on sorrow, transitoriness, and the absence of an abiding principle in things, that he won Arahatship[60] for himself."

The theme of reward and punishment working themselves out simultaneously in the same lifetime was obviously fascinating to the compilers of the birth stories, but sometimes led to extravagant flights of fancy, as in the case of the Spirit who is in paradise with thousands of nymphs each night because, formerly, as a king's chaplain, he had kept half a fast-day; in the daytime, however, this same Spirit is condemned to eat the flesh off his own back because, as the same chaplain, he had received bribes and made false judgements and indulged in "backbiting"! (JS 511). JS 531 tells a long and fascinating story about a king desperate to have a son. He finally consents to have his chief wife, Sīlavatī, "exposed in the streets". Because of her virtue, Sakka comes in disguise to carry her off to the heaven of the thirty-three, where he promises her, not one, but two sons. One will be wise but ugly, the other handsome but a fool; which will she have first? She asks for the wise one. Sakka causes her to conceive simply by touching her person with his thumb and she gives birth to the bodhisatta, who has just passed through a birth in the heaven of the thirty-three and "was longing to be born in a higher world". Sakka orders him to this human birth.[61] Why was the bodhisatta born so ugly? It appears that, in a former life, he had returned from the forest to discover that his sister-in-law had just given a "very dainty cake", otherwise reserved for him, to a paccekabuddha who had come to the door for alms. The bodhisatta was so angry that he "went and took the cake from the beggar's bowl". It was a punishment for this act that made him now so ugly.[62] But why was he born so wise? Surprisingly, we are not told. We are presumably meant to infer that the vast store of merit which the Great Being must have acquired in previous births accounted for his being well-endowed in all respects except his ugliness.

Apart from reward and punishment, present virtue and vice may be grounded in dispositions formed in earlier lives. A water-sprite who has been given permission to devour all who enter his pool except those who can correctly answer the question: what is truly godlike?, is told by the bodhisatta that his present evil disposition is "in consequence of your own evil deeds in times past" – though these are not specified (JS 6). On the other hand, "a certain holy man passing from the Brahma world was born again in the form of a young girl." She eventually marries the bodhisatta, though against the will of both parties. Though she is surpassingly beautiful, married, sharing the same room and bed, "they did not regard one another with the eye of sinful passion". Instead they both became ascetics and lived saintly lives together (JS 328). That rare thing in the Jātaka stories, a virtuous woman, owes her virtue to merit acquired in a former birth – as a male!

It occasionally happens that those who have lived virtuously and have gone to heaven, return from there in order to edify their descendants here below. In JS 450, the bodhisatta, having been very generous in donating alms as a merchant, is reborn as Sakka. His successors for five generations are similarly virtuous and are also reborn as gods. The sixth in line, however, is "without faith, hard-hearted, loveless, niggardly"; instead of feeding the beggars who come for alms, he beats them. Sakka, in league with his five generous successors, returns to earth and, disguised as a brahmin, proceeds to humiliate and eventually convert the miser. The conversion is achieved largely by pointing out how well-rewarded he and his successors have been for their charitable giving: "thus potent is giving of gifts; therefore wise men ought to do virtuously."

In JS 538 we find that the bodhisatta, "having reigned twenty two years in Benares, had been reborn in the Ussada hell where he had suffered for eighty thousand years, and had then been born in the world of the thirty-three gods" and was now wanting to go to the world of the higher gods. However, as in JS 531, Sakka comes and, instead of ordering, this time entreats him to take again a human womb, saying, "Friend, if you are born in the world of men you will fully exercise the perfections and the mass of mankind will be advantaged."[63] The bodhisatta accedes to this request and is born a prince. As he observes his father's cruelty, he recollects his former births and recalls the long years he had suffered in hell in order to atone for sins committed during his prior kingship. He thus determines not to become king but to become an ascetic instead.[64]

This story, apart from the bold admission that even the bodhisatta had, on occasion, sinned badly enough to have had to spend long years in hell, is also interesting in that it serves as an example of one's own memory of previous lives (rather than an ancestral visitation) enabling one to avert evil and, therefore, another evil destiny.

If memory or ancestral intervention can turn the past to good account, knowledge of the merit accruing to the performance of a given act can ensure a brighter future. Thus, in JS 543, we find the bodhisatta, dissatisfied with life as a Nāga prince, exclaiming, "What have I to do with this frog-eating snake-nature? I will . . . keep the fast and follow the observances by which one may be born among the gods."[65] This certainly introduces an ulterior motive into the performance of virtuous acts, but one cannot really complain that this is contrary to canonical teaching. The whole business of merit-making with a view to improving one's future lot is inevitably an ulterior affair. This, precisely, is what is wrong with it and is one of the main reasons why, if at all possible, it should be superseded. The man who is bent on acquiring merit and enhancing his position is still bound by fetters, still motivated by craving, and still destined to suffer.

A passage in JS 539 sets out to show that the Buddhist attitude towards the operation of Karma was more activist and less fatalistic than it was amongst Hindus. The bodhisatta had been shipwrecked. Other members of the crew "invoked their different gods", yet "became food for the fishes and tortoises". The bodhisatta, unlike his comrades, "never wept nor lamented nor invoked any deities" but daubed his body with oil, ate to capacity and then . . . rather disappointingly, the story now enters the realm of fantasy. The bodhisatta flew to an island and was rescued thence by a goddess. Before she rescued him, however, the goddess asked why he had striven so manfully when doom seemed inevitable and when there was apparently so little point in doing so. He replies:

> He who thinks there is nought to win and will not battle while
>   he may –
> Be his the blame what e'er the loss, 'twas his faint heart that
>   lost the day.
> Men in this world devise their plans, and do their business
>   as seems best, –
> The plans may prosper or may fail, – the unknown future shows
>   the rest.

Seest thou not, goddess, here to-day 'tis our own actions
    which decide;
Drowned are the others, – I am saved, and thou art standing
    by my side.
So I will ever do my best to fight through ocean to the shore;
While strength holds out I still will strive, nor yield till
    I can strive no more.

A very similar incident occurs in JS 442, though here the theme of self-striving is not emphasised.

What do the Jātaka stories have to say about the mode of operation of the law of karma? One might have expected that the popular tendency would be to personalise the working of karma and therefore to give Yama a much greater prominence than he has in the Nikāyas.

The rather surprising thing is that, apart from poetic references to death as Yama's "realm" or "flood" or "house" in some of the stanzas, there is only one reference to Yama in his role as judge and apportioner of destinies in the whole collection. This occurs in JS 240, where the bodhisatta is the son of an infamously cruel and wicked king, Mahā-pingala. When the king dies, everybody is jubilant except for a doorkeeper. Puzzled by this man's sadness amidst the general rejoicing, the bodhisatta enquires the reason. He learns that the porter's sorrow springs, not from grief at the king's death, but from fear that he might return: "For king Pingala, every time he came down from the palace, or went up into it, would give me eight blows over the head with his fist. . . . So when he goes down to the other world, he will deal eight blows on the head of Yama, the gatekeeper of hell. . . . Then the people there will cry – He is too cruel for us! and will send him up again." Underlying the humour of this passage is the genuine fear of a man who doubts the power even of superhuman jailers to keep his former tormentor out of harm's way. The bodhisatta manages to comfort the doorkeeper by convincing him that the law of karma is inexorable and cannot be bullied into submission. Doctrinally, it is a clever way of saying that there could be disadvantages if karma were administered more personally.

That the Jātaka has not exploited the opportunity afforded by canonical references to Yama to further personalise the mode of karmic operations might be explained along the lines that the stories take the law of karma very much for granted; there was very little curiosity about how the law worked. Alternatively, one could argue that the very form of the Jātaka tale focused attention on the simple narration of a story; it had very little interest in exploring the "why's" and "wherefore's" of the concepts it employed. A third possibility – and JS 240 seems to support this – is that there was sufficient monastic oversight of the doctrinal content of the stories to ensure that they did not stray too far down undesirable byways.

However, the description of Yama as "the gatekeeper of hell" in JS 240 is a reminder that the concept of hell or, perhaps more correctly, purgatory, was a very powerful sanction in the popular ethical climate generated by belief in karma and rebirth. We have already seen how even the bodhisatta spent part of his career in hell.

Description of life in various purgatories or hells, though less detailed, play a more prominent part in the Jātaka stories than in the Nikāyas. Obvious "baddies" like Devadatta sometimes make a dramatic descent into the nether regions. In JS 72, Devadatta shows shocking ingratitude to the bodhisatta who, living at this time as a fine white elephant, has just saved his life. The earth, "as though unable to bear the burden of all that wickedness", simply opens up, so that the flames of Hell are free to curl around the cruel ingrate and carry him off to his deserved punishment. Devadatta met a similar fate in this present life according to the Introduction of JS 466. Again "the great earth gaped" and he, together with five hundred families of his followers, was carried off to "the nethermost hell of Avīci". In the introduction to JS 530, we are told that he met this fate because he "was an enemy of the supreme Buddha". A similar fate befalls Ciñca-māṇavikā, the woman who feigned pregnancy in order to bring dishonour to Gotama and thus help the "heretics", who were "like fireflies after sunrise" in their annoyance at being so completely overshadowed by Gotama's success.[66]

We have already described, in the first chapter, the other occasions on which Devadatta earned torment in hell. In JS 422 he is being punished for being the first man to tell a lie. In this case, he sinks into the earth by stages each time he tells a lie, first up to his ankles, then to his knees, then his hips, his navel, his breast until finally "the earth opened and the flames of Avīci leapt up and seized him". In JS 518, his head is split into seven pieces and he meets his familiar fate of "disappearing into the earth" and being reborn in the Avīci hell – again for lying.[67]

Again, we encountered Mittavindaka's sojourn in hell in the first chapter. He goes to the Ussada hell for smiting his mother (JS 439) and is interviewed by the bodhisatta (Sakka in this story), who happened to be "making a round through the Ussada Hell" at the time. This is not the only time that the bodhisatta visits hell without himself being in residence. In JS 541, he comes to birth as King Nimi, the last of a line of 84,000 kings who have each spent 84,000 years in each of four roles: pleasure seeking youth, viceroy, king and ascetic.[68] The ascetic stage begins when a barber first discovers a grey hair on the king's head. While Nimi is king, he is so virtuous and holy, so assiduous in almsgiving, that the gods, when Sakka tells them of him, desire to see him. Mātali is sent to fetch the king in his heavenly chariot. Asked if he would like to see hell as well as heaven, and having said he would, Nimi is now taken on a horrifying tour. There follows a long verse dialogue between Nimi and Mātali in which, not only are the tortures of hell detailed but the sins of those who suffer these tortures are laid bare.[69]

In JS 530, the bodhisatta grows up in the family of the king's priest and is very friendly with the Prince – until the latter discloses to his friend his plan to murder the king and usurp the throne. Horrified, the bodhisatta goes off to become a Himalayan hermit. Meanwhile, his friend, having committed the murder, soon becomes terror-stricken and agitated with guilt. Fifty years later, his friend returns to "teach him the Law and remove his fears". He preaches a long sermon in verse in which the horrors of the eight major hells and the hundred and twenty eight minor hells are chillingly depicted. Particularly pertinent to his hearer would be the description of the fate awaiting a parricide; while his skin is peeled off in a boiling cauldron, he has steel shafts driven through him, is made to eat filth and is dropped in brine; goblins keep his jaws open with a hot iron ball whilst they pour in the filth; ravens and vultures with iron beaks tear his tongue apart whilst other goblins gleefully beat him. After all this talk of hell, there are a couple of stanzas describing the heavenly joys earned by the virtuous. Astoundingly, the king is comforted by the bodhisatta's sermon! The bodhisatta again preaches to a king the terrors of hell in JS 544,[70] but this time in order to warn the king of the terrible consequences of persisting in the false doctrine that there is no karma and no rebirth!

We have seen how, in JS 538, the bodhisatta himself has to suffer the torments of hell because of sins committed during his previous life as king. There is another occasion when he has had a narrow escape. This is in JS 94 when he "set himself to examine into the false asceticism". He becomes an *Ājīvika* (naked ascetic) and lives a life of solitary abstinence, enduring cold and heat, living in the jungle, feeding sometimes on cowdung. Yet, as he lay dying, "the vision of hell rose before the Bodhisatta". In the nick of time, he realises the worthlessness of his austerities, abandons "his delusions", and goes to heaven instead. This would be a sombre warning to "naked ascetics" and other "heretics" – and indeed to all pious listeners; if such things could happen even to the bodhisatta, how much more vulnerable were they.

It needs constantly to be borne in mind when reading the next chapters (4 to 6) that, underlying the ethical teaching which is there considered, there is always the powerful sanction of belief in karma and rebirth. The rewards of virtue are unashamedly described, but the penalties of wickedness are dreadful indeed.

4 Ethical Teaching: Non-Injury

This is the first of three chapters which deal with the specifically ethical teaching in our two sources. This chapter, as well as dealing in detail with what is in many ways the most important and distinctive of the ethical precepts, that of *ahiṃsā* (non-violence), also attempts a general statement regarding the ethical teaching both of the Nikāyas and the Jātaka. The next two chapters will concentrate on the sexual and social aspects of this teaching respectively.

(a) THE FOUR NIKĀYAS[71]

One of the most striking features of Gotama's teaching as set forth in the Nikāyas, is his general impatience with the ritual observances which had become a prominent feature of brahmanical religion and, in particular, his absolute abhorrence of animal sacrifice. Perhaps his greatest single contribution to Indian ethical life was that he caused animal sacrifice to fall into disrepute and, eventually, to be abandoned. Even when Buddhism as an institutionalised religion virtually disappeared from the land of its birth, an abhorrence of the ritual slaughter of animals remained rooted, at least in the caste Hindu ethos, an eloquent silent testimony to Gotama's lasting influence.

Before looking more closely at the early teaching on *ahiṃsā* – and it is this teaching which underlies the repudiation of animal sacrifice – it is necessary to see this teaching in the context of the ethical doctrine as a whole. It is not difficult to do this since *ahiṃsā* forms the first of the "five precepts" (*pañca sīla*), which summarises the main tenets of the Buddha's teaching.

The Five Precepts are as follows:

(1) *Pāṇātipātā veramaṇī sikkhāpadam samādiyāmi*
   (I undertake the precept to abstain from the taking of life)
(2) *Adinnādānā v. s. s.*
   (I undertake . . . not to take that which is not given)

(3)   *Kāmesu micchācārā v. s. s.*
      (I undertake . . . to abstain from misconduct in sensual
      actions)
(4)   *Musāvādā v. s. s.*
      (I undertake . . . to abstain from false speech)
(5)   *Surā-meraya-majja-pamādaṭṭhānā v. s. s.*
      (I undertake . . . to abstain from liquor that causes
      intoxication and indolence)[72]

As Tachibana has observed, four of these five (the exception
being the fourth, abstinence from wrong speech) occur frequently
in Brahmanical literature,[73] and are often grouped together as
being the four deadly sins for a high-caste Hindu. The significant
differences are, first, that the Hindu customarily regarded ritual
sacrifice involving animal slaughter as a legitimate exception to
the prohibition of taking life, whereas Gotama regarded slaughter
sanctioned by religion as especially culpable and, second, that,
whereas the Hindu tended to believe that performance of ritual
would purify him from sin, Gotama taught that one is answerable
for one's actions; there is no possibility of divine cleansing by ritual
means.

As regards the fourth precept, Tachibana has this to say:

Ancient Brahmans, in spite of their love and reverence for the
truth . . . allowed people to tell lies under certain circumstances.
. . . I think the Buddha has never made any concession in
telling lies. Truth-speaking in the case of the Buddhist is
absolutely demanded.[74]

We shall have more to say about the special importance attached
by the Buddha to truth-speaking in the sixth chapter.

All Buddhists, laymen as well as monks, are expected to observe
the five precepts. Although in the *Sigālvāda Suttanta* (DB III 173ff)
– which has been aptly termed the "layman's vinaya" – the
deleterious effects of alcohol are stressed, there are passages where
the five precepts are in fact reduced to four, the fifth being the
one that is omitted.[75] Consistent with this tendency to regard the
fifth precept as of less importance than the other four is the passage
where Gotama declares a recently deceased layman, Sarakāni, a
"streamwinner" even though he is said to be one who "failed in
the training and took to drink" (KS V 324ff). On the other hand,

Gotama is also recorded as saying that a woman may go to purgatory for a breach of any of the five precepts (KS V 164f).

There is a refreshing tendency in the Nikāyas, in spite of their general adherence to the doctrine of karma, to seek to avoid a strictly legalistic attitude to morality. It is not the mere observance or breach of a given rule that matters so much as the inner state that is being cultivated. Thus the value of morality is to be measured by the degree to which it increases profitable states and vice versa – and it is conceded that a merely formal moral observance may have the opposite effect of actually encouraging unprofitable states (GS I 204). Similarly, the seriousness of the consequences of a breach of morality diminishes as one's own spiritual development increases; the same act which, for an impoverished soul, could spell disaster, might be, for a monk "of great soul", negligible in its effects (GS I 227ff).

There is steady opposition to the performance of meaningless (i.e. amoral) rituals by contemporary brahmins. When Gotama encounters a young man (again in the *Sigālvāda Suttanta*) who, intent on obeying his father's dying request, has set out to worship the six quarters (i.e. the four major directions, the nadir and the zenith), the Buddha immediately gives this practice an ethical as opposed to a merely geographical content (though of course a Hindu would argue that the *intention* of the practice was a kind of sanctification of space and, as such, not *merely* geographical). When the man turns East, he is to think of his parents; South, his teachers; West, his wife and children; North, his friends; the Nadir, his servants; the Zenith, the brahmins and ascetics of his acquaintance. In this way, a ritual which could be performed mechanically is transformed into a device for recalling and revering all the people whose lives impinge most closely on that of the performer of the ritual.

The Buddha is depicted as a constant critic of those who take it for granted that the performance of ritual will automatically ensure salvation. The vedic brahmins are "bound to rite and rule" and consequently nourish a "low ideal" which will never "win to the beyond" (KS I 39f cf 128f). Trust in good works or ceremonies counts as one of the three bonds, or fetters, in DB I 200, III 209; GS I 221, and is one of the five bonds in DB I 201, III 225; MLS II 102ff; KS V 48f; GS IV 98f, V 13. In the same way, grasping rite and ritual (*sīlabbat-upādānaṃ*) counts as one of the four harmful graspings in DB II 53, III 222; KS IV 171ff, 47ff, and "inverted judgement as to rule and ritual" (*sīlabbata-parāmāso kāya-gantho*) counts as one of the four knots in DB III 222 and KS V 48f. Those who practise animal sacrifice in the pathetic faith that it is a pathway to heaven will discover to their cost that it is in fact the gateway to punishment (GS III 216f).

One of the most telling stories on the subject of the need for inwardness and for depth of virtue is that of the lady who had acquired a great reputation for gentleness. Her servant decided to put this reputation to the test and made the sad discovery that, when sufficiently provoked, in the privacy of her home, her mistress became uncontrollably angry (MLS I 161ff). The need for sincerity and depth is further attested by the singling out of "earnestness" or "seriousness" (*appamāda*) as the chief virtue in GS III 259f and as the chief good state in GS V 16f.

We should not let this blind us to the fact that, although the need for inwardness rather than mechanical observance of external rites and rules does seem to have been a vital element of Gotama's teaching, there are other elements in the Nikāyas which tended in just the opposite direction. As we observed in the previous chapter, the preoccupation with acquiring merit and the belief that merit could be acquired by the mere mechanical offering of gifts to a worthy recipient, were highly detrimental to the sort of teaching outlined above, yet these beliefs and practices had canonical sanction.

Reverting to the five precepts, these were the basis, not only of the layman's life, but also of the Arahant's.[76] The only difference in the latter case is that the third precept is taken to mean not merely abstaining from misconduct in sexual actions but abstaining from sexual intercourse (described disparagingly as the "village practice") altogether. In addition to the five, three other precepts are enjoined on the candidate for perfection. He must have only one meal a day, abstain from frivolous shows and the use of scents and ornaments and, finally, avoid sleeping on high couches. The layman desiring to grow more deeply in Buddhist virtue could participate in all eight of these precepts on sabbath days when he attended the monastery.[77]

The five precepts are also firmly embedded in the Noble Eightfold Path, which constitutes the fourth of the Buddha's Noble Truths and, as such, is guaranteed a perpetual place in the very forefront of Buddhist piety.

The Path is regarded as covering the three aspects of the

Buddha's doctrine, the foundation of which is morality (*sīla*). The stages concerned with morality are the third (Right Word – *sammā vācā*), fourth (Right Act – *sammā kammanta*) and fifth (Right Livelihood – *sammā ājīvā*). Next comes the stages conducive to meditation (*samādhi*), which are sixth, seventh and eighth (inculcating right effort, mindfulness and meditation respectively) and, finally, the two stages conducive to wisdom (*paññā*) which are the first and second (concerned with right view and right intention respectively) (MLS I 362f).

So far as the moral stages of the Path are concerned, it is noteworthy that, once again, speech, alone of the precepts, is singled out for special mention. The other four precepts are regarded as being collectively covered by the fourth stage of the Path, the one concerned with right action or behaviour. It is also noteworthy that speech and action should be carried over into one's mode of work. One's means of livelihood should not infringe any of the precepts. Five types of trade are specifically listed as wrong: trading in (1) weapons (2) other human beings (3) flesh (4) alcohol and (5) poisons (GS III 151f). Many other means of livelihood would also make it very difficult to observe the precepts. This was not disguised and was in fact advanced as one of the reasons why the earnest Buddhist should abandon all means of livelihood save that of living on the generosity of those still too unadvanced in the Path to feel their lay professions to be a stumbling block.

It may seem surprising that there are no specific precepts directed against pride, jealousy, covetousness, gluttony and laziness.

The reason for the silence regarding gluttony was probably the fact that the monk's enforced abstention from solid food after noon was a constant reminder to all Buddhists of the need for restraint in this respect. Nevertheless there are passages, like KS IV 63f, which do stress the importance of watchfulness and moderation in eating.

In the case of pride, jealousy and covetousness, these would be regarded by Gotama as matters of right view rather than of right conduct, though one has to admit that there is an element of smug complacency about some aspects of Buddhist morality which seems to nourish pride rather than counteract it. An example would be the passage in GS I 190 which talks seriously about the solace of contemplating one's own virtue.

The real root of pride, as of jealousy and covetousness, is, according to Gotama, a delusive notion of selfhood. These three undesirable traits are manifestations of grasping (*taṇhā*) which is essentially what keeps us enchained to the wheel of *saṃsāra*.[78] Grasping requires a centre; it is the idea of an enduring ego which provides such a centre. Pride is a chronic kind of self-centredness; jealousy is the resentment arising from seeing in other selves qualities which belittle or threaten or humiliate oneself; covetousness is the grasping at the property of other selves and the desiring to appropriate it oneself. The cure for these and kindred states (the favourite Buddhist trilogy being: 1. lust or greed (*rāgo kiñcanaṃ*) 2. hate (*doso kiñcanaṃ*) and 3. illusion (*moho kiñcanaṃ*[79]) is to demolish the idea of selfhood. This is done by realising in depth the truth of *anattā* (selflessness), and this realisation belongs to the wisdom born of meditation rather than to the morality on which the meditation is based.

With regard to sloth or laziness, this again tends to be treated in the Canon not so much as a moral defect as an obstacle to spiritual progress. It is, for instance, the third of the commonly listed "five hindrances" – *thīna-middha*. But in this case, the defect is not born of wrong thinking; it is an impediment to the kind of meditative discipline which leads to right thinking. For this reason, it tends to be treated under the meditative aspect of the teaching. Two of the seven factors of enlightenment, the third, energy (*viriyo-sambojjhaṅga*), and fourth, zest (*pīti-sambojjhaṅga*), are specific antidotes to laziness.[80] Along the same lines are the rather amusing "eight bases of slackness": one jibs at the effort of meditating either because it will make one tired or because one is tired already, is too hungry or too full, fears one will become ill or pleads that one is convalescing, etc.[81] The need for energy in the one who aspires to proficiency in meditation is stressed in many of the lists – the "five factors in spiritual wrestling",[82] the most commonly recurring of the lists of "five faculties",[83] the "seven powers",[84] etc. Also, it should be noted that cultivation of right effort (*vāyāma*) in the Eightfold Path – another antidote to laziness – is classed by the Canon as belonging to the group of stages conducive to meditation.[85]

So much then for the general content and context of the ethical teaching found in the Nikāyas. It is time now to look more closely at the aspect of this teaching which is the special concern of this chapter – the doctrine of *ahiṃsā* (not harming).

We have already seen that this doctrine was especially directed against animal sacrifice and was in fact largely successful in eradicating this practice.

The vow not to take life was the first of the five precepts. It was also the first provision of "the householder's *dhamma*" outlined in MLS I 343ff. Here, the teaching is ordered according to another very common tripartite arrangement, that of body, speech and thought, and can be summarized as follows:

BODY – no: 1. killing, 2. stealing, 3. illicit sex.
SPEECH – no: 1. lying, 2. slander, 3. harsh talk, 4. frivolous talk.
THOUGHT – no: 1. coveting, 2. malevolence, 3. wrong views.

It will be seen that the three bodily prohibitions correspond to the first three precepts; that the four prohibitions relating to speech are all an elaboration of the fourth precept; that the fifth precept is here again omitted; that the prohibitions under thought (the favourite trilogy of *rāga*, *dosa* and *moha* again), are not included in the five precepts at all because they are classed under right view rather than right conduct – confirming what we said with regard to them earlier in this chapter.

Something very important for an understanding of Buddhist ethical teaching now emerges. If we look at the arrangement of the householder's *dhamma* in MLS I 343ff, we see that it has something in common with the frequently repeated formula relating to the three "bodies of doctrine".[86] Let us set them out, one below the other, thus:

(a)	BODY	SPEECH	THOUGHT
(b)	MORALITY	MEDITATION	WISDOM

We have already seen that, when the Eightfold Path was classified under scheme (b) (in MLS I 362f), right speech was grouped, along with right action, under morality. Thus in classification (b), what comes in the second column of classification (a) is absorbed into the first column, leaving the second column of classification (b) free for the new ingredient, meditation. If we look at columns one and three, we see that they correspond very closely and are in the same sequence in their respective trilogies. It should also be noted that the division into body, speech and thought (in that order) occurs very frequently elsewhere in the Nikāyas.[87]

What is important, and I am not aware that this has been noticed before, is that the Buddhist order reverses the order with which we in the West are familiar. We normally talk of thought, word and deed; the Buddhist normally talks of deed, word and thought. It is not merely a matter of conventional ordering but of differing assumptions about the causal interrelationship within the trilogy. If we take the householder's *dhamma* as an example, and if we concentrate on the concept of *ahiṃsā*, where a Westerner would say, "root out hatred, and you will put an end to killing", the Buddhist says, "root out killing, and you will put an end to hatred". We have tended to assume that the thought is father to the deed, whereas the Buddhist tends to assume – and this is precisely why he makes morality the foundation rather than the fruit of the Path – that the deed is father to the thought. The interesting reflection to which this gives rise is that modern behavioural psychology, as far as I am conversant with it, seems to favour the Buddhist rather than the traditional Western causal sequence.

However that may be, it is very important to realise that, for Gotama (and, I suspect, the Indian tradition generally), the essential thing is to cultivate the right habits of conduct first; the right meditative and cognitive attitudes will follow. It is useless to attempt to cultivate the right habits of meditation and thought if one's habitual mode of behaviour is incompatible with these desired habits. Thus, where *ahiṃsā* is concerned, one should avoid, so far as is humanly possible, the killing or maiming of any sentient being. If this is one's practice, then the right dispositions of a "friendly mind" (*mettā*) and "compassion" (*karuṇā*) for all creatures can be cultivated. If, on the other hand, one's livelihood is dependent on hunting or fishing or trading in flesh, the right mental dispositions will prove elusive.

Regarding the rigour with which the principle of *ahiṃsā* is observed, Gotama adheres to his policy of adopting the middle way. Others in India, notably the Jains, have gone to much greater lengths to avoid killing or harming other creatures. They have swept the ground in front of them to avoid treading on ants and similar insects and worn a mask over their face to avoid inhaling living organisms. The Buddhist monk was not expected to go to these lengths – although one of his eight possessions was a water strainer, intended, rather naively, to prevent his swallowing living beings when he drank. However, he was not even expected to be a strict vegetarian. He incurred guilt if an animal was slain, with his knowledge, specifically to feed him, but otherwise, he was free to eat whatever was offered to him. This was a fairly radical departure from the normal practice of caste Hindus.

The Buddhist attitude seems to have been that, if guilt and demerit were incurred in slaughtering animals for food, the guilt attached to those who prepared the meal, not necessarily to those who ate it. So far as the sensibilities of caste Hindus were concerned, they should reform their attitude to the ritual slaughter of animals before being too fastidious about the "innocent" (i.e. unintentioned) eating of animal food.

(b) THE JĀTAKAS

We should not expect the Jātaka stories to attempt any systematic or comprehensive ethical teaching, though we should expect them to be, like folk tales in general, moralistic in tone. Many of the stories include references to the five precepts.

There is one, somewhat exceptional, story which has clearly been built around the five precepts. This is JS 459. It is in reality five separate stories which have, in a very contrived manner, been brought together by the device of making the hero of each story resolve to become a paccekabuddha.[88] Sure enough, these five paccekabuddhas eventually meet each other and together meet the bodhisatta, who at this time is king of Benares. The king asks each of the paccekabuddhas why he decided to embark on the ascetic life. It turns out that they have all been stricken with remorse after committing a sin; one has stolen, one has been the victim of lust, another has lied, one has permitted animals to be killed "to make offering to the Goblins", whilst the last has condoned a drinking festival at which many were eventually injured. In other words, they have each violated one of the five precepts – though at least not in quite the canonical order. Yet even here, it is only the first precept which has been rearranged; the others follow the canonical sequence.

On the other hand, in JS 468, we encounter a virtuous king (the bodhisatta) who, though we are told that "he kept the five virtues", preaches a sermon for the edification of his subjects which embodies ten virtues. Three of these virtues are familiar: they are 3. honesty, 4. respect for life and 5. sexual purity. These correspond to precepts 4, 1, and 3 respectively. Precepts 2 and 5, abstaining from theft and from intoxicants, are not mentioned. The remaining seven virtues in the bodhisatta's sermon are as follows: 1. acquiring wealth 2. acquiring learning 6. giving generously 7. caring for aged parents 8. honouring teachers 9. honouring ascetics and 10. practising austerity.

It is interesting that the three virtues alluding to the five precepts are mentioned consecutively, but not in the canonical order. It is also interesting that the remaining seven virtues seem to be echoing the *Sigālavāda Suttanta*, where the importance of acquiring wealth is implied by the large section warning against the "six channels for dissipating wealth" and all the remaining virtues are implied in the "Aryan" method of worshipping the six quarters, i.e. honouring and caring for one's parents, teachers and the ascetics one encounters, etc.[89]

These two stories, then, show quite disparate attitudes towards the ethical teaching of the Canon; the one follows it slavishly in a group of stories which are all highly contrived whilst the other is much more relaxed, simply recalling unsystematically what seem to the narrator to be the more important tenets of the ethical code. Even in the latter case, there is hardly a story as such. The whole *raison d'être* of this particular Jātaka is to "declare the Law" or, in other words, to give moral instruction.

JS 31, on the other hand, is very much a story in its own right, although the keeping of the "Five Commandments" plays an important part in it at a number of points. When explaining what these involve, the leader (the bodhisatta) of a band of workmen says, "not a man among . . . us destroys life, or takes what is not given, or misconducts himself or lies; we drink no strong drink; we abound in loving kindness; we show charity; we level the roads, dig tanks and build a public hall". Here, five positive qualities match the five abstentions. Later in the same story, the bodhisatta is also said to keep seven injunctions: 1. to cherish his mother and 2. father, 3. to honour his elders, 4. speak the truth, 5. avoid harsh speech, 6. eschew slander and 7. shun niggardliness. Three of these seven, it will be noticed, are concerned with right speech. Later still in this story, the bodhisatta (now Sakka) expels the Asuras from the realm of the thirty-three by making them drunk but, when pursued by the Asuras, who are bent on revenge, he stops his chariot to avoid mowing down trees and thus depriving young Garuḷas of their homes. "Let us not", he says, "for empire's sake, so act as to destroy life. Rather will I, for their sake, give my life as a sacrifice to the Asuras". Towards the end of this tale, Sakka meets a woman who, for lack of merit, has been reborn as a crane; he exhorts her to keep the "Five Commandments". To test the crane, he appears as a fish. When the crane, thinking the fish dead, takes it in its mouth, the fish wriggles and the crane releases it. For being thus virtuous, she is reborn in a potter's family and is rewarded with a cartload of golden cucumbers which Sakka, disguised as an old man, says he will give to anybody who keeps the Commandments. She is the only person who even understands what he means.

In JS 483, we learn of a king who goes in search of a stag (the bodhisatta) which has eluded his arrows. In the chase, the king falls headlong into a water-logged pit but is saved from drowning by his former quarry. Having rescued him, the stag "admonished the king and established him in the Five Virtues". The king becomes such a benign influence that many of his subjects attain to heaven. Sakka, in order to "declare the goodness of mercy and the Five Virtues", decides to put the king's virtue to the test by bribing him heavily – but unsuccessfully – to kill the stag.

In this case the five precepts are twice mentioned but never enumerated and, on the second occasion, are linked with mercy. There is a real story and the ethical content is subordinate to the story. Though the five precepts are mentioned, the one that is emphasised is the first, abstaining from killing.

The final example of a Jātaka relating to the five precepts is JS 512. This is really concerned with the otherwise somewhat neglected fifth precept, abstention from intoxicants. By an accidental natural process, fermentation takes place in some water beneath a tree. Birds, coming for a drink, become stupefied, then merry. A passing forester emulates them – and so on – until, by a chain reaction, the king himself acquires a taste for alcohol. Sakka (the bodhisatta) is afraid that if the king becomes addicted to strong drink, "all India will perish". He comes to the king disguised as a brahmin and preaches a long sermon on the evils of drink, whereupon the king breaks the drinking vessels, undertakes to keep the precepts, gives alms and goes to heaven. "But", the story mournfully concludes, "the drinking of strong drink gradually developed in India."

Here again we have a genuine story. It is told to demonstrate the wisdom of one specific precept. Yet it manages very unobtrusively to put the homily against alcohol in the context of canonical ethical teaching by referring at the end to the king's undertaking to keep the precepts.

There is another "story" which consists simply of telling how a precocious child came to the bodhisatta to enquire about the paths leading to spiritual welfare; in the Introduction, the same child, in a later birth, has come to the Buddha to ask the same question. The answer is given in the stanza:

> Seek Health, the supreme good; be virtuous;
> Hearken to elders; from the scriptures learn;
> Conform to Truth; and burst Attachment's bonds.
> – For chiefly these six Paths to Welfare lead.   (JS 84)

I know of no other occasion in Buddhist literature where just these six injunctions occur together, neither do I know of another occasion where health is classified as "the supreme good", though there are many occasions where good health is classified as one of the requisites for meditation and spiritual progress.[90] Here, the injunction to be virtuous is simply one of the six paths and is not spelled out in further detail. There is no mention of practising meditation. All in all, this seems to be an instance of folk wisdom which, because it coincides quite well with Buddhist ethical teaching, has been adopted into the Jātaka. Much closer to the five precepts are the "four virtues" of JS 220. These are defined as 1. not envying, 2. not drinking, 3. having no strong desire and 4. not being angry.

The introduction to JS 56 tells an engaging story about a monk who, though anxious to succeed, became quite nonplussed by the amount and complexity of the moral teaching he was given. "There is a tremendous lot of this Morality", he thinks to himself and is on the point of returning to the simplicities of lay life when Gotama, learning of the problem, tells him that he need concern himself with no more than three rules: guarding voice, mind and body so that he does no evil in word, thought or act. The Brother stays in the monastery and soon becomes an Arahant.

We have observed already, in discussing the teaching of the Nikāyas, that this triple division of moral teaching is very common. The order is interesting, however. Instead of the typical Buddhist order (body, speech, thought) or the typical Western order (thought, word, deed), here we have priority given to speech. This is unusual, but it does reflect a typically Buddhist attitude to right speech as being of paramount importance. Putting mind second and body third, however, is not only very unusual; it is quite unBuddhist. An interesting comparison is afforded by a passage in GS I 210 where the Buddha comes to the aid of a monk, who "cannot stand" the "more than 150 rules" he has been taught, by telling him that he need remember only three things; but in this case the three are the higher morality, thought and insight (*adhisīlaṃ, adhi cittaṃ* and *adhipaññaṃ*). This is the traditional triology (b), but with the substitution of "thought" (*cittaṃ*) for the more familiar "meditation" (*samādhi*).

At least forty of the Jātaka stories are concerned specifically with the doctrine of *ahiṃsā*. This is not surprising in view of the central emphasis which this doctrine unquestionably has in the ethical teaching of the Nikāyas. From many points of view, the most interesting set of stories within this group is the one which depicts the bodhisatta himself as being, in one way or another, involved in killing or injuring. The stories concerned are JSS 93, 128, 129, 152, 178, 233, 238, 246, 315, 319, 384.

The first of these (JS 93) is a very hard-hearted little tale about a wealthy merchant (the bodhisatta) who is annoyed by his herdsman's report that the cows are giving very little milk because they are afraid of a lion, which has taken to prowling in the vicinity. Learning that this lion has taken a liking for a doe, the merchant orders the doe to be smeared with poison so that, when the lion, in his fondness for the doe, comes to lick her, he will die. "Affection for others should be eschewed", says the merchant when he hears of the success of his scheme; "mark how ... the king of beasts ... was led by sinful love for a doe to poison himself". The stanza goes a step further in nastiness by pointing the moral that "trust kills".

It is noticeable that the merchant is absolved of responsibility for the lion's death; it was the lion's sinful love which led him "to poison himself". Nevertheless, in procuring poison and instructing his herdsman to use it, the merchant has infringed the ban on the traffic in poisons found in GS III 151f. The least likeable aspect of this story is that, in its anxiety to preach the folly and danger of attachment and affection, it cheerfully sets aside the principle of *ahiṃsā*. The fact that the lion has violated the "law of the species" in liking a doe rather than a lioness provides an excuse for this harshness – though the strictures of the merchant afterwards would apply to any form of trust or affection.

Two other stories (JSS 152, 178) should be linked with this one. In JS 152, there is a much more blatant breach of the "law of the species"; a jackal has the effrontery to fall in love with the queen of the lions – who nearly dies of shame: "this jackal here is mean amongst beasts, vile, and like a man of low caste. . . . How can I live after hearing such things said?" The enormity of the jackal's behaviour serves to justify the bodhisatta (a lion now) when he kills the jackal later in the story. Again the killing is indirect so that it could be said that the jackal had killed himself.

In JS 178, the bodhisatta is a potter who inadvertently, whilst digging for clay, breaks the shell of a tortoise, which subsequently dies. The tortoise has clung so passionately to its native lake that it missed its opportunity to swim with its mates into the river whilst there was still time to do this. Now the lake has dried out and home has become a grave. Again the moral drawn is the folly and danger of attachment, though in this case the story is much less hard-hearted than JS 93 and the bodhisatta is quite innocent of any intention to kill.

Another group of these stories which involve the bodhisatta in killing is really attempting to come to terms with the harsh, predatorial realities of the natural world. In JS 233, for instance, the bodhisatta is a benign king given to feeding fish. When a crocodile preys on the fish as they are feeding, the king orders the crocodile to be harpooned and captured – he does not order it killed. The crocodile is harpooned, is "mad with pain" and does in fact die. The stanza says in effect that this is the fate of anybody "who knows no law but his own will and wish".

One wonders whether this story might not have caused some uneasy questioning in the minds of at least some of its hearers. Is it reasonable to expect a crocodile to obey a higher law than that of its own will and wish? If the killing of the crocodile was justified by its having preyed on the fish, would not the crocodile have been justified in its habits if some of the fish it devoured had themselves preyed on smaller fish? Does killing in any case justify killing?

There is a somewhat similar situation in JS 384, where the bodhisatta is born as king of the birds. A wicked crow has come to his flock and, posing as a "holy person" who is in the habit of standing on one leg and eating only the wind, gains employment as egg-watcher and baby-minder to the flock. As soon as the coast is clear, the crow has a huge meal of eggs and birdlings. When the king-bird is sure of the culprit, he has him executed. The problems are much the same – except that the crow's posing as an ascetic introduces a fictitious element of guilt into the situation. Virtually the same story is told in JS 128, only this time the bodhisatta was king of the rats and the predator posing as ascetic was a jackal. When the rat-king discovered the jackal's guilt, he "sprang at the jackal's throat and bit his windpipe asunder just under the jaw, so that he died". Here, for the first time, the killing is done solely and unequivocally by the bodhisatta himself. JS 129 is again the same story, bodhisatta and predator-ascetic being rat-king and jackal respectively. This time, however, the jackal is burned almost bald in a forest fire. Looking at his reflection whilst drinking, the jackal notices that the bit of hair still left to him resembles a top-knot. Thinking to himself, "at least I've got wherewithal to go to market", he goes to the rats' cave and passes himself off as a votary of the Fire-God, with the familiar sequel, except that in this case we are told nothing about the fate of the jackal.

Two other stories should be mentioned in this connection, although they take us for a moment away from the group in which the bodhisatta is himself implicated. Both hinge on the same theme – that of the predator who is himself killed – but both are vivid stories in their own right. In one of them, JS 397, the bodhisatta is a lion whose son falls in with a jackal (Devadatta). The jackal persuades the lion's son to hunt and kill horses, even though horses enjoy royal protection and even though his father has warned him not to listen to the jackal. The young lion persists in hunting horses and is eventually shot and killed, whilst the jackal slinks away from his dying "friend". In the other, JS 438, the bodhisatta is a partridge who learns to recite the whole of the three Vedas from a learned brahmin. After the brahmin's death, the partridge continues to instruct the deceased teacher's disciples. All goes well until a wicked ascetic (Devadatta again, but this time with a prodigious appetite) kills and eats, all in one day, two young lizards, the partridge, a cow and its calf. A little later a lion and tiger go to visit their friend, the partridge, but find its cage empty and its feathers and other tell-tale remnants of that fateful day. Questioned by the tiger, the ascetic denies that he killed the partridge but, questioned later by the lion, he admits his guilt. When he tells the truth the tiger wants to release him but the lion insists that he be executed.

In the first of these stories, it is not *ahiṃsā* as such that is defended since the lion's son has been preying on other animals without censure before it turned to horses; it seems to be going beyond the natural bounds and cultivating forbidden tastes (as well as listening to bad advisers) that constitutes the crime. In the second, it is interesting that the telling of a lie greatly compounds the heinous offence of the wicked ascetic whereas, at least in the eyes of the tiger, telling the truth exonerated him. The lion seems to be upholding the law of karma. The crime must be punished; the virtue of truth-telling will doubtless bear its fruit in a future birth.

Reverting to the group implicating the bodhisatta, three stories relate to the guilt attaching to eating animal flesh. In JS 246, the bodhisatta is a brahmin ascetic. A wealthy man serves the ascetic with a fish meal and, when he has eaten, says, "This food was prepared on purpose for you, by killing living creatures. Not upon my head is this wrong, but upon yours!" The bodhisatta replies that if a wicked man serves the flesh of his own child to a holy man who is quite ignorant of what is going on, the latter is quite innocent of guilt.[91]

In JS 315, the bodhisatta, now the son of a wealthy merchant, obtains more venison from a deer-stalker than any of his three rivals because he uses terms of greater endearment in asking for it. Having thus befriended the deerstalker and his family, he settles them on an estate of their own and thus succeeds in taking the man away from "his cruel occupation". Here, it seems, the bodhisatta does not scruple to eat large quantities of meat if, by so doing, he can befriend and convert a hunter.

In JS 319, the bodhisatta, as a brahmin ascetic, gives pastoral advice to a partridge who has been trained by a fowler to act as a decoy to other partridges, who are then killed. The partridge tries keeping silent in its cage, but the fowler strikes him and the resulting cry of pain still lures other birds to their death. Troubled in conscience, the partridge asks the ascetic if it incurs guilt for involuntarily acting as decoy. It gets the reply, "He who plays a passive part from all guilt is counted free". Although the bodhisatta is not directly involved in the dilemma in this case, the advice he gives is so similar to the verdict given in JS 246 that I have included the story here.

The last of the stories implicating the bodhisatta, JS 238, is of rather a different order. The story is minimal. The bodhisatta, a rich merchant, is asked by his son to sum up the best means of gaining one's ends in a single word. The merchant replies that the one word is skill, though virtue and patience need to be added. If these three qualities are cultivated, he tells his son, "you will do good to friends and to your foes do ill". To employ skill to bring harm to one's foes is hardly consistent with *ahiṃsā*; this is a clear case of the bodhisatta's being made to speak out of character.

In sharp contrast is JS 371 where, in the person of Prince Dīghāvu, the bodhisatta refuses to slay the king who slew both his own parents, although he has an admirable opportunity to do so. The stanza here ends with a sentiment which is in striking contrast to that in the story we have just considered. Here we read:

> Not hate, but love alone makes hate to cease:
> This is the everlasting law of peace.

We have already considered some stories which touch on the theme of hunting. There is a little group of stories which has as its common theme the outsmarting of the hunter by a would-be prey that gets away. Thus, in JS 21, Devadatta is a hunter who traps and kills deer by building a platform in a fruit tree; the bodhisatta (an antelope) eludes capture by cleverly detecting the trap; in JS 38, a crab suspecting that a crane which pretends to be carrying fish away to a better pond is really eating them, and thinking, when the crane offers to transport him to this better pond, that it has similar designs on itself, declines to be carried in the crane's beak (the fish's undoing!), but clings to its neck with its claws instead. As soon as the crab's suspicions have been confirmed, the unsuspecting crane has its head pinched off by its wily "prey"; in JS 138, and again in JS 325, a lizard (the bodhisatta in both cases) escapes death at the hands of a false ascetic who has acquired a taste for lizard flesh; JS 277 is substantially the same story except that, in this case, the bodhisatta is a pigeon; in JS 142, a jackal (the bodhisatta) rumbles the plan of a drunken rogue who has feigned death but is really lying in wait with a club in his hand; by his shrewdness the jackal escapes. Two almost identical stories (JSS 249, 365) tell of a snake charmer who loses his performing monkey on account of his ill treatment of it.

All of these tales follow a very similar pattern. The prey, or, in the last case, the badly treated monkey, becomes the hero of the story and the hunter, normally thought of as extremely cunning and crafty, is made to look somewhat ridiculous. In all these stories, the hearer's sympathies will be entirely with the prey and entirely against the hunter. It would be difficult for a man to hear one of these tales approvingly and then go off on a hunting expedition without qualms of conscience.

In one story, JS 222, Devadatta excels himself in villainy. In the role of hunter, he comes across a thin, blind, old she-monkey (the mother of the bodhisatta and his brother, who are both in hiding nearby). When the bodhisatta sees that the hunter is bent on shooting his mother, he comes out of hiding and allows himself to be shot instead. Having killed the bodhisatta, the hunter again takes aim at the mother and this time the brother reveals himself and is shot. Not satisfied, the hunter still kills the mother-monkey. As the hunter is going home he learns that his family and house have been wiped out by a thunderbolt. He drops the pole on which he has been carrying the three dead monkeys, strips off his clothes and rushes naked into his ruined home, to be struck dead by a falling beam. To complete the melodrama, the earth now opens up and the familiar flames engulf the hapless villain. This story would doubtless enjoy enormous popularity but one doubts if it would be as effective in propagating the doctrine of *ahiṃsā* as the previous stories because the hunter of this story is so much more villainous than hunters normally are; hunters in the audience would be unlikely to identify with him.

There is another fairly large group of tales which all contain more or less explicit teaching or preaching on the theme of *ahiṃsā*. This group includes JSS 18, 19, 22, 50, 140, 276, 314, 347, 385, 418, 433, 482, 501, 502, 537, 542 and 543 (VIII).

Within this group there are seven stories which have to do with the ritual sacrifice of animals. JS 50 is a delightfully witty account of how the bodhisatta, having become viceroy to his father, King Brahmadatta of Benares, and having been repelled by the wide-spread practice of slaughtering "sheep, goats, poultry, swine and other living creatures" at popular festivals to gods, himself pretends to go regularly to worship the fairy inhabiting a certain banyan-tree. When he becomes king, he discloses to his ministers that he had vowed to the god of the tree that, if by its help he became king, he in return would offer to the god a sacrifice consisting of a thousand people "addicted to the Five Sins, to wit the slaughter of living creatures and so forth". Not surprisingly, the king is unable to find a single victim for his sacrifice since "not a soul persisted in the old wickedness". This might almost be termed a homoeopathic remedy – or threatened remedy – for the disease.

In JS 314, the king has been alarmed by hearing "four sounds uttered by four beings who dwelt in Hell". His brahmin advisers want to offer a huge animal sacrifice to avert the dangers which these cries might threaten. The bodhisatta, a brahmin ascetic, manages to get the sacrifice called off by interpreting the cries in a way which convinces the king that he is in no danger. Substantially the same story, though somewhat elaborated, recurs in JS 418, where it is specifically said that animal sacrifice "will cause rebirth in hell".

In JS 347, the bodhisatta, now King of Benares, issues a decree putting an end to the hitherto popular practice of sacrificing animals. The Yakkhas, "enraged against the Bodhisatta at losing their offerings", try to get the king murdered, but are unable to do so because he enjoys Sakka's protection. In this story, the battle for *ahiṃsā* becomes a mythological battle between the gods and the Yakkhas. It seems to imply that real powers are in fact placated by the sacrifice of animals, but these powers are inferior to the gods – and the gods endorse *ahiṃsā*.

In JS 433, the gods appear in rather a different light. Here we find that the bodhisatta has become a brahmin ascetic of such awe-inspiring virtue that Sakka feels threatened. Unless he can seduce the ascetic from his virtue, he fears that he will usurp his throne. So Sakka goes to the king, a former friend of the bodhisatta's, and asks him to send for the ascetic and command him to preside over an animal sacrifice. The bodhisatta declines to have anything to do with "this cruelty". Sakka now tells the king to send his beautiful daughter to the ascetic with the message that, if he does the sacrifice, she will be his wife. "Losing his moral sense", the bodhisatta, trembling "with the power of passion" agrees at last to the king's request – in spite of some popular protest at such a betrayal of his ascetic vows. It is only when the royal elephant lets out a piteous cry as the ascetic's sword is poised for slaughter that the bodhisatta is recalled to his true vocation. He realises that it is his lust that has made him willing to be cruel, renounces all lusts, preaches to the king and returns to his ascetical abode.

Section VIII of JS 543 contains a very spirited sermon by the bodhisatta against vedic animal sacrifice. Since this is in the context of a general critique of the caste system, and especially of the claims of the brahmins, it will be looked at more closely in chapter six.

The last story in this sub-group, JS 542, involves human as well as animal sacrifice. A king dreams of heaven and, enchanted by its memory, asks his priest how he can be assured of getting there. His priest (Devadatta) has conceived an insane jealousy against the king's son, and it is this which motivates his answer. A delightful note informs us that the king's question ought to have been put to a bodhisatta, not to Devadatta; the situation is compared to that of man who, having lost his way for a week, seeks direction from one who had been lost for a fortnight! However, "the king had little religious insight". The answer he gets is that the way to heaven is to offer a sacrifice comprising his sons, his queens, his merchant princes and his choicest elephants and horses. "And thus, being asked the road to heaven . . . he (the priest) declared the road to hell". It is only the Queen's "act of truth", resulting in Sakka's intervention, which prevents the slaughter.

Two other stories in the main group are concerned with justice rather than with *ahiṃsā*, though the latter principle is involved. In both cases (JSS 22, 140), the bodhisatta persuades the king to revoke an edict involving the wholesale slaughter of dogs (JS 22) or crows (JS 140) on the ground that it is not just to slay a whole species for an inconvenience caused by just a few members of that species.

Of the remaining stories concerned with animal slaughter, most are content simply to preach the doctrine of *ahiṃsā*. Such is the case with JSS 19, 385, 482, 501, 502. In each case this preaching causes penitence in the hearer and the resolve to abjure violence and killing.

JS 276 affords an example of great scrupulosity in the observance of *ahiṃsā*. A king shoots arrows to the four quarters. He sees where three land but fears that the fourth, which fell in water, might have killed a fish.[92]

The two remaining stories call for special comment. In JS 18, we read of a goat which, whilst being prepared for sacrificial slaughter by a brahmin, alternately laughs and cries. Asked why it does so, it tells the brahmin that it laughs because it knows that this is the last of five hundred births in which it has had to have its head cut off. This is a punishment for having, as a brahmin, five hundred births previously, cut off a goat's head in sacrifice; it weeps because it knows that this brahmin will have to suffer the same fate. The brahmin hastens to assure the goat that he has changed his mind about the sacrifice. The goat is set free but, that very day, whilst stretching its neck to feed from a bush, its head is struck off by a thunderbolt.

Two things are noteworthy here. First, the fact that the victim has been a sacrificer and the sacrificer, if he persists, is doomed to become a victim. This is an example of the way in which the doctrine of rebirth powerfully reinforces the doctrine of *ahiṃsā*. A man who is cruel, even to the lowliest of creatures, can expect that he himself will be reborn as that same lowly creature and have to suffer that same cruelty. Second, the fact that the goat loses its head anyway. The law of karma cannot be cheated, but woe betide the man who, even when he is the instrument of karmic necessity, violates the principle of *ahiṃsā*.

Finally in this group, JS 537 tells the lurid story of a king who accidentally tastes human flesh. The taste immediately "sent a thrill through the seven thousand nerves of taste" because the king in question happened to have been a yakkha, fond of human flesh, in his immediately preceding birth. The king is able to satisfy his rekindled cannibalistic taste by secretly eating the flesh of condemned criminals. When these run out, he instructs his cook to kill at random and secretly steal human flesh for the royal table. The story then becomes extremely ramified. When the truth about the king's eating habits leaks out, his commander-in-chief tries to dissuade him from persisting in cannibalism by telling a number of cautionary stories. He fails and the king is eventually banished. However, the banished king, armed with a spell, becomes more fearsome and voracious than ever. Sakka is asked to intervene and convert this monster. He says that this is beyond his power; there is only one man (the bodhisatta) who is able to convert the man-eater. It so happens that the bodhisatta, who is now King Sutasoma, had been friendly with the man-eater when the two of them had been student princes together. He comes to the man-eater but, in spite of their erstwhile friendship, the man-eater resolves to capture and eat him too. He accedes, however, to Sutasoma's request to be allowed, before he dies, to go to learn four verses which have been taught to a brahmin by the Buddha Kassapa himself. When Sutasoma keeps his promise to return, the man-eater is so awed that he spares his life and offers him four boons if he will pass on the mysterious four verses. The fourth boon for which Sutasoma asks is that the man-eater renounce his cannibalism. After a great struggle, he finally agrees to do so and is finally, with the bodhisatta's help, restored to his kingdom.

Even that rather convoluted summary gives little idea of the true complexity of this story. All sorts of themes enter into it and it is, of course, heavily overlaid with mythological elements. The most striking thing about it is that, although there is much preaching of *ahiṃsā* in the effort to convert the man-eater, the dominant interest is in the fate of the man-eater himself. When he does finally surrender his cannibalism, he is restored to his kingdom. In view of the law of karma, and in view of the extent and seriousness of the man-eater's crimes, this might seem to be a genuine miscarriage of justice. However the man-eater is always depicted as the slave of his appetites – rather like an alcoholic who does not so much will to drink as feel driven to it. The obsessive nature of his crime, which has a karmic cause, requires a process of behavioural therapy before moral instruction can be usefully imparted. Once the craving has been overcome, the will, which never was intentionally wicked, is set free to revert to the practice of normal morality. Throughout the story, the bodhisatta exhibits a spirit of sacrificial concern for others which seems much closer to Mahāyāna in its ethos than to Theravāda. This is particularly evident when, having converted the man-eater, he tells him to cut down some potential victims, all kings, he has strung up by their hands,

and the man-eater took his sword and severed the bonds of one of the kings, and as this king had been fasting for seven days and was maddened with pain . . . he fell on the ground, and the Great Being on seeing this was moved with compassion and said, "My man-eating friend, do not cut them down like this", and taking hold of a king firmly with both hands he clasped him to his breast and said, "Now cut his bonds" . . . and letting him down tenderly as though it were his own son [he] laid him flat upon the ground. Thus did he lay all on the ground, and after bathing their wounds he gently pulled the cords from their hands, just as it were a string from a child's ear, and washing off the clotted blood he rendered the wounds harmless.

It is very probable that this story has been much influenced by Mahāyānist ideas. Certainly, in the Mahāyānist collection of birth stories, the *Jātakamālā*, where a shorter version of this story occurs as number 31,[93] the qualities of loving compassion and redemptive concern of the bodhisatta – the qualities we tend to associate especially with the Mahāyāna – are not emphasised any more strongly than they are here. It is equally certain that we have passed well beyond the mere preaching of a principle; we have entered the world in which redemption, restoration, caring help have become much more important than the operations of the law of karma. It is important to notice this because it means that here in these stories, which have exerted far more popular influence in Theravāda cultures than has the canon itself, ideas are conveyed which never occur within the Nikāyas. By being thus conveyed, the difference between Theravāda and Mahāyāna at the popular level has been very much reduced.

Somewhat akin to this story, though at a less developed level, is JS 316, where Sakka, disguised as brahmin, comes to ask the bodhisatta, in the form of a hare, for food. The hare promptly offers his own body to be cooked and eaten rather than allow the brahmin to "break the moral law by taking animal life"; before running into the flames, the hare "thrice shook himself that if there were any insects within his coat, they might escape death". The flames have in fact been conjured up by Sakka and are quite unable to harm the bodhisatta or his parasites, but again, we see an almost Mahāyānist passion for self-sacrifice in this story.

In closing this chapter, brief mention should be made of a story which shows another side of the doctrine of *ahiṃsā*, and also another aspect of Mahāyānist influence. In this story (JS 288), the bodhisatta is with his brother on the banks of the Ganges. They each eat, but the bodhisatta throws a part of his meal into the river to feed the fish, "giving the merit to the river-spirit". The river-spirit enjoys an increase of divine power as a result of this donated merit and is so grateful that she later recovers the bodhisatta's inheritance for him after his brother has tried to cheat him of it.

Here it is the positive aspect of *ahiṃsā* that is stressed; not merely not harming but actually helping and caring for other beings. Also, there is mention of merit-sharing, a practice which is virtually unmentioned in the Four Nikāyas, but which was a popular feature of Mahāyānist piety and came, through the influence of Jātakas such as this one, to be a common feature of popular Theravāda practice.

5 *Sex and Marriage: Love and Friendship*

(A) THE FOUR NIKĀYAS

Anybody who has studied the Nikāyas will feel compelled to admit that they exhibit an overwhelming antipathy to each of the four words in the title of this chapter. That is not to deny that one reads a good deal about love (*mettā*) and compassion (*karuṇā*). When these words are used, however, it is always made quite clear that these dispositions should be general and undiscriminating; they should be free of the kind of attachment which characterises friendship and marriage.

A passage sometimes quoted in refutation of what has just been said is the following dialogue between King Pasenadi and Gotama. Pasenadi says that Ānanda has said to him:

> About the half, lord, of this life in religion consists in righteous friendship, righteous intimacy, righteous association.

Gotama replies:

> To Ānanda saying this, sire, I replied: "Not so, Ānanda! . . . Verily the whole of this life in religion consists in righteous friendship, etc".[94]

Unfortunately, Buddhism has suffered probably more than any other major religion from quotations wrested from their context in such a way as to give an entirely misleading impression. If the quotation stops here (as it does, albeit in a less ambiguous translation, in Saddhatissa, 1970, pp. 170f; Humphries, 1960 p. 91) one would naturally assume that the Buddha is talking about friendship in the ordinary sense. In fact, he is talking about the opposite, as he makes perfectly clear in the paragraph which follows the one just quoted:

Gotama goes on, "And how, Ānanda, does a bhikkhu who is a friend, an intimate, an associate of that which is righteous, expand the Ariyan eightfold path? He is taught, Ānanda, to develop right views based on detachment, based on passionlessness, . . . etc." (KS I 113).

In other words, the Buddha is not talking about righteous friendship in the personal sense at all; he is talking about friendship with that which is righteous, i.e. the doctrine of detachment, passionlessness, etc. Lest we should be in any doubt that these doctrines are inimical to friendship in the personal sense, we find, a little later in the same volume of the Canon, Māra's daughter, Craving, asking the Exalted One: "Why makest thou no friends among the folk?" She gets the following answer:

> Now that the host of sweet and pleasant shapes
> Hath been repulsed, I'm seated here alone
> And meditate upon the good I've won,
> The peace of heart, the bliss experienced.
> Therefore I make no friendship 'mong the folk;
> Friendship with anyone is not for me. (KS I 158)

Attempts have been made, as for instance by Mrs C. A. F. Rhys Davids[95] to say that such passages reflect a later, monkish distortion of the original, much warmer gospel of Gotama. However much sympathy one might have with such speculations, they are in a sense irrelevant, at least in the present context. Our concern is not with what the actual, historical Gotama said and did – which is, in any case, something we can never know with certainty – but with what the Pāli canon reports him as saying and doing because it is this last which is considered normative for Theravāda Buddhism, that is to say, the Buddhism within which the Jātaka stories came to birth. When references are made to Gotama's teaching in what follows, the question of the actual historical provenance of the teaching is therefore left entirely open.

When we look at the teaching conveyed by the Four Nikāyas, it is no surprise to discover that loving relationships form no part of this teaching. How could they? One of the main aims of the *Dhamma* is to annihilate the delusive concept of human personality as something stable, precious and cherishable. In GS II 37, we find the Buddha expounding the Four Truths with the significant substitution of "person-pack" (*sak-kāya*) for "suffering" (*dukkha*), thus:

Just so, monks, when a Tathāgata arises in the world . . . he teaches *Dhamma*: "Such is the person-pack (*iti sakkāyo*): such the origin of the person-pack (*iti sakkāyasamudayo*): such is the ending of the person-pack (*iti sakkāyanirodho*) . . .

The following paragraph informs us that even the devas, until then blissful in their ignorance, "fall to quaking and trembling" when they hear this teaching because they have realised that "we are impermanent, unstable, not to last, compassed about with a person-pack." (GS II 37).

The inference is unmistakable. The object of the Eightfold Path is as much designed to end delusions about personality as it is to end suffering. Indeed, from the point of view of the *dhamma*, there is no difference: the concept of personality and the experience of suffering are inseparably linked.

If there is no such thing as personality in any sense which has meaning or value, how could personal relationships possibly be regarded as anything other than a dangerous delusion?

Just as the antidote to suffering (*dukkha*) is to root out craving (*taṇhā*), so the antidote to delusive ideas about personality is to root out all sensual attachment (*kām-upa dānam*) to our own persons or other persons.

Thus Prince Siddattha forsakes his wife and child. In MLS III 176ff, there is a dialogue between the novice, Aciravata, and Gotama. The novice has been trying to explain to a Prince how a monk can attain to "one-pointedness of mind". The Prince simply refuses to believe him, saying, "This is impossible". When Gotama learns of this, he asks the novice how he could have expected a Prince "living as he does in the midst of sense-pleasures, enjoying . . . being consumed by thoughts of . . . burning with the fever of . . . eager in the search for sense-pleasures" to understand what he, the novice, was talking about. It is as if a man standing at the foot of a mountain, able to see only the mountain looming in front of him, should be told by a man standing at the top of the mountain what can be seen from the summit. The man at the bottom might well exclaim, "This is impossible". Gotama always seems to have taken it for granted that the renunciation of family was the price he had had to pay for enlightenment; having attained enlightenment, he always taught that the life of a solitary recluse is infinitely to be preferred to the life of the married householder.

In KS V 348 the layman Dhammadinna comes to the Tathāgata for instruction. Being told that this will involve him in that which is "deep in meaning, transcendental and concerned with the

Void", he protests, "Lord, it is no easy thing for us, living as we do in crowded houses, encumbered with children, enjoying the use of Benares sandal-wood . . . to spend our days learning these discourses . . . Let my Lord . . . teach us some other teaching", whereupon the Buddha teaches the "four limbs of stream-winning" (i.e. the Three Jewels plus the Ariyan Virtue – very much the rudiments of the Path).

The pleasure or pain arising from sensual experience stems according to the Nikāyas, from ignorance.[96] If a man desires to be free of pain – and the Buddhist assumes that anybody embarking on the Path has this as his prime object – he must be prepared to sacrifice pleasure as well as pain. The object of his endeavour is to dissipate the primeval ignorance which underlies his suffering. However, bearing in mind the Buddhist assumption, which was commented on in the previous chapter, that right bodily habits must precede right mental attitudes (and not the reverse), it follows that, before one can hope to overcome ignorance, one must *first*, so far as is humanly possible, cultivate a mode of life in which there is the minimum sensual experience, either pleasurable or painful. The Buddha's is the "Middle Way", eschewing the cultivation of pain as much as the cultivation of pleasure[97] primarily because both pleasure and pain depend on sensory experience, at least in the first instance. Just as ignorance feeds the senses, so the senses feed ignorance. By reducing sensory experience, whether painful or pleasurable, to the bare minimum, one deprives ignorance of its main source of nourishment and thereby stands the best chance of cracking it open with the blinding, enlightening wisdom of the *arahant*.

Thus it is that the meditative technique of the Four "trances" (*jhānā*) aims at a progressive withdrawal from the life of the senses, the very first of them leading to joy and ease born of detachment.[98]

Thus, by the same token, we find that, in the lists of undesirable states to be overcome, any form of sensory attachment is usually given pride of place. Thus, in the list of the five hindrances, the first is sensual desire (*kāma chanda*)[99] and in the list of the three obstacles, the first is lust (*rāgo kiñcanaṃ*)[100] and, most important of all, the first of the three (or, sometimes, four) fetters (*āsavā*) is lust (*kāmāsava*)[101]

A monk was committed to celibacy. Any kind of sexual intercourse whether with a woman, an hermaphrodite, a eunuch, another man or any animal[102] was a violation of one of the four rules which spelled defeat (pārājika), and incurred automatic exclusion from the Order. In order to guard against temptation, a monk encountering a woman had to adopt a triple defence. In the first place, he should think of her as his mother or sister or daughter (which she assuredly will have been in some previous birth): the powerful taboo of incest will then help to neutralise his sexual interest in her. Second, he should think of all the foul constituents of even a fair body and third, he should be generally watchful (KS IV 67–70).

The second line of defence, the contemplation of the foul constituents of the body (bile, phlegm, urine, spittle, snot, etc.) was commonly advocated[103] and widely practised. The monk was urged to think of the body as a boil, oozing with foulness, stench and filthiness and, therefore, he was to be "disgusted with this body".[104]

Indeed there was one occasion so damaging to the Buddha's reputation as a "peerless charioteer of men" that it is hard to think it would have been invented. I have never seen it referred to in any of the books on Buddhism I have read. In KS V 284, we read that the Buddha had commended "the unlovely" as a subject for meditation before he himself went off for a fourteen-day retreat. On his return, he found the Order sadly diminished because so many of the monks, contemplating "the unlovely" had "as to this body ... worried about it, felt shame and loathing for it, and sought for a weapon to slay themselves" – and had in fact, committed suicide. Ānanda suggests that in future it might be better if the Buddha "would teach some other method" of meditation. Gotama complies with this suggestion and advises his monks to base their meditation on their breathing in future.

Another example of this – at least to a Western reader – astonishing negativism occurs in KS IV 104–6 where we read a biting denunciation of the senses and all their work. Regarding the sixth, the mind, the monk is told that "It were a good thing, brethren, to be asleep. For sleep ... is barren for living things ..., one would not be applying his mind to such imaginings as would enslave him, so that ... he would break up the Order. ... "[105]

It seems to be unquestionably the case that the Nikāyas teach a doctrine of radical selflessness (anattā) which is designed, amongst other things, to anaesthetise the monk to pain. For this to be accomplished, the doctrine of anattā has, by a process of diligent meditation, to be realised at the profoundest levels of awareness.

Thus Upasena, although fatally bitten by a snake, suffered "no change for the worse in his faculties" because he did not nurse the illusion of possessing a body or being a body (KS IV 20–22). This is not, of course, a doctrine of bodilessness but of there being no "I" to possess the body (and therefore to suffer when the body suffers).

Much more important than this immunity to present pain, however, was the conviction that, by having fully realised this egolessness, by having stamped out the subjective centre of craving (or, perhaps better, having realised how ignorant one was to have thought there *was* such a subjective centre in the first place), one had escaped from the cycle of rebirth – for it is ego-yoked craving which supplies the fuel which keeps the wheel of *saṃsāra* turning (KS IV 280f). When there is no "self", any craving that remains will be purely a matter of biochemistry, it will have no repercussions on the "self" because there is no "self".

In all this, the distinction between the sexes is strictly irrelevant. Yet even the way in which this sexual equality is expressed often betrays a considerable element of male chauvinism, as when we are told that a nun, Gopikā, "having abandoned a woman's thoughts and cultivated the thoughts of a man" is reborn as a male deity in the heaven of the thirty-three, whilst three monks become mere *gandhabbas* (DB II 306).[106] When Ānanda prevailed upon Gotama to allow a separate Order for women, he is reported to have been very gloomy about this. It would, he said, halve the length of time for which the *Dhamma* would be preserved in a pure form.[107] Even so, Gotama made no attempt to argue that women were constitutionally unable to live the monastic life. Just as the Order did not discriminate against persons on caste grounds, there was no basis for it to do so on sexual grounds. Generally speaking, a woman's nature, though it does seem to be thought of as something of a handicap, is irrelevant if the Dhamma is rightly grasped (KS I 162).

At a more mundane level, a woman's lot is ambivalent. A woman may have five attractive qualities (a beautiful form, wealth, virtue, vigour, the ability to bear children), but, on the other hand, she is subject to five woes (having to leave her home to go to her husband's "at a tender age"; menses; pregnancy; childbirth; having to wait on a man) (KS IV 162f). A woman can get the better of a man by exercising her "five powers" (beauty, wealth, kin, sons, virtue) but a man may triumph over all these by his "one power" (authority) (KS IV 165f). A bride may become a *deva* by being diligent, attentive, gentle, respectful to her husband's circle, skilled in homecrafts and in running the household, and in guarding and spending her husband's earnings (GS III 29f, IV 175ff), yet, women never tire of sexual intercourse and childbearing (GS I 72) and they never sit in court or embark on business because "they are uncontrolled, envious, greedy and weak in wisdom" (GS II 92f).

In the secular field, it seems that a woman, by being a dutiful and virtuous wife (i.e. by being meekly submissive to the male), can attain to a heavenly rebirth. On the other hand, her own nature is such that her chances of qualifying, even in this rather unsatisfactory way, seem somewhat slender.

So far as the subject of this chapter is concerned, what it amounts to is that the Nikāyas say virtually nothing positive about love either in the context of friendship or of marriage.[107b] Insofar as one nourishes attachment for another human being, one is nourishing a "fetter", something which will impede spiritual progress and, when the time of death or separation comes (as it inevitably must), will bring acute pain. If this applies to the most "selfless" and other-regarding love, how much more must it apply to sex when this is dominated by animal lust and blind passion. The best that can be said for marriage is that it does provide an opportunity to fulfil one's social responsibilities (assuming one is still at the stage where these are considered important) in a manner both chaste and dutiful.

One would guess that, in spite of this rather forbidding theory, monks might sometimes get somewhat attached to each other in practice. Although, in the early days, the ideal was to go "from home to homelessness" (*agārasmā anagāriyaṃ*) and to live as a solitary recluse, an island to oneself,[108] in the rainy season at least, monks tended to congregate into smaller or larger communities. For a time at least they had a home again and were having regular, if temporary, intercourse with one or more of their fellow monks. Gotama himself seems, throughout his teaching ministry, to have been in regular contact with quite a group of disciples, many of whom are named. The relationship between himself and Ānanda seems to have been particularly close. However much the teacher might exhort his disciple to accept his death philosophically (DB II 152f), Ānanda could not prevent himself, in the event, from being greatly moved (DB II 177).

This causes us to wonder whether homosexual love, either covert or overt, existed within the Order. Its overt expression is bluntly forbidden by the Vinaya rule already referred to, which precludes any kind of sexual intercourse. We read in the Vinaya of two novices having intercourse with each other and, because of this, of the rule that no two novices should be attached to the same Elder. (Horner, 1951, Vol. IV pp. 99f.)

In the Four Nikāyas, however, I have been unable to discover any direct reference to male homosexuality. I think this may well be significant. We know from the Vinaya that the phenomenon was not unknown. We may surmise from the fact that the Order of Monks and the Order of Nuns were strictly segregated communities, committed to total chastity and having to move very circumspectly whenever in contact with the opposite sex because of inquisitive lay eyes, that the question of homosexuality must surely have presented itself. In view of the fact that so much in the Nikāyas is addressed specifically to Monks, and in view of the enormous amount that is said in stricture of or warning against heterosexual activity, is it not surprising that not one word is said, either in stricture or in warning, against homosexual activity? The only suggestion of such a warning I have found is in GS III 196f, where monks are counselled against devotion to one person. If a monk says of another monk, "he is dear and lovely to me", he is likely to be adversely affected should the beloved monk fall into error, go elsewhere, become mentally unstable or die.

This silence could be interpreted in a number of ways. I would be inclined to interpret it as follows: assuming homosexual emotions were felt and sometimes expressed within the Order, the knowledge that at least the expression of such emotion was contravening a major Vinaya rule would have made this a very sensitive area and would have given the monks, especially those involved, a strong motive for drawing a veil of silence over the whole topic. If, apart from that one occasion in the Vinaya, the Buddha was never held to have spoken against this kind of emotion or activity, it would be easier to condone it, either in oneself or in one's brethren. After all, in loving relationships of this kind, there was no temptation to forsake the Order, since both parties were equally committed to it; there was no possibility of producing children and, in consequence, becoming saddled with just those cares and responsibilities one had joined the Order to escape; on the other hand, there was the possibility, since both were committed to the same teaching and the same training, of keeping the mutual attachment within reasonable bounds and ensuring that it did not hinder what each considered to be more important objectives.

Arguments from silence are always hazardous, but in this case the silence is so eloquent that the argument seems to be justified. What we shall learn from the *Jātakas* certainly seems to support it.

(B) THE JĀTAKAS

In view of the fact that the Jātaka stories are concerned for the most part with the preoccupations of lay life and since the stories had their currency mainly within the lay community, it is not surprising that the themes of this chapter play such a large part in these tales.

It will be remembered that we stressed in chapter three that the basic premise of a Jātaka, namely that the same person goes from life to life in an endless succession, involves a complete setting aside of the doctrine of *anattā* (selflessness). Since, as we have seen in the preceding section of this chapter, the main basis for the Nikāyas' teaching about friendship and marriage is precisely this doctrine, we shall expect that the Jātakas will, on the whole, adopt a rather different stance. Whether consciously or not, the objections to marriage occurring most often in the Jātaka stories are very rarely theoretical. Instead, they are based on anecdotes about the practical disadvantages and disillusionments of the married state. Although this kind of story preponderates, there are some stories which help to balance the picture by presenting the married relationship in a much more favourable light than is usual in the Nikāyas. Clearly, the lay influence in the shaping of the stories was strong enough to prevent the celibate monk from having it all his own way.

There is such a wealth of material to include in this section that I propose to treat the two halves of the topic for this chapter separately. This was not necessary in reviewing the teaching of the Nikāyas, but in the case of the Jātakas I think it will be found helpful. The two parts, sex and marriage on the one hand and love and friendship on the other, are not mutually exclusive. Nevertheless, it is revealing to discover that the overlap is in fact very slight. Whereas we in the West are in the habit of making a

trinity of love, sex and marriage, the very marked tendency of the
Jātakas is to divide the sphere of inter-personal relationships into
the two doublets of our chapter heading.

(a) *Sex and Marriage*
Perhaps the best point at which to begin this review is the point
at which many of the stories themselves begin. There is a group of
twenty-four stories (JSS 30, 63, 85, 106, 147, 191, 207, 212, 262,
310, 327, 360, 383, 386, 401, 423, 425, 436, 443, 477, 523, 526,
531, 536), which all have a similar introduction, usually very brief,
though occasionally more extended. The common theme of these
introductions is that a brother has begun to hanker after the world
or to become "passion tossed" (*ukkaṇṭhita*). Upon enquiry, it emerges that this brother was formerly married and has recently been
assailed by thoughts of his former wife or, alternatively, has encountered a beautiful woman who has thrown him quite off
balance and made it impossible for him to meditate. The Buddha
then proceeds to tell a story "of former times" in order to deter
the monk from rushing back to or into marriage. It is interesting
to see the various ways in which this is done.

The blackest picture of marriage is suggested by those stories
(JSS 30, 85, 147, 386, 423), which say or imply that marriage is,
if not exactly a fate worse than death, then at any rate tantamount
to death. In JS 30, a monk is told that the lady who now en-
snares him was the cause of his death in a previous life since he was
the pig which was fattened up to provide her wedding feast. The
message of JS 85 is that sensual lusts are like the what-fruit – "very
fair to view . . . very fragrant and sweet; but when eaten, it racks
the inwards and brings death". JS 147 tells the sad story of a poor
man whose wife badgers him so much to get hold of some safflower
with which she could dye her dress, that he finally agrees to go at
night into the king's conservatory in search of some. He is caught,
arrested and impaled as a thief. Not only does he die in agony but
he is reborn in hell! JS 386 becomes somewhat ramified. A king
is about to surrender his life because he has agreed to his wife's
request to let her know a spell he has been given on the clear
understanding that, if he tells it to anybody else, his own life will
be forfeit. Sakka (the bodhisatta) manifests himself as a goat and,
in order to attract attention, copulates with a she-goat (really a
daughter of the *Asuras* in disguise) in full view of the king's
chariot. Having thus got into conversation, he cures the king of

his sacrificial intent by imparting such homespun wisdom as

> He who his own special treasure on his wife will throw away,
> Cannot keep her faithful ever and his life he must betray

and

> . . . no one is dearer than self: it is not good to destroy oneself
> and abandon the honour one has gained for the sake of
> anything that is dear

and

> . . . Life is the chief thing: what can man seek higher?
> If life's secured, desires need ne'er be crossed.

It will be observed how blatantly this self-regarding hedonism sets aside, not only the doctrine of *anattā*, but also the basic tenet of canonical teaching: that life, so far from being "the chief thing", is really suffering.

The last of the stories in the marriage–equals–death group (JS 423) is again somewhat ramified. The introduction tells us that a particular monk was tempted to return to his former wife, not so much for sexual reasons as to regain the comforts of home, his wife's cooking having been incomparably better than the repulsive scraps he was getting in his begging bowl. In a former life, we learn, this monk had been the ascetic Nārada. But one day, walking along a river bank, he saw "many beautiful courtesans tempting the men". One of them (now the brother's former wife) tempted him. He lost his power of meditation and was about to indulge his passion, when the bodhisatta told him a tale-within-the tale about a beautiful young man who became a victim to his senses (though *his* passion was the eating of deer-flesh) and, in the process, became, on his own admission, "the ghost of a man", wrinkled, ugly and joyless.[109]

Most of the stories addressed to the "passion-tossed" monk do not adopt quite such a bleak view of marriage. They use as their deterrent the alleged fact that a wife is so often unfaithful, is so lustful by nature and so fickle, that marriage will prove again, as it has in the past, a bitter disillusionment. The stories in this category are JSS 207, 212, 262, 327, 360, 401, 425, 436, 536 – nearly half of the main group.

In JS 212 the bodhisatta, who is an acrobat begging at a brahmin's door, reveals to the master of the house that his wife has hidden her lover in the store-room as soon as she heard the footsteps of her returning husband. JS 327 tells how the bodhisatta, when King of Benares, had his beautiful chief queen carried off by a *Garuḍa*[110] king, who had come disguised as a human being. When the king sent his musician in search of her, the latter, as soon as he found her, "enjoyed the lady's favours" before returning with his message to the king. The Garuḍa king, when he learned what had happened, returned the queen to her husband in disgust. The same story, slightly elaborated, is repeated at JS 360, but this time the bodhisatta is himself the Garuḍa king. A fickle chief queen features again in JS 401. The son of the king's priest, seeing the beauty of the queen, falls madly in love with her and takes to his bed, unable to eat. When the king learns of the state the young man is in, he allows him to have the queen for seven days in his own house. After having taken "delight with her" for a week, neither can bear to part, so they run away to another kingdom. The king is desolate at the loss of his wife until his adviser (the bodhisatta) gets him to see that "if she loved me she would not forsake her kingdom and flee away". We may note the intriguing double standard which obtains in this story. The king, presumably out of affection for his young courtier, is quite happy to lend him his wife; when she proves less adaptable, and wants to stay with her new lover – a lover not of *her* choosing be it noted – she is regarded as fickle. JS 207 also sets out to demonstrate the fickleness of women. A king's beautiful wife dies; he is so grief-stricken that he is immobilised, until the bodhisatta, an ascetic of supernatural insight, reveals to the king that the dead wife upon whom he has lavished so many tears is now, because of her vanity and lack of merit, a dung worm. Asked what her feelings for her former husband are, now that she is a worm, she replies, "Why, now I would kill king Assaka, and would smear the feet of my husband the dung-worm with the blood flowing from his throat!".

JS 436 tells the bizarre story of an Asura who, becoming enamoured of beautiful human lady, captured her and kept her safe in a box which he swallowed and guarded in his belly! He made the mistake of allowing her out for a bathe one day. While she was bathing, "a son of Vayu who was a magician" passed by, "walking through the air". "When she saw him, she put her hands in a certain position and signed to him to come to her". She managed to hide him in the box so that, when she climbed in and was swallowed again by the Asura, she had managed to secure a lover with whom to amuse herself whilst "guarded" in his belly. The bodhisatta (an ascetic) divined what was going on and enlightened the Asura, who promptly "threw up" the box and released the magician. The ascetic instructed the Asura "in the five moral precepts" and told him not to harm the woman. The Asura decided to let her go on the not unreasonable ground that, if *he* could not keep her safe, nobody could!

Somewhat similar is the story (JS 262) which tells how the bodhisatta, once again King of Benares, tries to keep his daughter and nephew apart. He knows the two are in love but intends his daughter to marry into another family. Although he keeps his daughter constantly under his eye, one dark, cloudy day, a pageboy "with soft hands", having had the daughter's bangles transferred to his own wrists, is substituted for her and led back by the hand by the unsuspecting father who thinks he is escorting his daughter from her bathe. Needless to say, the princess and her cousin have eloped. The father reflects ruefully that "not even if one goes along and holds hands can one guard a woman".

In JS 425, Ānanda and the bodhisatta have been born as a prince and merchant's son respectively and are the best of friends. When the prince becomes king, the bodhisatta lives close by but pays a daily visit to a beautiful courtesan. Every day he pays her a thousand pieces in return for the riches she bestows. At the same time, he pays three visits each day to his friend, the king. On one occasion he decides to go straight from the king to the courtesan. Since he has no money with him, he tells her he will bring two thousand pieces on the following day. Although his daily payments have amounted to eighty *crores* up to this time, because her lover cannot produce cash on this one occasion, she refuses to see him and has him thrown out. Thinking, "oh, womenkind are wicked, shameless, ungrateful, treacherous" he decides to become an ascetic.

Finally in this woman-are-fickle group is the Kuṇāla Jātaka. In introducing his separate edition of this Jātaka, W. B. Bollée observes that, although it falls into "the type of stories told by the Buddha to admonish monks whose ardour had flagged because they had fallen into the hands of women", it nevertheless "is distinguished from the other Jātakas of this kind by being not a single tale, but a collection of misogynous tales and strophes".[111]

This story is too long and too complex to be capable of summary here. Suffice it to say that women are presented as ungrateful creatures; it is wise to treat them harshly since kindness is bound to be exploited. They are all of them lecherous by nature and absolutely insatiable in their lust; they will abandon themselves to a hunchback or a cripple if there is nobody more attractive on hand. A nun is as easily seduced as any other woman. A woman's word can never be relied on since women have endless ingenuity when it comes to finding clever veils behind which to work their voluptuous will. By the time the conference of birds, which provides the framework for this little necklace of malice, is concluded, one would think that a virtuous woman had yet to be born.

Two stories addressed to the "passion tossed" monk take a milder line, one (JS 106) suggesting that the man who marries risks becoming henpecked and the other, JS 191, warning that some women come to despise their husbands and deliberately humiliate them.

A group of five stories (JSS 310, 383, 443, 523, 526) adopts a totally different approach. Although addressed still to the monk who has been assailed by sexual craving, these stories, instead of warning against marriage, point to examples of people who have been able to resist sensual temptation and therefore to achieve "higher" things.

JS 310 simply tells how the bodhisatta, being friendly with the king (Ānanda again), fears that he is about to be made king's chaplain. He wants nothing to do with the world, so he goes off to a Himalayan hermitage. Nothing his friend can say is able to coax him back to the pleasures of courtly life. In JS 383, the bodhisatta (now a cock) is wooed by a she-cat who hopes, having married him, to eat him. The cock is proof against her blandishments and retains his independence – and also his life.

JS 443 is more elaborate. The bodhisatta has been born into a brahmin family, having just descended "from Brahma's world". Against his will he is married to a girl of surpassing beauty – who happens also to have been in Brahma's world in her previous birth. Consequently, although they are each so attractive, "in the way of passion neither so much as cast a look at each other". They decide to become ascetics. The king (yet again Ānanda) comes across them and discovering that, although married, they live as ascetics, he decides, having fallen in love with the woman, to seize her by his "sovereign power". Though she cries out in distress, the bodhisatta "looked once but looked no more". Since the king is a previous incarnation of Ānanda, however, we should expect him to do the decent thing in the end. Sure enough, when he discovers the mistake he has made, he releases his unwilling bride and gives both ascetics the royal protection (cf JSS 328, 458).

In JS 523, an ascetic, tempted by Sakka to become enamoured of a beautiful woman, succumbs for a time but then, remembering the advice of his saintly father (the bodhisatta), is finally able to resist temptation and return to his meditation. JS 526 is virtually a repeat of the same story, the main difference being that here the father is still alive to advise his son in person.

Before we leave the "passion-tossed" monk and the stories directed specifically toward him, we should look at a rather similar cluster of three stories (JSS 348, 435, 477) only one of which (JS 477) is said to be addressed to a "passion-tossed monk". The three stories are virtually the same, however, and should obviously be treated together. They tell of a man who, after his wife's death, decides to become an ascetic along with his youthful son. While the father is away a young girl discovers the son alone and the two decide to elope, though the son says he must first ask his father's permission. When the father (always the bodhisatta) returns, he convinces his son that, if he follows his sensual lust, he will become involved in endless trouble and suffering. The girl has already gone ahead; the son opts not to join her but to allow his father to train him further in the ascetic life.

We shall now look at two stories, or rather one introduction and one story, which suggest that the monks had to be very careful to keep their reputation for celibacy inviolate. Any suggestion that a monk had defaulted in this respect could be very damaging.

In the introduction to JS 472, we learn of the plot of "heretics" to discredit Gotama by getting a nun to accuse him of having made her pregnant and then having disowned both her and the impending child. The plot has been so carefully laid that it requires the intervention of Sakka and four gods in the form of mice to expose it. The mice gnaw through the cords binding the wood she has concealed in her robe to simulate pregnancy. The crowd is enraged at her wickedness; she is rescued from their wrath only because the ground opens to carry her away to the lowest hell – a dreadful warning to anybody who might feel inclined to make false accusations of immorality against a monk.

In JS 391, the king of Benares learns that his wife is being "corrupted" each night by some villain who steals into her chamber and then slips away, having enjoyed her. The villain is in fact a wizard with magic powers who unfortunately disguises himself as a monk by day. When the king's men track down the culprit, he is wearing his robes, so the word immediately starts to go round that "these men go about by day in ascetic's garb and misconduct themselves at night". The king banishes all the monks from his realm – with the result that, bereft of spiritual mentors, the people grow savage and no new gods arrive in heaven. Sakka (the bodhisatta) decides to set the record straight and enlightens the king as to the real identity of his villain. The king is cured of his "heresy" and the monks return.

One cannot help feeling that a monk in a tight corner, whether guilty or not, would find this story useful. If somebody resembling him, and wearing the robes, was detected in some sexually incriminating situation, the monk could always argue that the real villain was a wizard disguised to look like him!

Perhaps we should at this point investigate the sexual record of the bodisatta himself since this also must have had considerable influence on popular ideas about monastic morality. It turns out to be a richly diverse, and in many ways a fascinating record. In order to introduce some degree of order into the account, I propose to classify the stories which bear upon the bodhisatta's sexual life under four sub-headings, as follows:

 (i) stories in which the bodhisatta proves vulnerable to sexual temptation and is admitted, within the story itself, to have violated the precept relating to sexuality: JSS 66, 251, 263, 431, 507.
 (ii) stories in which the bodhisatta seems to fall below accepted standards of sexual propriety but in which there is no censure within the story itself: JSS 360, 425, 487, 491.
 (iii) stories in which the bodhisatta has a sex life which conforms more or less to the canonical norm: JSS 527, 531, 546.
 (iv) stories in which the bodhisatta obtains children by para-sexual means: JSS 380, 497, 523, 526.

(i) This is probably the most remarkable of the four groups because all the stories in it frankly admit that the bodhisatta was capable of sexual misconduct, in all cases in intent, and sometimes in act. The stories in this group fall into two clusters. In the first (JSS 66, 251, 431), the bodhisatta is, in each case, an ascetic enjoying royal patronage. In each case the queen is asked to care for the ascetic during her husband's absence. Again, in all three accounts, the bodhisatta comes to visit the queen one day just as she has taken a bath; he comes 'walking' or 'passing' through the air and she, taken rather by surprise, rises in haste; her bath robe slips away, revealing her form in all its loveliness. Quite overwhelmed by "this unusual sight" (JS 66), when this "extraordinary object struck upon the eye of the Great Being" (JS 431), "he was as a tree felled by the axe" (JS 66). Now the stories diverge slightly.

In JS 66, we have a charming account of how the ascetic, all insight having deserted him, confesses to the king, on his return, that his heart is "fettered by lust" on account of the queen. The king immediately gives his wife to the ascetic but secretly asks her, before she departs, to try "to save the holy man". The queen, with splendid psychological insight, begins by making her would-be despoiler face the harsh realities of married life away from the luxury of the palace. They have been given a small hut which the queen orders her lover to clean and furnish before she will enter. When at last they are sitting together on the bed, "she took him by the whiskers and drew him towards her till they were face to face, saying, 'Hast thou forgotten that thou art a holy man and a brahmin?'" After the "cooling off period" she had organized beforehand, this is enough to cure the holy man of his infatuation. He regains his insight and passes through the air to the Himalayas.

In JS 251, the ascetic, similarly stricken and bereft of his mystical powers, has fallen to murmuring, "What a woman! lovely hands, lovely feet! What a waist, what thighs!" and so forth. But this time, when the king returns, the mere confession of his "wound" is sufficient to restore him to his former self. Again he flies away to the safety of the Himalayas.

In JS 431, however (the impious might be tempted to say, "third time lucky"!), "being unable to fix his thoughts he went and seized the queen by the hand, and forthwith they drew a curtain round them". Henceforth the ascetic is "misconducting himself" with the queen every day until the king returns. The king, having heard reports of what is going on, bluntly asks each in turn if these reports are true. The queen owns up immediately. The ascetic, having calculated that, if he told a lie, the king would believe him, nevertheless resolves to tell the truth, for "those who forsake the truth . . . cannot attain to Buddhahood".

Then follows a most revealing little note which lets us in on the rules of play as it were – rules which are, I think, faithfully observed throughout the Jātaka collection. We read:

> In certain cases a Bodhisatta may destroy life, take what is not given him, commit adultery, drink strong drink, but he may not tell a lie, attended by deception that violates the reality of things.

We have had occasion to notice before – and we shall be returning to this theme in the next chapter – that Theravāda Buddhism often gives a very special emphasis to the precept forbidding wrong speech.

As before, the ascetic now repents, recovers his meditative skills, bemoans the censure he has incurred through "dwelling in a place where I ought not", and flies away to the Himalayas.

The second cluster (JSS 263, 507) contains two stories which differ only in that the second is told mainly in verse. The three stanzas of JS 263 are identical with three of the stanzas in JS 507. The story concerns a prince (the bodhisatta) who has been born from the Brahma world and who cannot bear to see a woman – in JS 507 he is actually called Prince Anitthi-gandha (Woman Hater). "When they suckled him, they would milk the breast for him, or they gave him the breast from behind a screen" (JS 263) or, alternatively, "they must needs dress as men to give him the breast" (JS 507). When, as a youth, the prince is no better adapted to the fair sex, his worried father gladly agrees to let a very alluring dancing girl try to seduce his son. She succeeds. The prince "went the way of the world, and knew the joy of love" (JS 263). But now his passion completely deranges him. He runs amuck through the street vowing to kill all other men so that no other man shall possess this woman. The king, greatly alarmed, banishes his son, who goes, with his "wife" to live in a hut by the Ganges (JS 263) or by the sea (JS 507). A hermit comes flying through the air and rests in the hut. The prince is away and the hermit is brought down "from his mystic trance, making a breach in his purity" (JS 263) because he too is bewitched by the woman's beauty. When the prince returns and sees this other man, the old fury returns and he chases the hermit away with his sword. The hermit attempts to fly but soon plunges into the sea. The prince calls out to the hermit that it is a pitiful thing to see a holy man so stricken by passion. Women are

> Full of seductive wiles, deceitful all,
> They tempt the most pure-hearted to his fall,
> Down – down they sink: a man should flee afar
> From women, when he knows what kind they are.
> Whom so they serve, for gold or for desire,
> They burn him up like fuel in the fire.

(I have followed the translation of JS 263, but the identical verses occur also in JS 507.) The hermit, hearing these words, regains his loathing for the world, his mystic trance and his power to fly. The prince, impressed, asks himself: "Why should not I like him cultivate the trance, and pass through the air?" (JS 263). He sends the woman packing, becomes an ascetic and eventually returns to the world of Brahma.

In this story the fault lies not so much in the bodhisatta as in the human condition. A being born with a pure pedigree has a natural immunity to women; but, alas, a woman's charms are so powerful and so destructive that even this immunity can be broken down. If this happens, instead of becoming a happy sensualist, the pure being is utterly disoriented until some counter-stimulus restores him to his purity and his balance of mind. Exactly the same syndrome is repeated in the case of the hermit. The earlier cluster is much fairer to the fair sex. Although there too it is the sight of a beautiful woman's body which proves to be the bodhisatta's undoing, the woman is not blamed for this. She is quite innocent of any intention to seduce and it is indeed her virtue (in the first two versions) which saves the bodhisatta from falling.

(ii)   In this group we find the bodhisatta abducting another man's wife (JS 360), paying a daily visit to a courtesan (JS 425), having an illegitimate child by a slave-girl when he himself was a chaplain (JS 487), and, as a peacock, being ensnared by lust when a peahen makes a love call before he has had time to recite the charm which otherwise would have protected him (JS 491). The last case is somewhat marginal as one could hardly expect even an ascetically disposed peacock to be proof against the "snares of lust". In the other three cases, however, the bodhisatta is engaging in sexual activity which, by canonical standards, would not be above reproach even for a layman. In the case of the abduction he was certainly violating the precepts forbidding sexual misconduct – and perhaps that is why, for this story, the bodhisatta is depicted as a Garuḍa king disguised as a human being. Perhaps Garuḍas cannot be expected to observe the same sexual code as humans. At any rate, it is interesting that each of these incidents is recounted in a perfectly matter-of-fact way, without any hint of moral censure or any attempt to justify the bodhisatta's conduct.

(iii)   This group is the least remarkable of the four. In JS 527 we see the king (the bodhisatta) struggling with his passion for Ummadantī, a girl born intoxicatingly beautiful because of her virtue in a previous birth, but now the wife of his commander-in-chief. Although the latter is willing to divorce his wife and surrender her to the king, the king refuses to allow this to happen and eventually recovers from his passion. In the remaining two stories JSS 531 and 546, we see the bodhisatta falling in love and getting married in quite the normal way.

(iv)   Here are four stories in which, in each case, the bodhisatta, after becoming an ascetic, acquires a child. In each case the child is born by marvellous, para-sexual means, which render it unnecessary for the ascetic to break his vows. In JS 380 the bodhisatta, having become an ascetic, adopts as his own daughter "a being of perfect merit" who "fell from the Heaven of the Thirty-Three and was conceived as a girl inside a lotus in a pool". In JS 497 the bodhisatta is born an outcast, a *Caṇḍāla*. One day he inadvertently causes a merchant's daughter, who has looked at him, to have to wash her eyes with scented water because of the defilement the sight of him has brought to her eyes. Her companions beat him up for having caused her this inconvenience. He resolves to get his own back by having her for his wife – and "the resolve of the Buddhas is immovable". He parks himself on her father's doorstep and will not budge until given permission to carry off the daughter. Having been allowed to do this, he will not transgress the rules of caste by having intercourse with her, so he becomes an ascetic instead. Having quickly attained the "Eight Attainments and the Five Supernatural Faculties", he is able to transport himself to Brahma's heaven. On the night of the full moon he comes to his wife in the form of Brahma. "At that time", we are told, his wife "was in her monthly terms. His thumb touched her navel, and she conceived".[112] Never was fair lady so little defiled by outcast husband!

In both the remaining stories (JSS 523, 526) the bodhisatta is living the life of a brahmin ascetic when "a certain doe in the brahmin's mingeing-place ate grass and drank water mingled with his semen, and was so much enamoured of him that she became pregnant and . . . gave birth to a man child". One suspects that the poetic imagination has never devised a more ingenious method of providing a celibate father with his own son – though one is left wondering how it was that the ascetic's semen came to be mixed with the doe's diet!

These are all cases where the story requires that the bodhisatta, even after becoming an ascetic, be provided with a child. They afford an opportunity to show how wonderfully the bodhisatta's virtue can provide him with what would normally be the fruit of sexual intercourse without his having to become embroiled in so lust-begetting and so sanctity-destroying a process.

So far we have been concerned with stories which relate the theme of sex and marriage, in one way or another, to the life of the monk. The remaining stories are more general.

Some adopt a bluntly negative approach. JS 185, for instance, both in the Introduction and the story, tell of a brahmin youth who had diligently learned the Three Vedas by heart. When he married, however, he became "subject to passion, error, folly", "household cares clouded his mind", and he was no longer able to remember the verses.

This is obviously a reply to the Hindu who claimed that marriage was an honourable estate, in no way incompatible with the holy life, but indeed an important stage within it. The Buddhist is here asserting the contrary. The married state is inherently non-satisfactory – nothing but an impediment to the serious searcher for release from suffering This argument occurs explicitly in JS 509,[113] where a king tries to dissuade his son from renouncing the world at the age of sixteen. He implores him to

First learn the Vedas, get you wealth and wife
And sons, enjoy the pleasant things of life,
Smell, taste, and every sense: sweet is the wood
To live in then, and then the sage is good.

The son replies that truth does not come from the Vedas; no

amount of sensory indulgence can prevent the advent of old age; the path of wisdom is the path of release from the senses. Other stories are much less specific but nevertheless make little asides which suggest that sex and marriage spell only trouble as, for instance, JS 136, where the bodhisatta as a golden mallard has all his lovely feathers plucked off him by his greedy wife, or the incident in JS 330 where an ascetic observes a servant girl vainly waiting on the lintel all night for a lover who has promised to come to her. Only at daybreak, when all hope has gone, can she sleep. He muses,

> The fruit of hope fulfilled is bliss;
> How differs loss of hope from this?

In fact, something stronger is intended. Sexual passion might lead to bliss – but only for a time; if thwarted it leads to pain and when sated it will, sooner or later, lead to pain. The renunciation of sexual passion can lead to uninterrupted peace and freedom from pain.

One of the chief ways in which the Jātakas campaign against sexual involvement and marriage, as will already have become quite clear, is its teaching about the sinful, lustful, fickle, nature of women. Many other stories, apart from those already noticed, pursue this theme, notably JSS 61, 62, 63, 64, 65, 120, 130, 145, 193, 198, 199, 232, 266, 374, 402, 416, 446, 472, 481.

Some of those stories are relatively mild in their criticism. JS 266, for example, simply shows the foolishness of playing "hard to get"; the woman (in the introductory story) who does this, loses the man she really longs for. JS 232 tells of a girl who, having been told that a "cow with a hump" is a "right royal bull", assumes that the best of men will be a hunchback, and promptly elopes with one. This story may not have sexist overtones since there are also stories of rather dim-witted men (like the father in JS 211). There is no doubt about the sexist bias in JS 446, however, where a wicked wife persuades her husband to murder his own father. The murder is prevented only by the intervention of their child – a boy (the bodhisatta).

JS 62 is a really villainous story in which the bodhisatta himself is the real villain, however much the story tries to persuade us otherwise. The bodhisatta is a king fond of gambling with his chaplain. He always wins because he is in the habit of reciting a lucky stanza before throwing the dice. The last line of the stanza is, "All women work iniquity"! The chaplain thinks that if he can have a virtuous woman in the house he can break the charm – but the only way of finding a virtuous woman, apparently, is to have her born in the house and brought up in strict seclusion, only ever seeing women, never a man – other than the chaplain himself. The chaplain manages to avoid dicing until the girl has grown up. He then challenges the king to a game, and each time the king gets to the last line of his stanza, he interjects, "excepting my girl". Sure enough he turns the tables, leading the king to conclude that it must be the arrival of a virtuous woman which has caused his luck to change. He then decides to break the girl's virtue by hiring a "scamp" who, by a very devious plot, manages to gain access to the chaplain's protegée and enjoy himself "wrecking the girl's virtue". As soon as the king knows of this, he plays again and wins, in spite of the chaplain's interjection. The king then explains to his opponent what has happened to his ward's virtue and tells him how naive he was to think that, even by guarding a girl so carefully, albeit from the moment of birth, he could preserve her virtue. "Why, you couldn't be certain of a woman, even if you had her inside you and always walked about with her."[114] The storyteller then comes to the astonishing conclusion that "such, we learn is the wickedness of women. What crime will they not commit . . ."

Less damaging to the bodhisatta, and still relatively mild in its criticism, is JS 64, where the bodhisatta (a brahmin teacher) has a disciple who marries "a sinful and wicked woman", i.e. one whose mood is unpredictable. Expressing his puzzlement to the teacher, he is told, "on days when they have done wrong, women humble themselves before their husbands and become as meek and submissive as a slave-girl; but on days when they have not done wrong, then they become stiff-necked and insubordinate to their lords. After this manner are women sinful and wicked; . . . No heed should be paid either to their likes or to their dislikes."

In JS 130 the bodhisatta (again a teacher) has a pupil whose wife pretended to be sick and bed-bound whilst he was at home but no sooner the door shut on him, than she was in the arms of her paramours. JS 65 tells of a similar situation but, in this case, instead of the drastic remedy (a threatened beating) suggested in the previous story, the teacher simply advises a philosophical indifference for, as he explains to his pupil, "there is no private property in women: they are common to all". There seems to be a much graver accusation in these stories, which pave the way for the next sub-group. These are a good deal stronger and more sweeping in their denunciation of feminine wiles.

JS 402 tells us that a woman can never have enough of three things: "intercourse, adornment and child-bearing", and proceeds to tell of a brahmin woman who "being unsatisfied with intercourse, wished to put her husband away and do her sin with boldness". She sends her husband out to beg so that she can have the freedom she desires. In JS 145, two parrots, one of them the bodhisatta, are asked by their brahmin master to keep an eye on his wife during his absence. The woman has a constant stream of lovers and one bird is minded to interpose. The bodhisatta prevents him on the grounds that it would be quite futile: "You might carry a woman about in your arms and yet she would not be safe". At least the stanza here concedes that "wifely love", had it been present, might have curbed her lust. The conjunction of the words "wife" and "love" is extremely rare in the Jātakas! JS 198 is the same story except that here one of the parrots does interpose – only to have its neck wrung by the guilty woman. The following story (JS 199) shows us the bodhisatta, having discovered that his wife is committing adultery with the local headman, thrashing the man until he faints and seizing his wife by the hair, knocking her down, and threatening much worse if she dares repeat her adultery. A sense of outrage at the violation of the third precept seems to have bred forgetfulness of the first!

In JS 416 we read of a king who has to flee with his pregnant wife and servant. While the king is away, the servant gains sexual access to the pregnant queen, who then says, "If the king knows, neither you nor I would live. Kill him". She wants his head chopped off and his body hacked to pieces! Only slightly less monstrous is the behaviour of the consort of a king (in JS 472) who takes the place of the deceased mother of beautiful Prince Lotus (the bodhisatta). Whilst the king is away, the new queen becomes enamoured of the prince and tries repeatedly to entice him to her bed. When she realises that he is impeccably moral and may well tell the returning king, she decides to simulate rape and do a "Potiphar's wife". She hopes to have the prince executed but is thwarted by divine intervention – which also spells her own doom. It is noteworthy that the god who saves the prince from the woman's wickedness is identified as Ānanda; the eternal friend versus the fickle woman!

JS 481 is made up of a number of tales which all point to the same moral: "careless talk costs lives". The first of these concerns a king's chaplain, a tawny brown brahmin, who discovers that his wife is carrying on an affair with another man of very similar appearance. The chaplain thinks he will get rid of his rival by telling the king that it is crucial that a tawny brown brahmin be sacrificed before a certain edifice can be safely built. The king agrees and the chaplain returns in glee to tell his wife that, on the following day, her lover will die. He makes the mistake of disclosing his scheme to her. She promptly ensures that her lover and all other men of similar appearance flee the town so that, when the time comes for the all-important sacrifice to be made, it is her husband who has himself to be the unwilling victim.

In the remaining anti-feminist stories, the depiction of women reaches a crescendo of defamation.

JS 61 concerns a young brahmin who is inclined to lead a family life although his parents would prefer him to go to the forest in order to worship the Fire God. The son, as so often in the Jātakas, goes to Takkasilā to learn at the feet of a famous teacher. When he returns, his mother determines to bring him round to the parents' way of thinking. She asks him if his teacher instructed him in the "Dolour Texts". When he says "no", she sends him back to complete his education. The teacher, knowing that the "Dolour Texts" do not exist "concluded that his pupil's mother must have wanted her son to learn how wicked women were". This presents no problem at all. He instructs his pupil to take over from him the daily chore of bathing his hundred-and-twenty year old mother, but the pupil is to keep saying how well-preserved she is and what a beauty she must have been in her youth. The teacher's mother thinks this pupil has fallen in love with her and she becomes inflamed with lust for him. As soon as the pupil (following his teacher's instructions) declares his love, she orders him to kill her son so that there will be nobody to interfere with her desires. When the pupil refuses, she says she will kill her son with her own hands. The teacher, being informed of this, arranges a wooden image to be put in a bed and asks the pupil to take an axe to his mother with the message that his master is sleeping. She stumbles, almost blind with age, to his room, bares the dummy's head and brings the axe down on the throat. At the same time as she hears the crunch of the axe in the wood, her son appears and asks her what she is doing; the old hag drops dead of shock. The pupil returns to his mother, having made the decision that he will be very happy to "have nothing to do with family life"! He renounces the world and goes off to worship the Lord of Fire, having learned that "women are depravity incarnate". Perhaps there is something Oedipal about the fact that it is his own mother who has been so anxious for him to learn this horrid lesson.

In JS 63 we encounter a Treasurer's daughter so unpleasant that her attendants take advantage of a storm to leave her to drown in the Ganges. She does not drown however because an ascetic (the bodhisatta) risks his life to save her. He allows her to stay in his hut, where she determines to seduce him. He duly loses "his Insight" and settles down with her. One day the wife is carried off by robbers. The bodhisatta is not unduly worried, confident that she will return to him at the first opportunity. Sure enough, a message comes asking him to rescue her from the robbers because she is so unhappy as their captive. Actually the reverse is the truth; she is so happy with the robber chief as her lover that she has decided that she will feel more secure if she gets her husband killed. Accordingly, when the bodhisatta arrives, she hands him over to the robber chief who takes delight in beating him "to his heart's content". He repeats this treatment on the following day, then becomes intrigued that his victim's only response is to keep muttering something about "ingrates" and "traitors". He asks what all this is about and learns the truth about his lover. Realising that, if she treats her rescuer like this, she is capable of anything, the robber kills the wife instead of the husband and goes off with the latter to become an ascetic. This story needs to be compared with JS 73 which, in its main plot, is the same as JS 63, except that the villain has undergone a sex-change. Here, a wicked prince is left to drown by his servants, is rescued by an ascetic (the bodhisatta), later becomes king and orders the bodhisatta to be flogged and killed. The bodhisatta, at each flogging, recites a verse which makes the bystanders curious and leads to the revelation of the king's ingratitude and treachery. The king, not the bodhisatta, is executed and the bodhisatta is appointed king in his place. Since the villain is here a man, it seems very unfair that JS 63 (which is also addressed to a "passion-tossed" monk) should speak as if only women were capable of such wickedness.

The queen in JS 120 makes her husband promise never to have sex with another woman. Although he has sixteen thousand "nautch-girls", for love of the queen, he reluctantly agrees. When the king has to go off to fight, his wife wants to accompany him; finally accepting that this is impossible, she asks her husband to send a messenger to tell her he is safe at every league of his journey. Since the king travels thirty two leagues, sixty four messengers are dispatched on the return journey; as soon as each arrives, the queen orders him into bed with her. When the king is almost back, he asks his chaplain (the bodhisatta) to prepare the city for his return. While he was busy in the palace, "the sight of his great beauty so moved the queen that she called to him to satisfy her lust". When he refuses, she says sixty four others have had no scruples, so why should he? When he still refuses, she also does a "Potiphar's wife". When the king is about to execute him, the chaplain explains the true situation. The king confirms the story and now wants to behead all sixty four messengers and the queen. The chaplain (who has protested to the king that he himself has never broken any of the five moral precepts) restrains him on the ground that the men cannot be blamed; they were only obeying their queen. The queen cannot be blamed either because she was only following her nature, "for the passions of women are insatiate".

JS 193 is a gruesome tale about seven princes and their wives, banished by the king because he fears treachery. The banished couples stay together but are unable to find food and become ravenous. "They determined to save their lives at the women's cost." Starting with the wife of the youngest brother, they kill a wife a day and divide the corpse amongst the survivors. The bodhisatta is the eldest of the princes and he and his wife have, each day, saved one of their two portions. When his wife's turn to be killed arrives, he donates the saved portions instead. That night he leaves his brothers, carrying his wife on his shoulders. When she is dying of thirst and no water is found, he lets her drink blood from a self-inflicted wound in his knee. When they reach the Ganges all is well, until they hear the pitiful cries of a robber who has had hands, feet, nose and ears cut off and has been left to drift down the Ganges in a canoe. The bodhisatta rescues him and tends his wounds in the hut he has built. As the wounds heal, the wife's earlier revulsion turns to uncontrollable lust. On the pretext of offering a sacrifice with her husband, she goes with him to a hill-top and then pushes him over a precipice. The prince's fall is cushioned by some bushes and he is rescued by a friendly iguana (Ānanda, of course, in a previous life – never far away when needed!). The prince eventually becomes king and is able to punish his faithless, murderous wife and the ungrateful robber.

JS 374 is a variation on the familiar theme of the wife who murders her virtuous husband out of lust for a robber. In this case the robber deserts the wife (feeling she is too treacherous to be trusted). As she is weeping at the loss of both husband and lover, Sakka (the bodhisatta) comes, with two other gods, to enact a little morality play which brings home to her the folly of her cruel passion.

Why such a savage onslaught on the fair sex? I am convinced that JS 61 gives us the most reliable clue to an answer. The stories are designed mainly to discourage young men from family life and sexual involvement. Now, as we have seen, the canonical reason for turning away from the entanglements of family life is that these are "fetters", nourishing the illusion of "self" and of attachment to other "selves"; only in the detachment of the realisation of *anattā* (selflessness) can true peace be found. We have also seen that the Jātakas studiously avoid the doctrine of *anattā*, since this would undermine their basic premiss: that the same person moves on from life to life. Deprived of the canonical objection to marriage, they have to invent another. As we have seen, there are passages in the Nikāyas, though they are not very prominent, which suggest that a woman's nature, as opposed to a man's, is lustful, fickle and never tired of sexual gratification. Many of the Jātakas latch on to these passages and build them to such exaggerated proportions that they become, in themselves, a sufficient reason (as they never are in the Nikāyas) for eschewing marriage.

Thus women pay very dearly for the Jātakas' need to avoid the *anattā* doctrine. In becoming the scapegoat, they must have found it very hard to retain any self-respect. A Theravāda woman, bred on the Jātakas, must have felt the dice were very heavily loaded against her – as must a layman who hoped that his marriage, against all the odds, would turn out well.

At least the Jātakas breed an ethos which is permissive of sexual frailty. A man need never blame himself if he indulges his illicit passions; he has been lured by the wicked wiles of the archetypal woman. It is equally fruitless to blame the woman; she is simply following her abysmal nature. Whilst the situation might be lamentable, it is only to be expected.

Interesting light is thrown on the attitude to women in general in JS 31. Here, a group of workmen are engaged in all manner of good works under the leadership of the bodhisatta. Since "they had lost all desire for womankind, they would not let any woman share in the good work". The four sisters of the bodhisatta prevail upon their brother to get this altered by saying to his colleagues, "Save the Realm of Brahma, there is no place from which women are excluded". Thus, although the sisters prevail on grounds of simple justice, we again see the tendency of men engaged in well-doing to exclude women, presumably because they fear that they will distract them from earning merit and tempt them back to the perilous path of self-indulgence.

Fortunately for the fair name of womanhood and for the hopes of young lovers, there are stories, though not nearly so numerous, in which women emerge in a very different light. Let us now look at this group – JSS 66, 67, 194, 223, 239, 267, 281, 320, 359, 408, 419, 485, 519, 539.

JS 66 we have already looked at in connection with the bodhisatta's own sexual record. It is the very charming story of the queen who, with great tact and insight and enviable strength of character, saves the bodhisatta from his own relative weakness.

JS 67 presents a woman with a dilemma; she can take with her only one of three people, either her husband, her brother or her son; which will she have? Contrary to everything the misogynous stories would have led us to expect, the woman chooses her brother on the ground that he, alone of the three, is irreplaceable.

In JS 194 the bodhisatta (a householder) is blessed (for a change!) with a wife who is as "faithful, virtuous and dutiful" as she is beautiful. The king sees her and, though he discovers that she is married, is maddened with lust and determined to get her. He tries to get the husband executed on a trumped-up charge of robbery, but Sakka, in response to the desperate prayers of the distracted wife, intervenes. The king, not the bodhisatta, is executed and the bodhisatta is made king in his stead. JS 485 has a very similar theme except that here the bodhisatta is a fairy and the king falls in love with his fairy wife. This time the king shoots the bodhisatta but Sakka intervenes before he dies and restores him to his former vigour.

The bodhisatta has become the king's adviser in JS 223. When he notices the selfish and shabby way in which the king treats his wife he advises her, in the king's presence, to leave him unless his behaviour improves, for "union without love is painful". This is only the second time so far that we have noticed the conjunction of love with marriage in the Jātakas. JS 320 tells a very similar story.

In JS 234 we have a most welcome inversion of the usual theme. A prince is banished by his suspicious father. Though he goes off with his wife, he quickly leaves her for a "woodland sprite" who has caught his fancy. The wife, disgusted, goes to the bodhisatta (an ascetic) and becomes his disciple. The sprite proves elusive, so the prince returns to his wife. When she sees him coming, she rises in the air and, from this safe vantage point, assures her husband that she has not the slightest intention of exchanging the mystic rapture she now enjoys for her old estate.

The point of interest in JS 239 is the little note in the introductory story telling how, when king Bimbisāra was murdered by his son, "the queen very soon died of love for him" – the third mention of love in connection with marriage.

The fourth occurrence of the word "love" is in JS 267 where the bodhisatta, now an elephant, is able to vanquish a huge and lethal crab only because his mate stays with him and helps. "Mate! don't leave me – for you love me well", he implores; his mate replies that she will never leave because, for sixty years "none so dear as thou has been".

The introduction to JS 281 informs us that Gotama's wife, the mother of Rāhula, became a holy Sister. In the introduction to JS 359 a very devout girl, married to a heretic, converts her husband by inviting monks to the house for alms food. They both then decide to become ascetics. In the story which follows, the bodhisatta, as a stag, caught in a snare, owes his life to his doe-wife's willingness to die, if need be, to save him.

The ending of JS 408 again contains a welcome inversion of the usual sequence. The bodhisatta (a potter), after listening to the preaching of four paccekabuddhas, calls his wife and announces that he wants to become an ascetic. He asks her to look after the children. She announces that she also has become dissatisfied with lay life and, on the pretext of going for water, actually goes to get ordained. It is her husband who has to bide his time until the children are able to fend for themselves! The sequel, with its account of the bodhisatta's rather unsatisfactory cooking, seems to be censuring the wife's behaviour as showing lack of concern for her children; we are given no indication how the wife was to have managed without the support of her husband's frugal income had he gone off to the monastery first.

In JS 201 we actually do have the reverse situation. The bodhisatta (again a poor man) is pushed into marriage against his will by his mother. He decides to become a recluse, but his wife informs him that she is pregnant and wants him to stay until his child has been born. After the birth, she wants him to stay until the child is weaned. The bodhisatta refuses to wait any longer, however, and escapes overnight. The verses make a virtue of this renunciation but again seem to show complete disregard for the economic plight of the deserted mother, thus:

> Not iron fetters – so the wise have told –
> Not ropes, or bars of wood, so fast can hold
>   As passion, and the love of child or wife,
> Of precious gems and earrings of fine gold.
>
> These heavy fetters – who is there can find
> Release from such? – these are the ties that bind:
>   These if the wise can burst, then they are free,
> Leaving all love and desire behind!

JS 419 tells of a courtesan who falls in love with a robber about to be executed. She bribes the chief constable to set him free and goes to live with him, having entirely given up her wealthier, former lovers. Her husband gets restless after a few months but, realising that his wife has great wealth, decides to kill her and go off with her fortune. He lures her to a lonely place and announces his intention to kill her. She begs to be allowed to pay him her last respects, does obeisance in front of him, at the two sides and behind – but when she goes behind him, she pushes him over a precipice to his doom. A passing deity (the bodhisatta) observes:

> Wisdom at times is not confined to men:
> A woman can show wisdom now and then.

Again, the theme of the faithless husband is a welcome inversion of a much more familiar theme. JS 318 is an interesting variation on this theme. Here the robber is the bodhisatta and the courtesan is more ruthless. She delivers the bodhisatta from execution by tricking her former lover into taking his place. The bodhisatta, whilst being grateful for his escape, is horrified at the way in which it has been engineered and decides to leave the courtesan before she betrays him for some new lover; he robs her of all her valuables before he leaves and, though she pines for him, he shows not the slightest interest in her fate.

JS 519 really conflates two stories, one of similar type to JSS 194, 485 and the other very similar to JSS 223 and 320. The varying of the theme and the conflating of the stories is, however, done with considerable skill. This time the virtuous wife accompanies her husband, a prince, into the wilderness even though he has leprosy. A goblin falls in love with her and waylays her. She is distracted lest, as a result of this incident, "the love of my dear lord for me should fall away" (the fifth mention of love in connection with marriage). Sakka saves her from the goblin but the husband doubts her story. She makes an "Act of Truth":[115] if she is telling the truth, her husband will be cured of his leprosy. He is cured and, in consequence, takes the throne. Then (story two) he entirely neglects the wife who has done so much for him and goes off with other women. This gives the bodhisatta (her father-in-law, who has renounced his throne to become an ascetic when his son's leprosy is cured) the opportunity to denounce his son's behaviour as "an act of treachery to a friend". The king is made to realise the value of a loving wife and makes amends to her. What a far cry this is from many of the stories in the earlier group!

JS 539 is a long and, in many ways, most appealing story with a number of themes and incidents. The last part of it tells of a king (the bodhisatta) who has renounced the throne in search of the ascetic life but his wife, who has been exemplary in her devotion and fidelity to him throughout, refuses to leave him. When he finally forces a parting, she is utterly desolated, but eventually herself becomes an ascetic of some distinction.

One thing should be apparent by now; the Jātakas have little taste for an insipid neutrality of character. If a woman is not a monster of wickedness (which she usually is), she is very likely to be such a paragon of virtue that even the bodhisatta will stand in awe of her. Perhaps, in the microcosm of popular Buddhist literature, we are getting the scent of an ambivalence in the attitude to women which penetrates deeply into the Indian tradition, though, in the Hindu context, the attitude of reverent awe, expressed in the worship of so many goddesses, is considerably more prominent than it is in Buddhism.

Other stories illustrate some of the common concerns relating to marriage and its responsibilities. These include the need to care for one's aged parents (JSS 455, 484, 532, 540); the perennial problem of the bride domiciled with her mother-in-law (JS 417); the importance of a male heir, especially to a king (JSS 489, 531, 538); the need to guard the virtue of one's daughter (JS 102); the importance of marital harmony (JSS 306, 504).

Finally, we should look briefly at a cluster of stories illustrating something we have already commented on in this section, namely a marked tendency in the Jātakas to adopt a lenient attitude towards sexual aberration. JS 225 concerns a courtier who has been sleeping with a girl (or girls?) in the king's harem; the same courtier discovers that one of his attendants has been taking the same sort of liberty in his own household. When the courtier drags the offending servant before the king (the bodhisatta), the latter, who is aware of his courtier's misconduct, simply says, in effect "if you have a good man, you must bear with his weaknesses".[116] In the introduction to JS 118 some married men get a "charming girl", presumably a courtesan, to accompany a bachelor friend of theirs to a festival so that they can all "have a good time together".

As we have already noticed, courtesans feature in a number of stories. Sometimes they behave rather badly, as in JSS 318, 425, but not always. In JS 276, there is a courtesan who, tested by Sakka, refused all other clients for three years because he had given her a thousand pieces and said "I will come bye and bye". She is depicted as a woman of strict integrity,[117] like the dancing girls of a king, who are, in the introductory story of JS 497, very willing to sit at the feet of an ascetic when the king falls asleep.

In general one can say that the expectation of sex is low, but the strength of the sex drive is acknowledged and there is no undue concern about its indulgence so long as one has no illusions about the hazards – notably the dreadful depravity of most women. On the other hand, it is acknowledged – and one suspects that the lay voice is making itself heard at this point – that marriage may, in exceptionally fortunate circumstances, be a loving bond which is mutually enriching and ennobling. Even then, though this is not often stressed, there will come eventually the searing pain of separation.

(b) *Love and Friendship*

If love is a rare and fragile adjunct of marriage, it is the very essence of friendship, the paradigm case being the friendship between the Buddha and his most intimate disciple, Ānanda, which runs like a thread right through the Jātaka stories. There is no constantly recurring wife for the bodhisatta. When she is identified, she is usually "the mother of Rāhula", in which case she will have been a good, or at least an indifferent, wife. When the wife is wicked (as in JS 199) she is simply not identified. Very little interest attaches to the person of the wives because (a) they are few and far between; and (b) they are very variable in character. Since, in most of his human incarnations, the bodhisatta becomes an ascetic, the question of a wife never arises in these cases.

Where friendship is concerned, the situation is quite different. There *is* a constantly recurring friend for the bodhisatta and the friend, unlike the wife, always has a predictable fidelity. In story after story the bodhisatta's friend plays a significant part, and in nine cases out of ten the friend will be identified as Ānanda. We have already noticed a number of these stories. We shall now look at the most noteworthy examples in the remainder of this group.

Within this group there is a cluster of six stories (JSS 310, 378, 411, 498, 529, 530) only half of which definitely identifies the friends as Buddha and Ānanda (JSS 310, 411, 498), but all of which exhibit a strong family likeness, though with some fascinating variations.

Common to all six stories is the theme that, on the very same day as a prince is born to the ruling king (Brahmadatta, except in JSS 498 and 529), a son is born to the king's chaplain. The boys grow up together, go to Takkasilā together for their education (except in JS 498), are extraordinarily good looking (not mentioned in JSS 310, 498, 530) and are the closest of friends.

In four of the stories, the bodhisatta is the chaplain's son (JSS 310, 411, 498, 530), whereas, in the other two, he is the prince. On three occasions Ānanda is identified as the prince (JSS 310, 411, 498) but he is never identified as the chaplain's son, perhaps because it was thought improper for him to be cast in a more religious role than his Master. Hence the chaplain's son in JSS 378 and 529 remains unidentified. In JS 530, because of the needs of this particular variant, the prince is not Ānanda but Ajātasattu.

In three of the variations (JSS 378, 498, 529), the sequel is that, when the prince becomes king, the chaplain's son, not wanting preferment at court, decides to become an ascetic. After fifty years he returns to the king, reminds him of their former friendship, preaches on impermanence (JSS 498, 529) or suffering (JS 378), and the two go off together to become ascetics. In JS 310 the pattern is the same except that, in this case, the king tries to persuade his ascetical friend to return to court, without success.

The two departures from this sequel are JSS 411 and 530. In JS 411, the bodhisatta, although the chaplain's son, eventually became king. This is because, when his friend (Ānanda) became king, he appointed the bodhisatta to be his priest. One day the king rides through the city on an elephant, decked in great splendour; the priest is seated behind the king on the same elephant. The queen-mother looks out to see her son riding in the street below, but it is the man behind him who catches her eye. She becomes completely bedazzled by the priest's beauty and begins to pine away. When her son realises the cause of his mother's illness he, with the magnanimity of the true friend, makes the priest become king in his place, on condition that his mother becomes his chief wife; he himself steps down to the position of viceroy. Though "they lived all in harmony together", the new king hankers after the religious life. His wife, thinking it is the big age gap which makes her husband shun her, plucks out one of her own grey hairs and hands it to the king, pretending she has plucked it from his own head. She thinks that if he discovers signs of ageing in himself, he will be more disposed to settle down with her. What in fact happens is that the king, as in other stories[118] interprets the grey hair as a sign of the transiency of life and resolves there and then to become an ascetic. He restores the kingdom to his faithful friend.

In JS 530, the bodhisatta is again the priest's son. He leaves his friend after having done his best to dissuade him from his monstrous plan to murder his father.[119] The prince does the murder and assumes the throne, though quickly overcome by guilt and fear as he contemplates his deed. His friend, having become an ascetic, returns after the customary fifty years – but in this case to admonish him. After preaching the terrors of hell reserved for, amongst others, parricides, he comforts his friend with the thought that each good deed he does will at least help to mitigate his sin.

Of this cluster, JS 498 is the most interesting in the present context. Before the part of the story we have described, this tale begins by telling of the three former births of both the bodhisatta and Ānanda, first as two Caṇḍāla outcasts, then as two deer, when "they always went about together . . . ruminating and cuddling together, very happy, head to head, nozzle to nozzle, horn to horn", then as two osprey – behaving in much the same way, save the horns. In the fourth birth, depicted in the main story, although the bodhisatta has preached the impermanency of all things in order to draw the king away to an ascetic's life, the story ends by telling us that, having spent their last years as brother ascetics, "these two together became destined for Brahma's world".[120] This is very striking because it shows how determinedly the doctrine of *anattā* (selflessness) is ignored in the Jātakas and how friendship is so prized and idealised that it is portrayed as capable of surviving the otherwise universal ravages of *anicca* (impermanence).

The other stories in which the bodhisatta and Ānanda-to-be are depicted as friends include JSS 157, 389, 406, 425, 456, 460, 473, 476, 501, 502, 532, 533, 534.

The introduction to JS 157 tells how Ānanda is given five hundred robes by five hundred of the Kosalan king's wives to whom he has been preaching. The king, who had just given these robes to his wives for their own use, is annoyed because he thinks that Ānanda, in violation of the Vinaya rule that a monk should only have three robes, is stockpiling and "doing a little trade in cloth, I suppose" – the robes are worth a thousand pieces each. Ānanda explains to the indignant king that a monk is permitted to accept what he is offered so long as he does not keep it to himself; he has in fact distributed the robes amongst his five hundred brethren who have then turned their old robes into cloaks, their old cloaks into shirts, their old shirts into coverlets, their old coverlets into mats, their mats into towels and their old towels have been shredded into the clay used to build their houses. The king is so delighted to learn of this alms-cycle that he promptly donates another five hundred robes to Ānanda, who in turn passes them on to his attendant. Although the latter has distributed his robes amongst his fellow students, some monks complain to the Buddha that Ānanda has shown respect of persons in giving so lavishly to one person. The Buddha rules that one good turn deserves another and goes on to explain how, in a former life, he, as a lion, had got stuck in some mud for a whole week until Ānanda, as a jackal, helped to free him, thus saving his life. In gratitude, the lion had adopted the jackal's family, always sharing his prey with them. The lioness suspected that her husband must have an amorous interest in the jackal's wife, so decided to scare her off. The jackal, learning of the threats made to his wife, told the lion that perhaps it was time for him to be going; he did not want to "outstay his welcome". When the lion realised that his wife had misread the situation, he explained to her how he owed his life to the jackal. Not only is the friendship retained but it continues between the offspring of lion and jackal "through seven generations".

JS 389 explains how the bodhisatta, when a brahmin farmer, liked to bathe in a pool each morning. He had become very friendly with a crab "of golden hue, beautiful and charming" (Ānanda) inhabiting the pool. Before leaving the pool each day, he placed the crab on his outer garments to bask in the sun until he returned it to the pool each evening. One morning, he "felt a return of affection for the crab, and embracing it laid it in his outer garment". This was on the morning that a snake, to do a favour for a friendly crow, whose wife had suddenly been seized with longing to eat the brahmin's eyes – in which "were seen the five graces and the three circles very pure" – had determined to bite and kill the bodhisatta. As soon as the crab hears the farmer fall and sees the snake, he moves swiftly to the rescue, trapping crow in one claw and snake in the other. He refuses to let them go until the snake has sucked back the poison and then, with scant regard for *ahiṃsā*, kills both snake and crow. The she-crow flees in terror but "there was still greater friendship between" the farmer and the crab. It is worth noting how much less sympathetic is the depiction of the married crows, especially the wife, than is that of the two friends.

JS 406, like JS 532, shows that the course of true friendship does not always run smooth. In JS 406, the bodhisatta is king of Gandhāra and Ānanda – the bodhisatta actually calls him "Ānanda" at one point in the story – is king of Videha. Though they have never met, the two kings are great friends. When Videha hears that Gandhāra has forsaken his throne to become a Himalayan ascetic, he decides to do likewise. When the two hermits eventually meet and chance to discover each other's identity they are "exceedingly intimate and friendly" – until Gandhāra one day chides Videha for hoarding salt after renouncing a kingdom. Videha becomes estranged for a time and chides his friend for chiding him. Videha comes to see, however, that friendship must be based on "truth that will abide" and, since his friend's chiding has been prompted by his devotion to truth, he becomes reconciled. "So both, never leaving off meditation, became destined for the Brahma world".[121]

In JS 532 the bodhisatta and Ānanda, both fresh from the Brahma world, are born as brothers, Sona and Nanda respectively. Their parents are wealthy brahmins and, when they notice how handsome the boys have become, want to get them married. When Sona, the eldest, refuses, saying he prefers to become an ascetic, and Nanda, the younger brother, follows suit, the parents decide that they also will join their boys in the ascetical life. Both boys are solicitous for their parents' welfare. Each day "through his possession of the Five Supernatural Faculties" Sona would travel great distances to gather sweet, ripe food for his parents. Always when he got back, the parents had already been fed with the local unripe or semi-ripe fruit gathered by Nanda and were now fasting. Fearing that Nanda's harsh diet will shorten his parents' lives, Sona requests his brother not to offer food to his parents until he has returned each day. Nanda, "desiring merit for himself only", continues as before. Sona now exercises the prerogative of the eldest son: "My father and mother are my charge", and sends Nanda away. There follows quite a power struggle between the brothers, each vying with the other to impress wide-eyed kings with his magical prowess. At last Nanda is forced to acknowledge Sona's ascendancy, is forgiven, and charged not to feed his mother with sour berries again, for the mother has endured endless pain and hardship on her son's behalf and deserves the tenderest care in her old age. The spectating kings are established "in the five moral laws" by Sona and go off to rule their kingdoms righteously. Sona and Nanda become again "destined to the Brahma world".

JS 425 was reviewed in the group of stories addressed to "passion-tossed" monks. Its interest from the present point of view is that, when the courtesan, by her hard-heartedness, has driven the bodhisatta to renounce the world, it is Ānanda (then the king) who misses his friend, discovers what has happened and sends the courtesan, on pain of death, to seek out the bodhisatta and bring him back. The courtesan cannot win back her former client, nor Ānanda his old friend, but the courtesan obtains the bodhisatta's forgiveness and the king's pardon. The faithfulness of the friend is again in sharp contrast to the fickleness of the woman.

JS 456, both in its introduction and in its birth story, does not move on a very exalted level. The introduction tells how Gotama has had a number of attendants, none of them satisfactory. Now he is getting on in years he needs somebody reliable to attend on him permanently. All volunteer – and are rejected – except Ānanda. Ānanda agrees to the job on eight conditions: The Blessed One must not (i) give him a robe offered to himself; (ii) give him his food; (iii) share his cell with him; (iv) ask him to go where he is invited; on the other hand, the Blessed One must (v) accompany Ānanda where he is invited; (vi) allow him to introduce important visitors; (vii) allow him to come to the Master whenever he has a doubt; and (viii) repeat for him on his return any discourse he has missed. All eight conditions are granted. In the story, a prince (the bodhisatta) accidentally bumps into a brahmin (Ānanda) and breaks his begging-bowl. He is unable to pay for the damage at that time but tells the brahmin to come to him when he is king. The brahmin comes and asks for a number of quite substantial favours, all of which are granted, for

> trusty men cannot forget the past,
> Their friendship and acquaintance ever fast.

It is this rather hard, contractual bargaining which disfigures so much marriage arranging in India. It is mercifully absent in most Jātaka tales about friendship, though this story is a reminder that it does occur.

In JS 461, the bodhisatta and Ānanda are again brothers, the eldest and youngest respectively of the thousand princes born to the King of Benares. When the bodhisatta, having discovered the evanescence of dew to be a parable on the nature of life, decides to become an ascetic, his youngest brother joins him and, once again, they both become "destined for the world of Brahma".

All the remaining stories, bar one, are strikingly similar. In four of them (JSS 476, 502, 533, 534) the bodhisatta is born as a goose, and in one of them (JS 501) as a stag. During three of the goose-incarnations, Ānanda is also a goose and, each time, is called Sumukha (JSS 502, 533, 534).

Of the goose incarnations, the first (JS 476) is rather different from the others. Here, the king (Ānanda) became very friendly with the goose. The goose expressed the mutuality of the relationship by coming one day with water on one wing and sandalwood on the other, sprinkling the king with each in turn. "From that time the king used to long for the Great Being; he would linger, watching the way by which he came." One day, when the goose had come to the king, who had "anointed him under the wings with unguents" and given him "sweet rice and sugared water in a golden dish, and talked with him in a voice of honey", the goose first tells the king, then demonstrates for him, the incredible swiftness of his flight. The king asks the goose if anything could conceivably be quicker than this. "Yes", replies the bodhisatta. "Swifter than my swiftest . . . a hundred thousandfold, is the decay of the elements of life in living beings." The king, made to realise the transiency of all things, is stricken with fear of death and asks the goose to stay with him permanently to teach and comfort him. The goose says that the king might get drunk one day and order his friend to be broiled for the royal table. The king vows that, if the goose stays, he will be a strict teetotaller. The goose then says that a friend is a friend, however far away, but the man who is near at hand may be a foe and not a friend. Then, with a note of sad realism which is seldom allowed to dull the normally idealised Jātaka picture of friendship, the goose says,

> Who stay too long, find oftentimes that friend is changed to foe;
> Then ere I lose your friendship, I will take my leave and go.

The goose holds out the hope that, while they both live, they can continue to meet occasionally.

This rather sad note of realism at the end of JS 476 includes the verse,

> The cry of jackals or of birds is understood with ease;
> Yea, but the word of men, O king, is darker far than these!

In the remaining goose-incarnations (JSS 502, 533, 534) and in the stag-incarnation (JS 501), Ānanda is also born as an animal of the same species. Without the sad possibility of human faithlessness to mar the picture, the view of friendship is again restored to its lofty ideal, though, even at the animal level it should be noted that the friends concerned are always male.

In each of these stories, the bodhisatta gets caught in a trap and owes his life to the fact that his friend (Ānanda) refuses to leave him when the hunter comes, even though he is risking his own life.

In JS 534 (alone of the four stories) the bodhisatta, who is the king goose and has been taken captive by the fowler, begins to pine for his wife. He tells his friend Sumukha that he fears she might take her life in her grief at his non-return. Sumukha snorts with disgust to think that his friend, though good at admonishing others, can now "under the sway of passion" babble like boiling water. He decides "to make clear to him the vices of the female sex", and proceeds to make the usual charge of licentious lust and deceit. It is gratifying to note that the bodhisatta, "in his infatuation for the female sex" will have none of this. Women are the producers of life; it is from them that we draw our own breath and we should not disdain them. This little interchange[122] beautifully epitomises the ambivalent attitude to women already noted.

There is no ambivalence in the attitude to friendship. The last story in the Ānanda group introduces a little cluster of stories whose main purpose is, in a highly didactic way, to sing the praises of friendship. Before passing to this group, however, mention should be made of one other story which, though not in the Ānanda group, affords another personal illustration of the bliss of true friendship. The introduction of JS 27 tells of a monk who, even after joining the Order, would go to his friend's house for a meal every day. His friend would then "accompany him back to the Monastery, where he sat talking all the livelong day, till the sun went down". The monk always went back with his friend as far as the city-gates in the evening. The Buddha comes into the Hall when the monks are discussing "the intimacy of these two". He does not attempt to censure their behaviour but explains how they were thus intimate in a former life when the brother had been a royal elephant and his lay friend a dog. At first the dog went to the elephant's stall just to pick up scraps of food but, by frequenting the place, the two animals became very dear and, indeed, inseparable friends. When somebody took the dog away, the elephant refused to eat or drink until the king, having learned of the "warm friendship" that existed between the two, and having been advised by his minister (the bodhisatta) to find the dog immediately, restored the dog to him. "The elephant took the dog up in his trunk, and placed it on his head, and wept and cried, and . . . saw the dog eat first and then took his own food."

The last Ānanda story (JS 473), along with JSS 162, 187, 486, and part of 544, is a sermon on friendship rather than a story about friends. What we learn about friendship from these stories is that it is indiscriminate – the black hind will lick the faces of lion, tiger and panther alike (JS 162); it can be extended to beings of quite a different order from oneself – the tree-sprite and two geese in JS 187; it has distinguishable marks – the true friend remembers his friend in absence, greets him on return, has the same friends and foes as his friend, will not allow his friend to be slandered but is glad to hear him praised; true friends share secrets and guard them, speak well of each other, rejoice to hear of each other's welfare but sorrow at bad reports, always think of each other when one alone enjoys some pleasure in the other's absence (JS 473); everybody needs friends, especially at times of crisis – the hen-hawk is very thankful that she insisted her husband should find friends before she would agree to marry him; it is they who save her chicks from the hunters (JS 486); since one becomes like one's friends, it is important to choose them carefully (JS 544 – see JS VI p. 119). This last piece of wisdom about friendship is imparted by Rujā, a very devout princess "possessing great merit" because she "had offered prayer for a hundred thousand ages"; she turns out to be Ānanda again – in his only female incarnation recorded in the Jātakas.[123]

In what is said about friendship in the Jātakas it is fairly clear that a good deal of homosexual emotion is operating, though no oriental would wish to describe it in this highly Westernised, self-conscious way. Anybody who has observed the way in which men in Eastern countries will hold hands, embrace each other and generally show physical warmth and affection, must surely realise that there is an ocean of difference between Eastern (particularly Indian) and Western cultures in this respect. The East has not been afflicted with the Judaeo–Christian taboos which have made the homosexual emotion, at least for men, such a stunted and neurotic travesty of itself in the West. The Indian tradition has never seen warm, tender, loving feeling between males as anything but good – so long as the males concerned were mutually motivated towards the good and were not, either one of them, gravitating towards the evil. In a Buddhist context, it was the Five Precepts which served as the ethical touchstone.

There was no problem about the homosexual emotion then; what about overt homosexual practice? In JS 211 we are told that a young brahmin lad (the bodhisatta), after going to Takkasilā for his education, became the king's attendant "and he grew very dear to the king and became a favourite". Since kings were so little given to sexual restraint, it would be hard to suppose that the favouritism and the "dearness" were other than sexual. Yet there is no suggestion of censure in the story and the bodhisatta seems quite happy with the situation. In JS 253, the bodhisatta and Ānanda have again been born as brothers. When their parents die they were both "so deeply pained" that they became anchorites. A serpent king (and the serpent in the Jātakas is always, as Freud would have been gratified to learn, associated with voluptuousness) assumes the form of a man and comes to the young brother's hermitage. Ānanda (for the younger brother has no other name in the story) and the serpent talk for a while and presently "such friends did they become, that there was no living apart for them. Often and often came Jewel-throat [the serpent] . . . and when he left, so much did he love the man, he put off his shape, and encircled the ascetic with snakes folds, and embraced him, with his great hood upon his head; there he lay a little, till his affection was satisfied". Ānanda likes his friend well enough in human form but is petrified of the serpent hug he keeps getting. He grows thin and yellow, with protruding veins. The bodhisatta is worried by these signs of ill-health in his brother and, learning the cause, he simply asks, "do you like him to come or not?". The absence of any moral censure at this point is very striking. When Ānanda replies, "No I don't", his older brother shows him a way of keeping the serpent away. He is to ask the serpent to hand over his jewel. But this, though it succeeds so far as the serpent is concerned, is no cure for Ānanda. "Not seeing his beautiful serpent-king", he grows yet thinner and yellower. When the bodhisatta sees what is happening, he rather self-contradictorily sings,

> Importune not a man whose love you prize,
> For begging makes you hateful in his eyes.

The older brother counsels the younger not to grieve and together they yet again become "destined for the heaven of Brahma".

In JS 346 the bodhisatta is born into a brahmin family and is called Kappa. After being educated at Takkasilā he becomes an ascetic and studies under Kessava, becoming the senior of his five hundred pupils. The bodhisatta "shewed a friendly feeling and affection for Kessava. And they became very intimate one with another". After Kessava has visited the king of Benares (Ānanda) – for once he is not the bosom friend – with his disciples, the king persuades the old teacher to send his disciples back by themselves to the Himalayas so that the king can personally look after the sage. The arrangement does not work. "Kessava was unhappy at being deprived of the society of Kappa, and in his desire to see him got no sleep"; the sleeplessness induces dysentery and the king's physicians cannot help. There is no help for it. Kessava has to go back to the Himalayas and his beloved Kappa. "By the mere sight of Kappa, Kessava's mental disorder ceased and his unhappiness subsided." Kappa lovingly tends his aged teacher and, soothed by Kappa's bland diet, Kessava's dysentery is instantly assuaged. The king is a little hurt. He wants to know what Kappa has that he lacks; in particular what efficacy there is in Kappa's poverty-stricken meal compared with the luxury of the royal table. The answer he gets is,

> The food may coarse or dainty prove,
> May scanty be or much abound,
> Yet if the meal is blest with love,
> Love the best sauce by far is found.

Sex and marriage; love and friendship; there can be no doubt that this is the way in which the Jātakas, on the whole, see it. Sex and marriage on the whole are bad; love and friendship on the whole are good and, if one has correctly read between the lines, if sex enters into a loving friendship, there is no cause for alarm. When one remembers the enormous amount that is said in warning of the dangers of forming heterosexual relationships in the Jātaka stories, it is quite remarkable that there is not one word warning of the dangers of a homosexual relationship. The only reservation ever expressed is with regard to the corrupting influence of an evil friend. But whereas the corrupting influence of an evil woman is the norm in the Jātakas, virtuous women being merely exceptions which prove the rule, the possibility of a friend's becoming a corrupting influence is so remote that it is hardly ever mentioned.

This differs from the canonical position. There, unquestionably, sex and marriage are bad, but so are love and friendship, since these involve one in personal attachments and painful (or potentially painful) emotions. The only love or friendship which the canon can bless is that which is quite detached and general; a "boundless friendly mind for all creatures".

From the layman's point of view the Jātaka stories have one big advantage over the canon. Insofar as the main characters in a birth story are identified with people still living, it follows that they cannot have attained *nibbāna*; it further follows that, in their previous lives, they cannot have behaved themselves in such ways as would have brought them to *nibbāna*; in particular they cannot have realised in any depth the socially chilling doctrine of *anattā*. The Jātaka characters, even when holy ascetics, have thus been free to form personal attachments and enter into loving relationships in a way that brought them close to the ordinary layman. What we could regard as the solid core of the teaching of the Four Nikāyas, on the other hand, is undeniably addressed to aspiring *arahants*, i.e. to men whose ambition it was never to be reborn and who therefore wished to live in such a way that they would be carried right beyond the sphere within which the Jātakas operate.

Nevertheless, the Jātakas reflect the canonical aversion to marriage, though they tend to make misogyny rather than a high doctrine of detachment the basis of their objection. The Jātakas also exploit to the hilt the marked silence of the Nikāyas regarding homosexual attachments. They fill the canonical vacuum with a warm ideal of male friendship, which, if canonically unsupportable, is humanly very attractive.

6 Social Teaching

This is the third and final chapter dealing with the ethical teaching of our two sources. Taking the five precepts as our framework, the two previous chapters have dealt in detail with the first and third of these. This leaves us with the second, fourth and fifth precepts, i.e. those forbidding theft, false speech and the consumption of intoxicants. These three can be said to have a more emphatically social reference than the other two because *ahiṃsā* extends to all sentient life, not just to human society, and sexual conduct, whilst it obviously has social ramifications, belongs to one's private rather than one's social life. Private property, speech and liquor, on the other hand, necessarily imply human beings in inter-action but do not extend beyond the sphere of human society.

Along with material relating specifically to these three precepts, this chapter will consider other aspects of social teaching, e.g. the principles of good government, as they occur in our sources.

(a) THE FOUR NIKĀYAS

Trevor Ling has recently[124] drawn attention to the fact that the Buddha came from a ruling family. The business of governing and giving one's mind to matters of social concern were in his blood. Even after his renunciation of courtly life, Gotama never lost his interest in government and its problems. The fact of his having been a prince made it natural for the kings in Sāvatthī and Rājagaha,[125] Kings Pasenadi and Bimbisāra, to come to Gotama not merely for spiritual comfort and guidance but also for wise advice in matters of state. In fact, Gotama, with his princely background, did not make a rigid distinction between the two spheres. A king's spirituality and a king's mode of governing were inseparably yoked together. If the one was sound, so would be the other – and vice versa. The same was true of the community at large. The state of the nation in a secular sense was inseparably yoked to the state of the nation in a spiritual sense. Gotama never saw his monks as a "gathered" community, a spiritual "ghetto" divorced from the society which supported it. He did not think of church and state as two separate entities. He saw the function of the state as being to provide a framework of social living based on righteousness as summarised in the five precepts. This moral fabric was not regarded as a secular (as opposed to a spiritual) concern. It was the basis upon which *sīla* (morality) – the first and basic segment of the three-fold Buddhist *dhamma* – could be laid. Unless the state observed the principles of *sīla* and ordered its life in accordance with these principles, it was highly unlikely that individuals would attain to great moral stature.[126] In the righteous state, the righteous individual would be a natural outcrop and the monk would be seen, not as an isolated segment of society, but as the man who had risen to the top of a ferment of righteousness which ran right through society. He in turn would be seen as leavening the rest of the lump. It was along these lines, at least in theory, that the Empire of Asoka, the first great Indian empire, was conducted. Although Asoka never became a Buddhist in any partisan or exclusive sense, his whole way of thinking, both as an individual and as a ruler, was permeated with Buddhist teaching.[127]

According to Buddhist tradition, the marks of the Buddha are also the marks of the *cakravartin* (wheel-turning monarch). The one who has these marks will either turn the wheel of state in accordance with the principles of cosmic righteousness (with a heavenly wheel to signal cosmic approval) or he will become a great enlightened Buddha, setting in motion the wheel of the Dhamma according to the principles of cosmic wisdom (with various natural portents to signal the cosmic approval – see GS II 134f, IV 209). Again, there is no hard line between sacred and secular. It is precisely the same kind of person who is needed to excel in either sphere. GS I 71 states that there are two persons born into the world who bring profit, happiness and welfare to many folk, are extraordinary men, whose death is regretted by many folk and who, being enlightened, are worthy of a relic-shrine. "What two? A Tathāgata, an Arahant who is a Fully Enlightened One, and a world-ruling monarch."

Nevertheless, it should never be forgotten that Gotama *did* renounce the throne. However important he considered affairs of state to be and however willing he remained to give advice upon them, they were not important enough. Ultimately they were to be renounced. Affairs of state were affairs to do with this transitory space-time world in which the laws of karma and rebirth and the fact of *dukkha* (suffering) held sway. The cosmic wheel of the *cakravartin* was, when all was said and done, the eternal wheel of *samsāra*; it was a web of suffering. The cosmic wheel of the *dhamma* was the wheel of release, the wheel that span right out of space-time and broke entirely clear of the web of suffering spun by that other wheel. The core of Gotama's teaching is concerned with the second wheel, not the first. He claims to have been born as a *cakravartin* many times before,[128] but his present state is infinitely superior. In KS V 296f it is said that the "Ariyan disciple" (i.e. the one who has attained to arahantship) is sixteen times superior to the *cakravartin* ruling the four kingdoms. The reason given is that, whereas the *cakravartin*, for all his magnificence and virtue, is still not freed from *samsāra*, the Ariyan disciple is.[129]

Yet, though affairs of state cannot be said to touch the real core of Gotama's teaching, which was reserved for those who had "dropped out" of ordinary society altogether, these matters were not forgotten. People have to start somewhere. For Gotama, the starting place is always virtuous conduct, and this begins with the ruler. If the king mercilessly plunders his people, how can he expect them not to steal from each other? If the king is constantly fighting and killing, how can he expect his subjects to shed no blood? If the king is deceitful and treacherous, how can truth and right speaking prevail in his domains? If he is a drunkard and a wastrel, how can his people be sober? Villainy breeds villainy and violence violence. Harsh laws do not breed virtue; only virtue can do that. The king is not there to tax and exploit his subjects in order to satisfy his own ego or pander to his own lusts; he is there to serve his people and to provide them with the fabric of righteousness within which they can grow and flourish.

If it all sounds somewhat utopian, it should be remembered that, apart from its enormous impact on Asoka's India, this teaching has proved – and still is proving, in spite of tremendous counter-pressures – a powerful and stable social philosophy in Theravāda countries. One should not underestimate that which, for over two thousand years, has, barring periods of foreign, un-Buddhist interference, proved so practically effective. Gotama understood what many opportunist politicians forget: there is a great deal of utopian idealism in ordinary people. The "man in the street" is capable of standing much taller than the cynic would allow.

Yet Utopias do not come. If they did, Gotama would not have renounced his throne. Righteous rule, like anything else, is impermanent. One may have it for a while, but it will be supplanted.

There is a kind of momentum in human affairs which works counter to the ideal. Thus, in the *Cakkavatti-Sīhanāda Suttanta* (the Lion-roar on the turning of the Wheel; DB III 65ff), Gotama tells a story which follows a typically Indian, contra-evolutionary cyclical pattern. Long, long ago, King Strongtyre ruled the world with perfect righteousness for thousands of years. When he heard that the Celestial Wheel had begun to sink in the sky, he knew that the time had come for him "to seek after divine joys". He accordingly handed his kingdom over to his eldest son, shaved his head and became a recluse. The Celestial Wheel disappeared. The young king consulted the royal hermit and enquired how he could get it back. He was instructed in the "Ariyan duty of a wheel-turning Monarch" – which consisted mainly of honouring holy men and having a proper concern for all his people. The king governs accordingly and the Wheel returns. The Celestial Wheel, "with its thousand spokes, its tyre, its navel and all its parts complete", now moves in turn to each of the four directions. The king follows it each time and meets all the kings in each direction, instructing them (at their request) in the Five Precepts and making them his vassals. This entire process repeats itself, without any apparent loss of momentum, through seven long reigns, each lasting many thousands of years.

Then comes a king who does not consult the royal hermit but governs "by his own ideas". His ministers and officials come to him in alarm and tell him how vital it is for him to observe the "Aryan duty of a sovran king", which they "keep". After being duly instructed, the king partly conforms to the Ariyan duty but, by neglecting to bestow wealth on the destitute, poverty becomes widespread. In this situation, a certain man steals for the first time. Brought before the king, he explains that it was dire necessity which drove him to theft. The king does not punish him but provides him with money. As news of this gets round, stealing becomes a popular pursuit. When the king realises what is happening, he does a complete *volte-face* and starts beheading thieves. Thieves consequently start beheading their victims and, when caught, start denying their crimes. Thus stealing, killing and lying have become commonplace, meaning that three of the precepts have been violated already. Soon evil-speaking, adultery, abusive and idle talk, covetousness and ill-will, false opinions, incest, wanton greed and perverted lust, lack of filial and religious piety and lack of regard for the head of the clan have grown apace.[130]

During this process of degeneration, the people's lifespan has gradually shrunk from eighty thousand years to a mere hundred years. Eventually, says Gotama, it will shrink to ten years and maidens will become mothers at the age of five – and by this time the very word "moral" will have disappeared; human beings will wallow like swine in a morass of promiscuity and incest; they will delight in cruelty and violence. A few will escape to the jungle to escape the holocaust which eventually ensues. As they emerge, they will begin, by a process of natural revulsion, to seek to restore the lost rudiments of morality until eventually, countless thousands of years hence, we are back at the wheel-turning king, ruling the world from Ketumatī, the new name for a renewed Benares. Then will come Metteyya, the next Buddha, and he will have a thousand followers for every hundred of Gotama's.[131]

What is suspicious about this story is that it ends on this eschatological note. This is the only mention of Metteyya in the whole of the Four Nikāyas. The story does not tell us that the process does not stop there; the rest of the Canon assures us that it does in fact go on to another period of decline – and so on, world without end. This is why Utopias do not come and why no saṃsāric goals are ultimately satisfying. Nevertheless, the concept of the ruler's central role in establishing a morally sound state is entirely typical of canonical teaching.

If we look more closely at the specific content of Buddhist social morality, the thing which is most striking is the peculiar emphasis given to speech.

In MLS I 224ff, Gotama lays down the basis of monastic morality. He begins with the five precepts (except that the fifth is again not mentioned). The first three are hardly elaborated at all, but the fourth becomes:

> Abandoning lying speech, he is one who abstains from lying speech, a truth-speaker, a bondman to truth, trustworthy, dependable, no deceiver of the world. Abandoning slanderous speech, he is one who abstains from slanderous speech; having heard something here he is not one for repeating it elsewhere for (causing) variance among these (people). . . . In this way he is a reconciler of those who are at variance, and one who combines those who are friends. Concord is his pleasure, concord his delight, concord his joy, concord is the motive of his speech. Abandoning harsh speech, he is one who abstains from hard

speech. Whatever speech is gentle, pleasing to the ear, affec-
tionate, going to the heart, urbane, pleasant to the manyfolk,
agreeable to the many-folk – he comes to be one who utters
speech like this. Abandoning frivolous chatter, he is one who
abstains from frivolous chatter. He is a speaker at a right time,
a speaker of fact, a speaker on the goal, a speaker on *dhamma*, a
speaker on discipline, he speaks words that are worth treasuring,
with similes at a right time that are discriminating, connected
with the goal.

None of the precepts which follow are elaborated at all. It is
thus apparent that speech is singled out for special treatment. We
notice exactly the same emphasis when Gotama outlines the
dhamma for the householders of Sala in MLS I 344ff. This layman's
dhamma is divided under the headings of body, speech and
thought,[132] but the section relating to speech is longer than the
other two. It counsels against lying, bearing false witness at a trial,
slander, sowing discord, harsh speech, frivolous or illtimed or
inaccurate speech or speech not relating to the goal, the *dhamma*
or the discipline. It is almost identical with what was said to monks
in the discourse quoted above.

In KS I 293f, Sakka discloses that he attained to his present
position by living a previous human life in accordance with seven
rules. Of these seven, three had to do with speech, viz, speaking
gently, not indulging in slander and being truthful.

The concern for truth is indicative of something central to
Buddhism. Gotama's teaching does not depend on faith in a
divine being or on the performance of sacrificial rituals or on
prayers for divine grace and favour; it claims to be the truth –
hence the "Four Noble Truths". Applying this teaching "works for
the welfare of gods and men", not because of any supernatural
resources being tapped, but because to live in accordance with the
teaching is simply to live in accordance with the truth. The teaching
works because this is the way the world works. In social affairs, the
truth is all-important because only when men's lives are organized,
both corporately and individually, in a way which corresponds with
the truth, can there be any possibility of spiritual progress.

One corollary of this is that caste is seen to be baseless. There
is nothing in the nature of things corresponding to the caste
divisions which had already become an important feature of
Indian life in Gotama's day. The alleged superiority of the

brahmin depends on his privileged access to Vedic mantras and rituals. Since Gotama entirely denied the efficacy of such things, the brahmin was deprived of his claim to privilege. In reality, all men (and gods) are equally subject to the law of karma. They all, prince and pauper alike, grow old, get sick and die (KS I 125ff). They all fare according to their deeds.[133] A brahmin who commits a crime is as liable to punishment as anybody else, just as a brahmin recluse is as worthy of respect as any other recluse (MLS II 273ff). Superiority derives from merit, not from any inherited factor like caste (DB III 79f). The true brahmin is the man "who stands on dry land", who has crossed the stream and attained the further shore, i.e. *nibbāna* (GS II 5).

What is so offensive about animal sacrifice is that it is based on two lies. It assumes that such sacrifice is efficacious whereas, according to Gotama, it simply isn't. It also assumes that wanton slaughter of animals, even for religious purposes, is not a flagrant violation of a natural law whereas, according to Gotama, it surely is. The principle of *ahiṃsā*, being part of the teaching, is simply the expression of the truth which outlaws such lies.

The social teaching of the Nikāyas is thus based very firmly on the other aspects of the teaching, the whole *dhamma* being integrated around the concept of truth, regarding which Gotama seems to have espoused a predominantly correspondence theory. That is to say, he believed the truth of his teaching to reside in its correspondence with objective fact. It did not depend on an act of faith or on an elaborate metaphysical theory; it invited each man to test for himself, in the crucible of his own life and experience and of his own intellectual scrutiny, whether or not it corresponded with the "way things are" (*yathābhūtaṃ*).

This claim does not, of course, *establish* the truth of the teaching, but it does make plain how it wishes to be judged and how it sees itself. It also establishes the criterion for all social life and for government legislation. These also have to be in accordance with the truth; they must not, in any degree, compromise with unreality. This means, quite simply, that, from the point of view of the Nikāyas, social life must be regulated by the *dhamma* and, pre-eminent in all this, is the virtue of truth-speaking itself.

(b) THE JĀTAKAS

On the face of it, the approach of the Jātaka stories to social teaching is strictly in accordance with that of the Nikāyas. It will be apparent from stories reviewed in previous chapters that the theme of the king who renounces his throne in order to become an ascetic is very common. Particularly striking is the cluster of stories relating to the chaplain's son who, though born on the same day as the prince and though so friendly with him, yet decides to avoid entanglement with courtly life by becoming a recluse as soon as the prince becomes king. After fifty years, he returns to his friend and persuades him too to join him in the ascetic's life (JSS 378, 498, 529; cf 310, 411, 530).

Another very interesting example is JS 10. The plot is the same as that of JS 346, the story of Kappa and Kesava, which was mentioned in the previous chapter. Here, the roles are reversed. The elderly ascetic is now the bodhisatta and it is his senior pupil who pines for him. Instead of the master returning to the Himalayas, it is now the pupil who returns to court and, having greeted his master lovingly, just reclines on a mat beside him "crying with passionate earnestness, 'Oh, happiness! Oh, happiness!' ". Even when the king arrives, he just stays reclining like this. The older hermit excuses his pupil, explaining, "Sire . . . of old this ascetic was a king as you are. He is thinking how in the old days when he was a layman and lived in regal pomp . . . he never knew such happiness as now is his. It is the happiness of the monk's life, and the happiness that insight brings, which move him to this heartfelt utterance". This admirably expresses the canonical order of priorities. A king is, when all is said and done, simply a layman enjoying regal pomp, a man with many cares and duties; the recluse, being "freed from slavery to lusts" is the happier of the two. Whilst establishing the canonical order of priorities, however, the Jātaka subtly alters the emphasis. Where the canon would say that the recluse was superior in wisdom, the Jātaka says he is superior in happiness.

JS 181 is a fantasy on the theme of kingly renunciation. Prince Peerless (the bodhisatta), although the heir, declines the throne of Benares in favour of his younger brother. He goes to a neighbouring kingdom where the king and courtiers "showered gifts and honours upon him like rain" because of his prodigious skill as an archer, enabling a second arrow to overtake and slice the first, even though the first has travelled so high that it reached the heaven of the Four Great Kings.[134] When they see this, the people go wild with delight and respond as Jātaka crowds usually do to such spectacular feats: "they cheered and clapped and snapped their fingers, thousands of kerchiefs waving in the air". Prince Peerless now has to hurry back to Benares to rescue his brother, encircled by seven hostile kings. Sending an arrow into a golden dish from which the seven kings all happened to be eating, Peerless warned them of his return and of their fate unless they retreated immediately. "Thus did our Prince put to flight seven kings, without shedding even so much blood as a little fly might drink; then, looking upon his younger brother, he renounced his lusts, and forsook the world". This story is, in comic strip fashion, making the point that the super-hermit is also the superman. If he could be bothered with secular affairs – which he can't – he would not only be superlatively wise but superhumanly skilful and invincible. JSS 229 and 230 express the same idea. The bodhisatta, in one story the king of Takkasilā being besieged by the king of Benares, and, in the other, the king of Benares being besieged by the king of Takkasilā, deflects a mighty army simply by the display of his superhuman magnificence.

Another theme, which recurs very regularly, is that of the recluse or the wise mentor who preaches to the reigning monarch the five precepts and/or the ten duties of kingship.[135] Apart from these special occasions, the king is in the habit of consulting his chaplain before making any important state decisions. We saw in the table in chapter one[136] that the bodhisatta himself appears as king's chaplain or son of the king's chaplain twenty times; he is the king's minister or adviser even more often (thirty times). This oft-recurring theme of advice to the throne from the man of religion (or, even if from a secular source, the bodhisatta as king's adviser) reinforces the principle that secular affairs are strictly subordinate to the preoccupations of the monk and holy man. It is only through the guidance of the holy man that secular affairs can be properly and rightly conducted.

In some stories there are bad kings, though sometimes reclaimable, who are hostile to holy men. JS 149 is a tale about a king who asks a very holy ascetic (the bodhisatta) to try to reclaim his "fierce and passionate" son, Prince Wicked. The ascetic manages to do this by getting the prince to taste the leaf of a seedling Nimb tree. It is so bitter that he immediately spits it out, with the comment that what is now merely unpleasant will probably be deadly poison when the tree is full grown. The bodhisatta gets the prince to see that his future subjects will think likewise and, if he continues to develop in the same hateful way, will hound him out of the kingdom rather than risk a tyrant on the throne. From this time forward the prince "grew humble and meek, merciful and overflowing with kindness". He eventually becomes an exemplary king. In JS 396, the king's councillor (the bodhisatta) manages to convert a king who had been "set on the way of the evil courses" by finding similar homely parables with which to teach the importance of royal rectitude.

JS 202 tells of a King Brahmadatta who could not stand anything old. Old women are sent for "and beat upon the belly, then stood up again" and given a "scare". The whole court takes to this obscene geriatric-baiting, so that soon all the king's subjects are having to hide their old folks away. Because of the depravity at court and the inability of the people to care for their aged parents, Sakka (the bodhisatta) observes that there are "no new-comers among the gods" but, on the contrary, "as men died, they filled up the four worlds of unhappiness" (i.e. they were born in one of the hells or as animals, *petas* or *asuras*). Sakka comes to the king, disguised as an old man, and, after thoroughly humiliating him, warns him that he will cleave the king's head with a thunder-bolt unless he mends his ways, which, of course, he promptly does. Part of Sakka's rebuke consists in reminding the king that he also will grow old; he should ask himself how he would like it if he were treated, in his old age, as he treats others. Sadism is another form of untruth since it treats the other person as a non-person in defiance of the actuality. This particular form of sadism in the monarch upsets the whole fabric of the state, since it incidentally undermines the principle of caring for and reverencing one's aged parents. Somewhat similar is the story (JS 228) telling how the bodhisatta (again as Sakka) cures a king of his greedy lust for riches by appearing in human form and enacting a little morality play.

The fault is not always in the king. JS 213 tells of a quarrel between two bands of ascetics, one of them led by the bodhisatta himself. The quarrel is to do with who has the right to sit in the shade of a certain banyan tree. The king rules that the group who first sat under this tree have the right to it. The rival group "looked about them with divine vision, and observing the body of a chariot fit for an emperor to use, they took it and offered it as a gift to the king, begging him to give them too possession of the tree". In other words, they use their supernatural faculties (in a typically far-fetched manner) in order to bribe the king for their own advantage. The bodhisatta's group retaliates in a similar manner, but the ascetics are then stricken with remorse: "to think that we, who have overcome the love of riches and the lust of the flesh, and have renounced the world, should fall to quarrelling by reason of a tree, and offer bribes for it!". They speed away to the Himalayas to avoid being tempted to further sin. The "spirits" dwelling in the kingdom are so angry with the king for accepting bribes that they cause a flood in which the king and all his subjects perish, the latter "for the sake of the king of Bharu alone". In this case, the entire state perishes because the king had been seduced into immoral behaviour through the shortcomings of ascetics.

The prince in JS 247 is described as "an idle lazy loafer".[137] When the king dies, his adviser (the bodhisatta) counsels against consecrating this prince until his fitness has been tested. The courtiers hold a trial in the prince's presence; first they make a deliberately wrong judgement and then a manifestly right one. Each time they ask the prince what he thinks of their judgement. When they discover that he reacts in exactly the same way on both occasions, they decide that he is a "blind fool" and make the bodhisatta king instead. Here is a case of a potential king being set aside in favour of his adviser because of the importance attached to royal wisdom and integrity.

JS 257 is a fantasy on the same theme. Here the bodhisatta (Prince Mirror-face) succeeds to the throne at the tender age of seven because he demonstrates, in various fanciful tests, his precocious maturity of judgement. As king, he rapidly acquires a reputation for his phenomenal wisdom. This story really amounts to a distortion of canonical teaching because the king's wisdom is so magical and exaggerated that one tends to lose sight of the canonical reason for urging royal wisdom, which is simply the need to ensure the maintenance of a righteous social fabric.

The canonical view is better maintained, though still in a somewhat fanciful way, in the story (JS 276) of the king of Indapatta (the bodhisatta), in the Kùru kingdom. Not only the king, but also the fifteen people most closely associated with him, observe the "Kuru righteousness" (i.e. the five precepts). When a neighbouring kingdom, Kāliṅga, is afflicted by drought and when none of the king's desperate attempts to bring rain (including the borrowing of the Kurus' state elephant) have been of any avail, the king learns that the real secret of the abundant rainfall enjoyed

by the Kurus is the meticulous observance of the Kuru righteousness by the Kuru king and his entourage. The king of Kāliṅga
sends for details of this righteousness. He gets the five precepts
inscribed for him on a plate of gold but he finds that the king and
all the members of his entourage are so scrupulous in their
observance of the precepts, that they all fear that they may have
infringed one of them at some time or another. The theory underlying this story, namely that complete social righteousness can
even ensure an adequate rainfall, however much it may stretch
our credulity, does nevertheless enjoy canonical support, as was
shown in the first section of this chapter.[138]

There is an even more far-fetched claim in JS 334, where an
ascetic (the bodhisatta) demonstrates to the king that, when a
ruler is unjust, even the ripe figs taste bitter! JS 520 is much more
realistic. The bodhisatta is here a tree-spirit regularly worshipped
by an otherwise evil and reckless king. The tree-spirit decides that
he owes it to the king to admonish him and get him to save his
decaying kingdom from collapse. He appears to the king one
night for this purpose and, on the following day, the king, accompanied by his chaplain, tours his kingdom to learn with shame of
the suffering his corrupt rule has brought to all his subjects. The
king returns having resolved to rule righteously hereafter.

Fantasy again takes over in JS 281 so that (as is fairly often the
case), the didactic element in the story becomes blurred and confused. Sakka feels so threatened by the holiness of a certain sage
(the bodhisatta) that he promises the barren queen a son who
will become a *cakravartin* if she obtains a "middle mango". This
is an elaborate device to disturb the ascetic and to prevent him
from having "tranquillity of mind". With the aid of parrots and
goblins the queen gets her "middle mango" – but still no son!
The ascetic is undisturbed. In this story, a scheming Sakka fails
in his plan and fails to redeem his promise, but no point of
substance seems to emerge.

JS 479 is a fantasy on the theme of the *cakravartin*, King
Kāliṅga (Ānanda). Even this great king finds that his state elephant is quite unable to approach the bo-tree, for, as his chaplain
(the bodhisatta) explains, it is "the throne of victory of all the
Buddhas, which has become the very navel of the earth". No
secular pomp, not even that of the *cakravartin*, can penetrate it.

JS 309 is a fascinating story in that, although the bodhisatta is
here an outcast in the process of stealing from the royal mango

grove, he admonishes the king and his brahmin teacher because he has overheard the king learning sacred texts from the brahmin whilst sitting in a higher seat than the brahmin; he tells them that they are both wicked in that neither of them recognises the superiority of the sacred over the secular. The king is so pleased with the pariah's "exposition of the law" that he makes him lord protector of the city by day and king by night, adding that, but for his outcast birth, he would have made him sole monarch.

The most flagrant case of a king who flouts the "law" (i.e. the moral precepts) is furnished by JS 313. Here, the drunken King Kalābu (Devadatta), enraged that, whilst he had fallen into a stupefied sleep, his dancing girls had gone to listen to a wise ascetic (the bodhisatta) in order to snatch the opportunity to hear "something worth hearing", has the ascetic arrested and, hoping to prove the superficiality of his holiness, tortures him by whipping him, then by cutting off his hands, feet, nose and ears. The ascetic does not become angry, but this monumental wickedness earns for Devadatta yet another long sojourn in the Avīci Hell. History repeats itself in JS 359 where Devadatta is again a cruel king, though this time his wrath is provoked by his own seven-month-old son. Sensing that the boy already has a much dearer place in his wife's affections than he himself enjoys, he has his son's hands, feet and head cut off and corpse mutilated. Needless to say the earth opens up and the king makes his familiar journey to the Avīci Hell.

JS 353 recounts how a king, though instructed by a good and wise teacher (the bodhisatta) in his youth, has, as his teacher had predicted of him, been reinforced in his own cruelty by heeding the advice of his cruel priest (Devadatta). The king sets out on a path of conquest and gouges out the eyes of a thousand captive kings before tearing out their entrails and sacrificing them. The king gets blinded himself and eventually goes to hell as, one feels certain – though we are not explicitly told this – does his priest.

JS 487 presents us with an interesting study in the relationship between sacred and secular. This is the story in which the bodhisatta, as chaplain to the king, "a wise, learned man" we are told, falls in love with a slave-girl by whom he has a son. He will not allow the child to be named by his family name because "it can never be that the name of a noble family should be given to a slave-girl's bastard". As the son grows up, having learned from his mother that the chaplain is his father, he falls in with a group of ascetics amongst whom he rapidly establishes himself as the most learned and best equipped to lead the company. The king hears of his eminence and comes to visit him in company with the bodhisatta. The king is duly impressed by the learned ascetic but the chaplain, even after discovering that this is in fact his son, tells the king that the ascetics are knaves and deceivers and would be better employed as soldiers in his army. He asks for his son to be employed as chaplain under himself. In this story, the bodhisatta is himself a rather worldly holy man and his son is even more compromised. The father apparently takes it for granted that his son, whose parentage is so deeply infected by wordly passions, can never, no matter how earnestly he tries, break through to true sanctity.

We observed, at the beginning of this section, that the theme of the king's renouncing his throne to become an ascetic occurs very commonly in the Jātakas. In some of the later stories, this theme could be said to have run riot. Hence in JSS 70, 505, 509, 510, 522, 525, 538, 547 we find that accommodation is provided for a retiring prince or monarch by Vissakamma, the heavenly architect, on the express orders of Sakka. In JS 70, the king (Ānanda) is seized with a desire to lead the anchorite's life after listening to a great sage (the bodhisatta) preaching. When the people of Benares hear of the king's renunciation they all decide to follow suit. "A train twelve leagues long" sets off for the Himalayas and, in order to accommodate this massive exodus, Sakka orders a hermitage of matching proportions to be built in a demesne from which "all the noisy beasts and birds and fairies" had been driven away. In JS 505, on the other hand, Prince Somanassa is provided with a simple leaf-hut by the heavenly architect, though he is attended by a retinue of deities in human shape. Equally modest accommodation is provided for the great Prince Vessantara and his family in JS 547.[139] The remaining stories (JSS 509, 510, 522, 525, 538) all follow the pattern of JS 70, accommodating huge numbers of ascetics in vast hermitages.

If a king is righteous but retains the throne, he acknowledges the superiority of the ascetic's life by being generous in his patronage and support of holy men and by listening attentively to whatever wisdom they impart. This theme recurs so often that it would be tedious to record instances, though one instance is of particular interest since, in this story (JS 421), the king's barber becomes an ascetic and eventually attains to the rank of a paccekabuddha. When he returns to court, he calls the king by his family name – much to the indignation of the queen-mother ("This low-caste shampooing son of a barber does not know his place; he calls my kingly high-descended son Brahmadatta") and other courtiers. The king rebukes the critics, however, and shows great deference to the ex-barber, adding,

> One who bowed before us all,
> Kings and lords must now salute.

Two heroic instances of royal generosity occur. These are the stories of kings Sivi (JS 499) and Vessantara (JS 547). The stories have a good deal in common and both go a good deal beyond the "middle way" advocated in the Nikāyas. Canonical giving is a means of acquiring merit and of advancing along the Path, but it is supremely the means of maintaining the Order. In these stories, which are but extreme examples of a tendency discernible in many of the Jātakas, giving has become much more than the provision of the basic needs of the *sangha*; it has become a challenge to scale the heights of self-sacrifice and to realise the extremest form of self denial.

Both Sivi and Vessantara (the bodhisatta in each case) make the same vow.[140] They are dissatisfied with gifts, however lavish, which "come from without". They vow that if anybody asks for part of their own bodies – heart, eyes, flesh, blood – they will, without a moment's hesitation, give it. In each case Sakka hears the vow. He comes to Sivi in the guise of a blind old brahmin and asks for an eye. Sivi gives him both eyes. One of his courtiers asks him what he hopes to gain by this sacrifice – is it "life, beauty, joy or strength"? Sivi replies that it is none of these things, neither is it glory, sons, wealth or kingdoms, but

> This is the good old way of holy men;
> Of giving gifts enamoured is my soul.

It turns out that his action is not as disinterested as this would suggest, however. Having donated one eye to the brahmin, Sivi says to him, "the eyes of omniscience is dearer than this eye . . . a thousandfold: there you have my reason for this action." Sivi is wanting to exchange his ordinary human vision for "the eye of omniscience"; sure enough, Sakka returns to him undisguised and restores his eyes, not mere "natural eyes", "but these eyes are called the eyes of Truth Absolute and Perfect".

The story of Vessantara is told in the last and best-loved of all the birth stories. After making his vow, Vessantara is married to Queen Maddī, becomes King and, soon afterwards, the father of a son and daughter. When there is drought in a neighbouring kingdom and when the monarch there is unable, by his austerities, to produce rain, he sends eight brahmins to Vessantara to ask for his white state elephant, which has the reputation of bringing rain wherever it goes. Vessantara not only donates the elephant but also the priceless jewels with which it is adorned, together with five hundred attendants, and grooms and stablemen. Generosity on this scale so alarms his subjects that they go to Vessantara's father and beg him to banish his son before the kingdom is ruined. Before he departs, together with his devoted wife and children, Vessantara indulges in more extravagant giving, even donating the chariots and horses he had been given to take him into banishment. All these spectacular gifts are accompanied by earthquakes and other portents. When Vessantara and his family are living in the hermitage provided for them by Vissakamma, an old brahmin (Devadatta) comes to the banished king and asks for his children to be his slaves. The children, overhearing the request, run away. The brahmin taunts Vessantara with the accusation that, whilst he has said he will gladly give his children, he has at the same time signalled to them to run away. Vessantara calls to his young son to come out of hiding, saying,

> Be thou my ship to ferry me safe o'er existence' sea,
> Beyond the worlds of birth and gods I'll cross and I'll be free.

The son dutifully returns and then the daughter. The father is joyful, "thinking how good a gift he had made", and prays, like Sivi, that he may attain omniscience: "dearer than my son . . . a hundred thousandfold is omniscience". The brahmin ties the children together and drives them away, whipping them cruelly. Twice they escape and return to the father, begging him not to let this cruel old brahmin take them away. But Vessantara, though he is greatly moved, knows that a righteous man will never retract a gift once given. Though he grieves for his children he realises that "all this pain comes from affection and no other cause; I must quiet this affection and be calm". He drives away the "keen pang of sorrow" "by power of his knowledge". His wife had been away when the children were given to the brahmin. On her return, Vessantara sits silent as she becomes increasingly distraught at not finding her children. When she faints away, "although for seven months past he had not touched her body, in his distress he could no longer keep to the ascetic's part". Putting her head in his lap, he soothes her and tells her the truth, begging her not to grieve; "We'll get them back alive once more, and happy shall we be". Maddī rejoices at her husband's generosity,

> For you, the mighty fostering king of all the Sivi land,
> Amidst a world of selfish men gave gifts with lavish hand.

She begs him to go on giving. On the next day, Sakka comes to Vessantara disguised as a brahmin and asks for his wife. Without hesitation, the gift is made, for Vessantara reflects:

> Not hateful is my faithful wife, nor yet my children are,
> But perfect knowledge, to my mind, is something dearer far.

Maddī is prepared to go uncomplainingly with the brahmin – and there are the usual natural signs and portents to celebrate this signal act of generosity. Then Sakka reveals himself, restores Maddī to Vessantara and grants him eight boons. Vessantara asks 1. that his father restores him to the throne, 2. that he may never condemn a man to death, 3. that all his people may look only to him for help, 4. that he will always be content with just his own wife but never subject to a woman's will, 5. that his son may live long and victoriously, 6. that celestial food will be provided each morning, 7. that he may always have the wherewithal to give without stint and 8. that he may go directly to heaven at death and never again be born on earth. These eight boons are granted, though, of course, the eighth is inconsistent with his being re-born as Gotama! There is thus a totally happy ending to the story.

Although the extravagance of the giving of Sivi and Vessantara is greatly lauded by the poet, and although this theme of totally unreserved generosity is such a popular theme of Indian poetry generally,[141] it does nevertheless have some very disconcerting features. The canonical basis for giving, especially from the throne, is that this establishes the well-being of the monks and ensures the supremacy of the *dhamma* in the administration of the state. In these stories, giving has become almost a self-indulgence. It is on such an extravagant scale that it bears little relation to the actualities of life, neither does it consider the possibly harmful effects of such lavish generosity on its recipients; it shows a total disregard for personal feeling and it retains a rather distasteful ulterior, contractual character. The giving is not really disinterested. It is a *quid pro quo*, material "goods" (including one's family in this category) being exchanged for spiritual benefits. Though the giving seems so costly at times, its costliness is largely offset by the donor's bland confidence that it must pay off.

One is compelled to say that at this immensely popular point, the Jātaka tales are moving very markedly in the direction of the Mahāyāna, where the quality of sacrificial self-giving, often in the most extravagant terms (see Matics, 1971, for instance), is one of the most emphasised of the boddhisatva's qualities. This Mahāyānist extravaganza is also, as we have noted, a return to a very popular Hindu theme, though a departure from the "middle way" of canonical Theravāda, in that it turns giving into a mechanism for merit-making which is essentially a substitute for the rejected vedic sacrifices. Giving becomes almost like gambling; the higher the stakes, the higher the potential winnings – though the Jātakas assure us that there is really no gamble involved. By sheer karmic necessity, giving *must* have its reward. The canonical view is that giving is a means to an end, the means by which the *sangha* can be nourished and maintained, but that it should not be allowed to get out of hand. The monk must constantly be on guard against being corrupted by the generosity of merit-seeking donors; the donor must never forget that his is the inferior position. To receive is more blessed than to give since one's highest good depends on one's willingness to forsake all worldly possessions and oneself depend on the generosity of others. The magnification of heroic giving into an end in itself, a supreme expression of spiritual eminence, is a clear distortion of the canonical teaching.

So much, then, for the question of the relation between the roles of king and ascetic, of the passage from the one to the other and of the relation between state and *sangha*. As we have seen, this is one of the major concerns of the Jātaka collection. There are a few stories which look at things more from the viewpoint of the individual, but which stress the extent to which the individual is influenced by his environment.

JS 26 is a naive little story about an elephant which, through repeatedly overhearing the talk of burglars conspiring in its stall, becomes as vicious as the burglars, taking all the men who approach in its trunk and dashing them to death on the ground. The king (Ānanda) sends his minister (the bodhisatta) to investigate the elephant's change of character. Learning of the evil influence the burglars have had, he counteracts this simply by sending good men to converse in the elephant stall. JS 184 tells of a horse that started limping only because it was imitating a lame trainer. At the end of JS 186, we are told of a gardener who deliberately causes the fruit of a sweet mango tree to become bitter by planting sour-leafed nimb trees and creepers around the mango. The stanzas end with the line: "And so you see bad company will make the better follow suit". As we noted in chapter one,[142] JS 503 tells how the bodhisatta and Devadatta were once born as brother-parrots. In spite of their having the same parents, a whirlwind carries the bodhisatta to a hermitage and Devadatta to a robber village; their characters develop accordingly.

This is not the whole story, however. There are other tales, notably all those which recount great acts of renunciation, wherein individuals successfully resist the pressures of the environment. Along similar lines is JS 183, which contrasts the quiet behaviour of thoroughbred horses, even after drinking strong drink, with the disorderly behaviour of donkeys fed on a much milder brew. The second stanza moralizes thus:

> The low-born churl, though he but taste and try,
> Is frolicsome and drunken by and by:
> He that is gentle keeps a steady brain
> Even if he drain most potent liquor dry.

The need for a righteous state is emphasised by the stories showing how individuals are affected by their environment; the limitations of the righteous state spring from the fact that, whatever his environment, the "low-born churl" is very easily led astray.

What constitutes a righteous state? As we have seen, this is primarily dependent on the ruler's personal integrity. He should genuinely respect the *dhamma*, honour the *sangha* and seek to administer his kingdom in accordance with the five precepts. In this chapter, it is with the more specifically social precepts, the ones prohibiting theft, wrong speech and intoxicants, that we are mainly concerned.

Stories which concentrate on the wrongness of theft are not very common though, as we have seen, robbers quite often appear in the tales. There are even two occasions when the bodhisatta is born as a robber. One of these, JS 279, includes the apologetic note that "the Bodhisattas, even though they are great beings, sometimes take the goods of others by being born as wicked men; this they say comes from a fault in the horoscope". In these cases, it seems, in spite of the law of karma, one's destiny is decided by one's stars rather than by one's deeds! This is one of the gratuitous details which constantly enliven the Jātakas since this story is not really about theft at all but about the importance of being able to distinguish friend from foe. The other story in which the bodhisatta is a robber is JS 318. In JS 164, where he is a vulture, he takes to thieving in order to repay a merchant for saving his life. In JS 168, as a quail, he all but loses his life for poaching on another's territory.

JS 305 is the tale perhaps most specifically concerned with the second precept. Here a father, who is also a teacher, tests the virtue of his students to see which of them is most eligible for the hand of his daughter. He asks his students to steal dresses and ornaments for his daughter, adding that he will only accept those articles the theft of which has escaped notice. Only the bodhisatta refuses to steal. When asked why, he says it is because no act of sin is ever hidden; even when no human eyes see, there are wood spirits and similar powers to observe and record the sin.

Perhaps those stories in which a king is admonished for discarding faithful servants who have grown old (JSS 409, 413) can be regarded as an extension of the precept against stealing. These people (or animals) have rendered the king faithful service for which he is now indebted to them. If he simply casts them off in their old age, he is failing to honour his debts and robbing them of that which is their due.

Although the fifth precept is quite often passed over in the Nikāyas, there are a few birth stories which are concerned with the evils of drink. The introduction to JS 81 tells the sad story of an Elder, Sāgata, who, having "won such supernatural powers as a wordling can possess", is able to subdue a fearsome nāga when sober but, when given "clear white spirit" by followers of the "Wicked Six", becomes so drunk that he could not "master even a harmless water-snake". In the story itself (JS 81), the bodhisatta is a brahmin ascetic whose five hundred pupils ask permission to "go to the haunts of men and bring back salt and vinegar".[143] They are given permission to go on their own for the duration of the rainy season. When the king hears of their arrival he gives them royal hospitality. All is well until, on the day of a drinking festival, the king sends them "a large supply of the best spirits", thinking that this will relieve the customary austerity of their lives. They get drunk and indulge in dancing, singing and horseplay. On the morning after, they are filled with remorse for this lapse and hurry back to their teacher, determined not to go off alone again or to frequent the haunts of men. As well as counselling against drink, this story is fairly typical in the stress it lays on the importance of staying with one's teacher, the corrupting influence of even well-disposed laymen and the vulnerability of an uncloistered virtue.

In a sub-story of JS 537,[144] we are told a story illustrating the hazards of lay life. A young Brahmin boy, born into a family "which kept the five Moral Precepts", falls in with a group of friends who eat meat and fish and enjoy strong drink, though the boy himself abstained from all these things. His friends resent this on the ground that "this boy because he takes no strong drink does not pay his reckoning". There is thus an economic as well as a social motive for getting the boy to conform to his friends' habits. This is achieved by tricking him into drinking alcohol disguised as lotus nectar while they are all at a festival. The boy loves the taste (and also the taste of the meat fed to him by his friends when he is drunk) and rapidly degenerates into alcoholism. His parents despairingly try to wean him away from his vice but, when they realize that it is hopeless, they disinherit him and leave him to die in squalor.

JS 466 is an interesting story, though its main point is to caution against greed and attachment rather than to inveigh against alcohol. Nevertheless, the latter theme plays quite an important part in the plot. A thousand carpenters with their families arrive by ship at an island where food and fruit grows in abundance. When they encounter the only human inhabitant of the island, he assures them that they have come to an idyllic spot; the only thing they have to be cautious about is that "the isle is haunted by demons, and the demons would be incensed to see the excretions of your bodies". They are cautioned to dig holes in the sand and cover their excrement whenever they relieve themselves. Eventually they decide to have a celebration and brew some toddy from the wild sugar-cane. They get drunk and relieve themselves all over the island, making it "foul and disgusting". The demons are furious and determine to send a tidal wave to drown these wretched despoilers of their playground. A good deity, not wanting to see them destroyed, goes to warn the carpenters of their impending doom whilst an evil deity, wanting them all to be destroyed, tells them that the first deity is merely wanting them to leave and that there is no real danger. Amongst the carpenters, there are two leaders, one wise (the bodhisatta) and one foolish (Devadatta). The wise leader says that, in case the first deity was right they should, Noah-like, build a ship and wait in it on the day for which the disaster was forecast. The foolish leader says this would be a waste of time and laughs his rival to scorn. Of course, he and the five hundred families who have followed him are drowned in the deluge, whilst the bodhisatta and his followers sail away in the safety of their ship. Their lives are saved because they have not grown so attached to the pleasures of the island that they have been unwilling to entertain the possibility of having to leave it. For all the families, it is their night of drunkenness which brings disaster.

In JS 220, the rather unlikely reason given by Chattapāṇl for including abstention from wine in his "four virtues" is that

> Once I was drunken, and I ate
> My own son's flesh upon my plate.

JS 512 is the story already referred to[145] where Sakka (the bodhisatta) comes to the king (Ānanda) specifically to warn him against the dreadful dangers of drink.

The remaining precept, the fourth, which prohibits wrong speech is, as we have already noticed, one to which the Pāli Buddhist literature gives especial prominence. It has already been noted that, in JS 431, we are specifically told that, whilst the bodhisatta can, on occasion, violate all the other four precepts, he can never tell a lie, since this would violate "the reality of things".[146]

There are many other instances which show the peculiar

importance attached to this precept in the birth stories. In JS 261, the bodhisatta is one of three brothers who try to get an old, noseless lake-keeper to give them some lotuses which grow on his lake. The two brothers hope to put "the old lacknose" in a good mood by telling him that his nose will quickly grow back again; they get no lotuses. The bodhisatta says that this is the babble of fools since a nose, once lost, can never be regained; he gets his lotuses.

JS 322 is a marvellous tale about the need for an objective realism, an unshakeable truthfulness, if the panic based on a wild rumour is to be allayed. A somewhat neurotic hare has just been thinking, "if this earth should be destroyed, what would become of me?" when a fruit falling on a leaf convinces him that the end is indeed at hand. The hare, terror-stricken, begins to fly away and soon gathers a host of other animals, equally terrified, and equally anxious to flee, because of the first hare's cry that "the earth is breaking up". A young lion (the bodhisatta) sees this mad, headlong flight and, guessing that it is based on some unfounded fear, determines to stop a stampede which could have tragic consequences. He stands in the path of the fleeing column and brings it to a halt. When informed that the animals are rushing away because the earth is collapsing, he asks for the evidence: "who saw it collapsing?" Animal after animal has to admit that it only knows of the disaster by hearsay. When the rumour is finally traced to its source, the lion says he will return with the hare to its starting place to see for himself what the position is; the other animals are to stay put. When the falsity of the rumour has been established by the lion, the herd is told to return to the forest.

In JS 332, the bodhisatta, as Lord Justice to the king, admonishes the king for sentencing a village to be punished simply on the basis of one man's report – which turns out to be false. In legal disputes it is especially important that every effort be made to obtain the truth impartially and patiently by probing every available source of information and then sifting conflicting reports with critical rigour.

JS 422 is the story already referred to[147] in which Devadatta as king of Ceti goes to the Avīci hell by degrees because he repeatedly tells a lie at a time when lies were unheard of and nobody knew what sort of thing it was, even asking each other, when first told that their king was intending to lie, "what kind of a thing is a lie?

is it blue or yellow or some other colour?" In this story, the telling of a lie becomes a kind of Fall from primeval virtue and innocence; once the lie is told, "right" is destroyed and other vices ensue.

JS 432 is a curious tale about a young man (the bodhisatta) who obtains a spell which enables him to trace footsteps even after twelve years. The king hears of this and, to test the boy's powers, himself steals and hides some royal treasure, then, pretending innocence, asks the boy to find both treasure and thief. The treasure is recovered without difficulty but the boy is reluctant to name the king as thief, telling stories which hint at the thief's identity instead. The king, however, insists that the thief be plainly exposed, with the result that, when the boy yields, the people are outraged, club the king to death and put the bodhisatta on the throne. The king's offence seems to have been his deviousness; in his anxiety to test the boy's skill, he had told lies and confused the truth. As in the previous story, it seems to be implied here that it is a particularly wicked thing for a king to compromise the truth since, by so doing, he undermines the foundations of the righteous state.

Devadatta again comes to grief by compromising with the truth in JS 474. Here he is a young brahmin who discovers that an outcast sage (the bodhisatta) has a charm enabling him to grow and sell fruit out of season. He manages to obtain the charm only by promising the bodhisatta that, if at any time the king should ask him how he came by this charm, he will on no account attempt to disguise the lowly origin of his mentor. As we should expect – and as the bodhisatta has predicted – when the test comes and the brahmin is questioned, he does lie and he does lose the charm. JS 518 is yet another instance of Devadatta's inability to honour his word. In this story, he poses as a sham ascetic and is thus able to get the snake-king to divulge the reason why the garuḍas are unable to capture snakes and carry them off.[148] Before divulging his secret, the snake-king has obtained the sham-ascetic's solemn promise that he will never disclose this secret to anybody else, least of all the Garuḍa-king. The ascetic promptly betrays his snake friend to the garuḍas and pays for his sin by going once again to the Avīci hell after his head has been split into seven pieces.

Apart from the merit accruing from right speaking, an "Act of Truth" can also act as a magical charm to accomplish some world-ly goal or to obtain divine assistance in times of crisis. In JS 35, the bodhisatta, as a young quail abandoned in the path of a forest fire, is in a desperate plight until he recalls that there is great efficacy in goodness and in truth, as there is also efficacy in the attributes won by previous Buddhas. He invokes all these efficacies, along with the efficacy of compassion, purity of life and faith, to make an Act of Truth; in their name he "conjures" the fire to retreat. In JS 491, a paccekabuddha's Act of Truth sets at liberty all creatures held in bondage. In JS 539, a wrongfully imprisoned prince sets himself free by his "solemn asseveration" of his innocence. In JS 444, two parents come to an ascetic (the bodhisatta) imploring his help to cure their son of a snakebite, saying, "Sir, religious people know simples and charms; please cure our son". The ascetic says he does "not ply the physician's trade", whereupon the parents beg him to perform an Act of Truth. He does this and asks the parents in turn to do likewise. With each declaration, the boy improves until he is finally quite well again. The idea here seems to be that an Act of Truth differs from a charm in that it releases power accumulated by one's own merit.

In JS 463 also, the bodhisatta's Act of Truth restores a boat to its proper course without any suggestion of divine intervention – though here a bath in scented water and the donning of new clothes seem to be necessary supplementary rituals. In JS 519, which we shall be looking at in a moment, the Act of Truth is accompanied by the sprinkling of ordinary water.

In JS 499, the story of king Sivi, when Sakka appears to the blinded king, he tells him that his eyes will be restored if he makes an Act of Truth. Sivi says he thinks his gift of his eyes should be enough to enable Sakka to restore his sight without any other means. Sakka replies, "Though they call me Sakka, king of the gods, your majesty, yet I cannot give an eye to any one else; but by the fruit of the gift by thee given, and by nothing else, your eye shall be restored to you". There seems to be a good deal of confusion here. If an Act of Truth is efficacious by itself, there would seem to be no reason for Sakka's presence. At the same time, it is clearly stated that gifts are not divinely bestowed but are merely the karmic fruit of one's own virtuous deeds. It looks as if there has been some tampering with the story in an attempt to change an act of divine help into an act of karmic reward, though the magical effect of this Act of Truth can hardly be said to be consistent with canonical teaching in any case.

There is a similar confusion in JS 540 where four marvels

(including the extraction of poison from a wound) are accomplished by an Act of Truth. A goddess, moved by pity, also makes an Act of Truth, but the story goes on to say that the marvels are accomplished "by the goddess's supernatural power".[149] Similarly, in JS 544, the princess (Ānanda), seeking to convert her father from heresy, prays for divine assistance – but adds "if they (the gods) have no power in themselves, then let them come by my power and virtue and drive away this heresy".[150]

In JS 519, the virtuous wife of a leprous king accompanies him into the forest. One day she is waylaid by a goblin who has fallen in love with her. "By the efficacy of her virtue", Sakka comes to her rescue. Her husband asks her why she is late returning and doubts her story. She makes an Act of Truth saying that, if she is indeed virtuous, his leprosy will be cured – which it promptly is. At the end of JS 518, it is the snake-king's Act of Truth which splits Devadatta's head into seven pieces – a reminder that the power of an Act of Truth can be used destructively as well as constructively. JS 537 furnishes another example of an Act of Truth being used curatively[151] but, in this case, the bodhisatta (who makes the Act of Truth) combines it with some business with the pounded bark of a tree – further evidence of the non-Buddhist, folk-cultural ethos to which the Act of Truth belongs. Though Sakka's aid has been granted earlier in JS 519, there is no mention of it in connection with the Act of Truth. In JS 538, however, when a barren queen requests, in an Act of Truth, that if she has never broken the commandments, she be granted a son, Sakka's dwelling becomes hot and, having ascertained the cause, he gives the queen a son. Here, there is a combination of karmic virtue and divine assistance. This comes out even more clearly in JS 75, where the bodhisatta, as a fish, makes an Act of Truth and thereby, "as a master might call to a servant", commands Pajjuna, king of the devas, to send rain. In JS 513, a prince's mother, sister and wife make an Act of Truth with the refrain,

> And by this Act of Truth I've charmed
> The gods to bring thee home unharmed

Here it is quite clear that the Act of Truth has the theurgic properties of a charm, compelling the gods into one's service, something quite over and above the karmic fruit of one's own deeds. In JS 542[152] a queen's Act of Truth (the truth in question being that a villainous priest has ordered human sacrifice), combined with an appeal to "ghosts, goblins, fairies . . . all ye gods", again wins Sakka's attention and timely intervention.

There is really nothing Buddhist about this idea at all. It is pure Indian folk religion. It is far, far away from the lofty canonical concept of truth as that which corresponds with "things as they are" (*yathābhūtaṃ*) and respect for which is therefore the necessary prerequisite for any aspirant to enlightenment.

This canonical respect for truth underlies the Buddhist attitude to caste. A man must be judged according to what he is, not according to the family into which he was born – however much his previous acts may have pre-determined the circumstances of his birth. Once born, a man or woman is capable, in large measure, of deciding his own destiny regardless of caste.

The highly discursive introduction to JS 465 tells a most interesting story, amongst others, about a deception practised by the Sakyas in order to preserve their purity of caste. The monks complain to the king of Kosala that, although his hospitality is lavish, the food is served with little friendliness, so that the monks are reluctant to feed at the palace. The king asks Gotama where the monks do find friendliness and obtains the reply, "with their kindred, great king, or with the Sakya families". The king then determines to get a Sakya girl to be his queen and sends to Kapilavatthu, Gotama's birthplace, for this purpose. The Sakyas think it will break "the custom of their clan" (i.e. their caste restrictions) to allow such a marriage but, on the other hand, are subject to the king of Kosala and afraid to anger him. They compromise by offering a girl who, though her father is a Sakya prince, has a slave girl for her mother. This is kept quite secret, but the Kosalans, knowing that "these Sakyas are desperately proud in matters of birth", decide to test the girl by seeing if the Sakyas will eat with her. She passes the test because of a trick; they seem to be eating with her without actually doing so. The son born to this Sakyan wife eventually discovers the truth about his parentage and, after experiencing the proud disdain of the Sakyas for himself, he vows that, when he is king, he will wreak a bloody revenge. The introduction ends by saying that he eventually "slew all the Sakyas".

It is hard to know how much credence to give this story because other elements in the same introduction are very fanciful. Since it reflects badly on Gotama's own caste, however, it is very unlikely to be pure invention. Insofar as it does have a factual kernel, it suggests that Gotama must have found it very difficult to overcome caste prejudice. JS 487 suggests that, in at least one of his incarnations, the bodhisatta himself showed similar pride of caste. He regards his child by a slave-girl as a "bastard" and will not allow his family name to be given to it. The ironical thing is that, later in this same story, the bodhisatta denies that caste, including his own brahminhood, has any true validity: "when men are purified . . . the good perceive that they are saints, and never ask their birth". Indeed, the ascetic himself must be indifferent about his own caste pedigree – or lack of it; JS 490 tells of an ascetic (the bodhisatta) who "was unable to induce the mystic ecstasy because he was full of pride for his noble birth".

The bodhisatta again shows caste scruples in inverted form in JS 497 when, as an outcast Caṇḍāla married to a woman of nobler birth, he refuses to consummate the marriage in the ordinary way on the grounds that this would involve "transgressing . . . the rules of caste".

In the last section of JS 543,[153] however, the bodhisatta preaches a sermon in verse to refute "the false doctrine" of a brahmin who has claimed descent of all brahmins from the creator Brahman and has maintained the efficacy of vedic ritual, especially sacrifice by fire.

The bodhisatta's sermon says that sacrificial fire is no more efficacious than a cook's fire or the fire that burns refuse. If Brahman is the creator,

> Why are his creatures all condemned to pain?
> Why does he not to all give happiness.

The brahmins themselves are accused of being mercenary:

> These Brahmins all a livelihood require,
> And so they tell us Brahma worships fire.

They dupe the credulous with strange rituals and mysterious mantras but,

> A clever low-caste lad would use his wit,
> And read the hymns nor find his head-piece split.

If no crime attaches to animal sacrifice and the victim is assured of heaven,

> Let Brahmins Brahmins kill – so all were well –
> . . . We see no cattle asking to be slain.

The whole theory of caste – and indeed of karma – is challenged:

> It was no lack of merit in the past,
> But present faults which made them first or last.
> . . . For after all, loss, gain and glory, and shame
> Touch the four castes alike, to all the same.

This poem is more vituperative and polemical than anything we read in the Nikāyas but, in all its main points, it is, as reference back to the first section of this chapter will confirm, asserting the canonical position.

7 *Doctrinal Teaching*

The title of this chapter needs to be understood in a limited sense because, of course, the preceding three chapters, concerned with the ethical teaching, have been doctrinal in a sense. *Sīla* (morality; conduct) is one of the three planks of Buddhist *dhamma* (teaching). From the point of view of the Jātakas, it is the most important of the three since it is the one which impinges most on the life of the ordinary layman. The second of the three planks is *samādhi* (meditation). This aspect of the *dhamma* only crops up incidentally in the present work since it never figures at all prominently in the Jātakas. When a recluse retires from the world to meditate, the usual Jātaka formula is contained in a single sentence informing us that he attained the "(Eight) Attainments and the (Five) Supernatural Faculties ((*aṭṭha*) *samāpattiyo* (*pañca*) *abhiññā*.)". Alternatively, we may be told that the recluse meditated "in the four stations of brahma" (*cattāro brahmavihāre*), but again without being told any further details.

The third plank of the *dhamma* is *paññā* (wisdom). It is the part of the teaching belonging to this category which forms the subject of the present chapter. *Paññā* is in fact at two levels, the first intellectual and the second experiential. It is not difficult to understand Buddhist wisdom at the first, intellectual level but it is taught that the second level will only be attained as the result of a gradual maturing resulting from disciplined meditation and control of the senses. We shall now investigate this aspect of the *dhamma* in each of our two sources.

(a) THE FOUR NIKĀYAS

According to MLS I 362f, it is the first two stages of the Noble Eightfold Path (*ariyo aṭṭhaṅgiko maggo*), Right View (*sammādiṭṭhi*) and Right Intention (*sammā-saṅkappo*), which are concerned with Wisdom (*paññā*), whilst the next three, right speech, conduct and means of livelihood (*sammā-vācā, -kammanto, -ājīvo*), are concerned with Morality (*sīla*), and the final three, right effort, mindfulness and meditation (*sammā-vāyāmo, -sati, -samādhi*), are concerned with meditation (*samādhi*).

In view of the fact that the three branches of *dhamma* are always put in the order, morality – meditation – wisdom, it might seem strange that the Path is arranged in the order, wisdom – morality – meditation. In fact, we are here dealing with a typically Buddhist circle or wheel (*cakka*) – and in this, Buddhism is simply following the Indian tradition. As has frequently been pointed out by other writers, the Western tendency has been to think in a linear way, starting at point A and travelling by route B to destination C. The Indian tendency is to think in a cyclical way whereby one starts at point A and travels by route B to destination C, which turns out to be point A again – and so on. There is a cycle involved within the Four Noble Truths (*cattāri ariyasccāni*). The fourth truth is the eightfold path, but the first stage of the path is pre-eminently the four truths (i.e. the summary of that which constitutes the right view).

In order to understand the cycle involved in the ordering of the eightfold path, one needs to bear in mind what was said just now about *paññā* being at two levels, the intellectual and the experiential. In order to embark on the Path at all one would need to have had some knowledge of the wisdom-aspect of the *dhamma*; one would need to have agreed that this was indeed the right view. Yet, in order to *realise* this right view, one would have to be prepared to embark on a daily discipline involving first, as its indispensable foundation, right conduct, and second, a carefully regulated series of meditations. Only in this way could the wisdom to which one had first given intellectual assent become a deeply ingrained part of one's own being. The order of the path thus implies this sort of cycle:

$$wisdom^1 - morality - meditation - (wisdom^2) -$$
$$wisdom^2 - morality - meditation - (wisdom^3) - \text{and so on.}$$

The theory is that, by constant practice of the path, there is a gradual maturing of the wisdom attained, culminating in the final goal of *arahantship*. The circle is in fact completed in MLS III, 113ff, where the "ten attributes of the arahant" are the eight stages of the Path plus 9. right knowledge (*sammāñāṇaṃ*) and 10. right freedom (*sammāvimutti*).[154] The difference between what we have called wisdom[1] and wisdom [2, 3 etc.] is well expressed in KS II 82f, where it is stated that "the ceasing of becoming is *Nibbāna*". Gotama goes on to explain, however, that one may know this without being an *arahant*, just as one may know that there is water in a well without having the means of drawing it up. Wisdom[1] represents the conviction that there is water in the well; wisdom [2, 3 etc.] represents the gradual perfecting of the means by which one is enabled to draw the water up. Patience is as essential as is practice. To wish for *nibbāna* without being prepared regularly to sit and meditate would be, according to GS IV 82f, 120, like a hen wishing for chicks without being prepared to sit and brood on her eggs. Obedience is also required: MLS III 55f asserts that, whilst the way to *nibbāna*/the Buddha as adviser about the way/ *nibbāna* itself/all exist, a given individual will only attain *nibbāna* if he follows the directions he is given with great care, just as Rājagaha exists, and roads to it and reliable guides, but only the meticulous following of the directions will actually get one there.

The content of the wisdom, at the intellectual level, is summed up in the first three truths: 1. life is suffering (*dukkha*), 2. suffering is caused by craving (*taṇhā*) and 3. suffering is cured by the quenching of craving.

The first truth depends for its acceptance on recognition of the three marks (*tilakkhaṇaṃ*) of all conditioned things: 1. impermanence (*anicca*); 2. suffering (*dukkha*); 3. the absence of an abiding self, soul or substance (*anattā*).[155]

Life is suffering because, like everything else, it is scarred by impermanence. However young, beautiful, lucky in love, gifted, etc., we are, nothing can stop the relentless ticking of the clock. We shall grow old, beauty will fade, loved ones will leave or die, our gifts will decline into senility, etc. The reason for the great emphasis on sickness, old age and death in the stories of Gotama's renunciation of home to become an ascetic is that these (with the possible, very rare, exception of sickness) are universal. In the long run, it is not the case that pleasure and pain are equally balanced since life never does end "happily ever after". Life *always* ends in old age and death. In the long run, therefore, life, all life, is ultimately *dukkha*.

For a modern Western humanist, acknowledgement of the truth of this fact would be no reason at all to embark upon the Buddhist Path, any more than it would have been for the ancient Chinese sages who produced the *Tao Te Ching* and the *Chuang Tzu*. They, both ancient Chinese and modern Western, would argue (though in slightly different ways) that, even if it is true that "all good things come to an end", that is no reason for not enjoying them whilst they are here. The beauty of the rose may fade, but it is no less beautiful whilst it lasts – and there are and will be other roses. Our life may fade and ebb away, but there are and have been and will be the lives of other people to delight in. The ancient Chinese sages had the advantage over the modern humanist in that they were not as gloomy about their own death as the humanist tends to be. How do we know, asks Chuang Tzu, that we shall not be infinitely better off after death than we are now?[156]

In any case, it might seem puzzling that, even if Gotama was right in thinking that all life is *dukkha*, it should be thought necessary to renounce the world and embrace the relatively austere path (albeit a "middle way" between the extremes of self-indulgence and self-torture) of the monk. If life is *dukkha*, death will end both life and its *dukkha*.

It is at this point that it becomes essential to the acceptance of Buddhist *paññā* that one should also accept the traditional Indian cyclical theories of karma and *saṃsāra*, which involve a given individual, not just in one life with its sufferings, but in a virtually endless cycle of lives, implying a virtually endless cycle of suffering. KS II 120 gives, as one of a number of illustrations of this, the alleged fact that the tears shed in one individual's course through *saṃsāra* would outweigh the four oceans. It is in order to escape this vicious circle of suffering that one follows the Path and possibly becomes a monk.

The curious thing, as we saw in chapter three, is that Gotama annihilated the Hindu basis for belief in *saṃsāra*. Whereas the Hindu[157] believed in an essential self, or *ātman*, which transmigrated from life to life (according to its karmic deserts) unless and until it found release from *saṃsāra* by realising its mystical unity with the cosmic self (*brahman*), Gotama denied, by a relentless analysis, that there was any such entity as an eternal *ātman* or an eternal *brahman*. Had he left matters there, he would have been in much the same position as the modern humanist. There would have been no need for his Eightfold Path or his Order of monks. It is very doubtful whether we should ever even have heard of him.

Gotama did not leave matters there, however. For reasons he could never state theoretically without infringing his veto on any form of metaphysical speculation, he still retained belief in the doctrines of karma and rebirth (*saṃsāra*). The only reason he ever gave for this retention was a moral one. Unless there was some correlation between the way one lived and the measure of joy or sorrow one experienced, it would be a matter of complete indifference how in fact one did live. Gotama always insisted that it mattered a great deal how one lived and *therefore* (although logically a *non sequitur*) the law of karma *must* operate. The only attempt to vindicate this intellectually was by resort to the doctrine of dependent co-origination (*paṭicca-samuppāda*) but, as we saw in chapter three, this can never be successful without illegitimately incorporating some kind of pseudo -*ātman* into the scheme in the shape of an evolving consciousness, or something of this sort, for which the ruthlessly analytical doctrine of the *khandhas* allows no place at all.

The Nikāyas leave us in no doubt, however, of the fact that Gotama did retain the doctrines of karma and *saṃsāra*. In the present context, it is that fact which matters. Having retained this belief but having, at the same time, rejected belief in the *ātman/brahman* concept, there was no possibility of teaching release from *saṃsāra* by the Upanishadic means of realising the mystic unity of one's *ātman* with *brahman*. Gotama's way of release was simpler and less speculative. It consisted in the profound realisation of *anattā*. Once one was convinced that one had no soul or enduring self, *saṃsāra* lost its sting because there was no longer anybody to be reborn. We seem to be back at the modern humanist's position, but we are not. There is no *ātman* to be reborn but there is, however inscrutable the doctrine might be, a kind of pseudo-self which is the product of craving (*taṇhā*) and which *will* go on from birth to birth unless and until this craving is quenched. One cannot help feeling that Gotama is wanting to both have his cake and to eat it, but this does seem to be the truth of the matter.

What it seems to amount to is that Gotama, although he could not subscribe to the idea of a transmigrating *ātman*, did retain the Hindu concept of karma and *saṃsāra* more or less unchanged. He seems to have done this for moral reasons, never providing any adequate theoretical substitute for the rejected *ātman* concept but taking shelter in the view that speculative theories not conducive to release were to be avoided. When it came to a doctrine of release from *saṃsāra*, however, Gotama did decisively reject the Hindu doctrine of *moksha* or *mukti* (release by realising the unity of *ātman* and *brahman*) on the ground that this doctrine was based on speculative theories for which there was no basis and about which there could be endless debate "not conducive to release".

In place of *moksha*, he taught *nibbāna*, the cooling of craving and the consequent dissipation of the pseudo-self, leaving no residue and no self (*anattā*) to be reborn. If it were simply a matter of realising that one had no self, there would be no need for the Path at all, as we have seen; one would simply make the best of one's fleeting life whilst one could, untroubled by the spectre of having to go on indefinitely enduring all the ills that flesh is heir to. It is the need to dissipate the mysterious "pseudo-self" and to quench the craving that nourishes it which makes the Path and the sober austerities of a life of renunciation necessary.

What is the nature of the "pseudo-self"? The Nikāyas, as we have seen, are so reluctant to tell us that they refrain even from mentioning it. What I have called the "pseudo-self" exists only by implication; there is no Pāli equivalent for it.[157b] Yet clearly, if unquenched craving leads to rebirth, there must be some kind of "pseudo-self" to be reborn; if there were not such a "pseudo-self", the doctrines of karma and rebirth would utterly collapse and we should be back at a humanist position. The most one would be able to say would be that there were causal links between one's behaviour and its happy or unhappy consequences within the space of one lifetime. It is quite clear that the Nikāyas say, and need to say, much more than this.

The essential attribute of the "pseudo-self" is its impermanency. If it were permanent, like the Hindu *ātman*, the only possibility of release would be for it to discover a blissful state of unity with *brahman* which utterly transcended all the changes and chances of this mortal life. By denying these concepts of permanence and insisting on a radical impermanence (*anicca*), Gotama closed the door to this possibility of release. His way of escape was by applying the principle of impermanence even to the *ātman* so that it only had a quasi-existence – and only that so long as it was nourished by craving. Gotama is reported as saying: "If the getting a self-hood as small as this (little pellet of cowdung), brother, were permanent, stable, eternal, by nature unchanging, then the living of the holy life for the best destruction of suffering would not be set forth". (KS III 122, cf 125, 127, 132.) One realised *nibbāna* by realising *anattā*;[158] *saṃsāra* was transcended, not in an eternal monistic unity of *ātman* and *brahman*, but in the dissolution of the pseudo-*ātman* through the cessation of the craving which gave it sustenance.

There may seem to be a contradiction here; in craving for

release one is craving for the cessation of craving. GS I 93f assures us that there is really no contradiction because, although one may long to attain *nibbāna*, one who has attained "has done with longings". Arrival at the goal quenches all attachment, including attachment to the goal itself. This is analogous to the teaching that *dhamma* itself is but a raft to ferry one across to the further shore of *nibbāna*; once it has served its purpose, one does not carry it on one's back but one discards it (MLS I 173f). Perhaps even more pertinent are those passages which assure the monk that striving is unnecessary on his part since, if he diligently practises the discipline without mishap, it is as certain that he will attain *nibbāna* as it is that a log floating down the Ganges will, if it escapes mishap, find the ocean.[159]

If one had attained *nibbāna*, then one merely had to allow the karmic forces which sustained this present life to work themselves out until death. This death would be no ordinary death because it would be the prelude to no other life of any sort whatever; it would in fact be *parinibbāna*. Thus we get many similes contrasting the smallness of the ill remaining to an *arahant* with the vastness of the ill from which he has been for ever freed – e.g. a tiny grain of dust contrasted with "the whole mighty earth".[160]

Thus it is that the goal achieved by the *arahant* is synonymous with *nibbāna* and with the realisation of egolessness consequent upon the cessation of craving.

It has frequently been maintained that *nibbāna* is in fact something more positive than this, a kind of blissful, transcendent state of being which can only be known in experience and which is quite unamenable to any kind of description. If this is the case, I can find no basis for it in the Four Nikāyas. So far as I am aware, there is not one word in the Four Nikāyas which lends support to the idea of *nibbāna* as some positive, transcendent state of bliss. If Gotama intended *Nibbāna* to have such a meaning, it would be hard to explain why he was so reluctant to say so and even harder to see what basis such a meaning could have in the rest of his teaching; it would also be hard to escape the conclusion that the entire Buddhist enterprise had ended up almost precisely where it began – which would contradict its claim to be distinctively different. Even if *nibbāna* does have this transcendental connotation, however, this would not make as big a difference as is sometimes imagined; a state so utterly transcendent that it bears no resemblance to any ordinarily experienced state is not much different, for all practical purposes, from a simple state of non-being; it is certainly no more attractive to those who are attached to their ordinarily experienced states.[161]

It seems to be self-evident from the fact of Gotama's own act of renunciation and from the life of controlled austerity enjoined on his monks that Buddhism has been, from its inception, a *via negativa*. It flees sorrow by fleeing life itself. Even Mahāyāna Buddhism, with its great emphasis on the doctrine of the void (*śunyatā*), has been unable to escape the negativism of its origins. If it is maintained, as it sometimes is, that, because the *dhamma* is a "middle way" betwixt, amongst other things, the extremes of eternalism on the one hand and annihilationism on the other, it cannot therefore be purely negative, this is to completely misrepresent the canonical passages concerned. In KS IV 282, for example, it is made perfectly clear that the refusal to say that there is no self to survive death (i.e. the opposite of eternalism, which has *also* been rejected) is due simply to the desire to avoid the confusing impression that "formerly indeed I had a self, but now I have not one any more". It is wrong to say "no self survives death" because, to Gotama's enlightened eye, there simply is no self. If one were to say to a child "there are no unicorns in London", the child might well think that there are unicorns, but not in London; the correct information would be, "there are no unicorns". For precisely similar reasons, Gotama refuses to say "no self survives death"; in his view, the correct information is simply, "there is no self".[162]

(b) THE JĀTAKAS

One of the favourite ways of preaching *dhamma* in the Jātaka stories is the employment of polemic. This is usually more a matter of counteracting other views, condemned as heretical, than of positively presenting the Buddhist view. The favourite views for attack are (i) the reliance on vedic sacrifice for salvation, (ii) the practice of extreme asceticism as a way to salvation or (iii) various "heretical" doctrines.

(i) Stories attacking the offering of animal (or even human) sacrifice have already been reviewed in the section on *ahiṃsā* in chapter four.[163] Two other stories (JSS 144, 162) deserve mention here since, in each of them, the bodhisatta is a brahmin youth who opts not to get married but to go into the forest in order to tend the sacred fire with a view to attaining to Brahma's realm. In the one case (JS 144) he has an ox given to him and decides to offer it to the "Lord of Fire". He leaves it tethered whilst he goes into the village for the salt required in a meat offering. He returns to find that hunters have killed and cooked the ox in his absence, leaving only remnants behind. The boy throws these remnants in the fire in disgust saying, "as this Lord of Fire cannot so much as look after his own, how shall he look after me?" He then goes off to become a recluse, winning "the Knowledges and Attainments" and, thereby, the Brahma realm. In the other story (JS 162), he offers rice and ghee which has been presented to him "to Great Brahma". The "sacred" flame, thus fed, suddenly leaps to the ceiling, promptly burning down the hermitage he had gone to so much trouble to build. The boy rushes off feeling he has been betrayed by "a false friend" and buries himself in the mountains where he embraces "the true religious life, cultivating the Faculties and the Attainments, until at his life's end he passed into Brahma's heaven".

With the significant difference that the goal sought for and attained is not *nibbāna* but heaven, these stories reflect the canonical view that vedic sacrifices are useless, and proper meditation very useful, to the seeker for salvation.

In the introduction to JS 544, we are told of the conversion to Gotama's teaching of Uruvela-Kassapa who had formerly worshipped the sacred fire. He gives as the reason for his conversion that "the sacrifices only speak of forms and sounds and tastes, and sensual pleasures and women; and knowing that all these things, being found in the elements of material existence, are filth, I took no more delight in sacrifices and offerings".

(ii)   In the introduction to JS 94, we learn of a monk who had become a disciple of Kora the ascetic and started to defame Gotama, saying that there was nothing supernatural about him and that his system was "the outcome of his own individual thought" and had no saving efficacy. When Gotama learns of this defection, he vigorously maintains "the superhuman nature and power which existed within him". A person who denies these must "change his belief, and renounce his heresy, or he will without ado be cast into hell". The ensuing story tells how, in a previous birth, the bodhisatta had "set himself to examine into the false asceticism" by becoming a naked ascetic, recanting and laying hold of the "real truth" just in time to prevent rebirth in hell. The introduction to this story is significant because it introduces an element quite foreign to the Nikāyas, namely the assertion that denial of Gotama's superhuman qualities will earn rebirth in hell.

After an introduction telling how "certain heretics . . . lost their former gains and glory" on account of Gotama's popularity, JS 339 tells how a crow (the Jain, Nāthaputta), which had enjoyed great fame in Bāveru because, prior to its advent, there had been no birds there at all, retires in great indignation to a dunghill because it has been entirely overshadowed by the arrival in Bāveru of a beautiful peacock (the bodhisatta).

In JS 544, the king has been persuaded by Guṇa, a naked ascetic, that the performance of good works is utterly fruitless. In order to be purified, every being has to pass through "eighty four great aeons"; nothing can be done to accelerate or to hinder this gradual process of purification. Having been persuaded of this, the king decides to give himself up to pleasure and to abandon any attempt to perform righteous deeds. His virtuous daughter, Rujā (Ānanda), is greatly dismayed by this change in her father's way of life since, after various sufferings in hell and as various castrated animals then birth as a woman, she has been atoning for sins committed long ago, when as the son of a smith in Rājagaha (s)he had fallen into bad company and gone about "corrupting other men's wives". She tells her father that she will not be free of her female sex and regain the form of a man until she has completed six births. She thus knows the falsity of Guṇa's teaching but she points out to her father that Guṇa is also inconsistent: "If a man is purified by the mere course of existence, then Guṇa's own asceticism is useless; like a moth flying into the lighted candle, the idiot has adopted a naked mendicant's life".

(iii) In JS 487, a chaplain (the bodhisatta) disputes with his own illegitimate son, who has become leader of a band of heretical recluses. The debate hinges on the merits of vedic study and sacrifice as opposed to the merits of righteous living. The father says,

> A thousand Vedas will not safety bring,
> Failing just works, or save from evil plight.

The son accuses him of saying,

> The Vedas then, must be a useless thing:
> True doctrine is – control yourself, do right.

The father retorts,

> Not so: the Vedas are no useless thing:
> Though works with self-control, true doctrine is.
> To study well the Vedas fame will bring,
> But by right conduct we attain to bliss.

The Vedas are not useless but their usefulness, it seems, is confined to this-wordly goals. Those seeking other-wordly bliss must cultivate the Path that begins in morality, not in external scripture or sacrifice.

JS 405 is concerned simply to refute the heresy that life, even though it is a heavenly life lasting aeons, is permanent. A heavenly life is simply the reward for merit accumulated. It may last a very long time, but it is not permanent.

In the introduction to JS 279 and in JS 528, we are confronted with a number of heresies within the one story. In the first case we are simply informed of six heretics who refuted Gotama's teaching, but no details are given. In JS 528, the bodhisatta is being persecuted by five heretical councillors who are also corrupt and given to taking bribes. The bodhisatta, although he is an ascetic, shows himself capable of giving much fairer judgements when people bring disputes to court. When the king asks him to judge cases each day, he demurs on the ground that, as an ascetic, acting as judge is "not our business". He yields to the argument that he ought to do this "in pity to the people" but, by accepting this office, he incurs the implacable enmity of the five "heretics". He decides to refute their views by appearing in court one day with a monkey skin. He says that, though the monkey has been useful to him, he has killed it and eaten its flesh. The five councillors immediately accuse him to the king of "an act of treachery to a friend and of murder". The bodhisatta deals with each "heretic" in turn as follows:

The first teaches that actions, good or bad, are involuntary, springing from "natural causes". He is told that, in that case, nobody should be censured for doing anything since nobody is responsible for his actions.

The second believes that everything, including the creation of the world, is brought about by a Supreme Being. He is told that, in that case, the Supreme Being, not mere mortals, must accept responsibility for all our actions.

The third believes that everything happens by the karmic

determination of previous deeds. He is told that, in this case, the monkey's death is due to its own karma and not to the bodhisatta's action.

The fourth is an annihilationist who teaches that all, good and bad alike, come to the same "ruin". He is told that, in this case, no action is culpable because no action is of any consequence.

The fifth maintains the "kshatriya doctrine . . . that a man must serve his own interests, even should he have to kill his own father and mother". He is told that he obviously cannot blame anybody for doing anything he regards as being in his own interest.

The story ends with a warning to the king to be wary of all false teachers, who are wolves in sheep's clothing and bring dishonour to the robe.

The introduction to JS 359 simply tells how the daughter of a pious Buddhist family, married into an "heretical" family, manages to convert her husband by repeatedly inviting monks into the home for almsfood. The influence of the monks' deportment and teaching not only converts the husband but persuades both husband and wife eventually to renounce the married state and each join the Order.

The Jātakas are not without a polemical element, therefore, and frequently claim to be the champions of orthodoxy. Nevertheless, there are a number of stories in which the bodhisatta acts in ways which the Nikāyas or the Vinaya would condemn. We have already noticed, in earlier chapters, occasions when the bodhisatta takes lives, steals property and commits adultery, etc. The only ethical precept he never violates is the one forbidding wrong speech.

On the doctrinal front, the bodhisatta is also capable of occasional lapses. We have already seen him embracing the "heresy" of naked asceticism (JS 94). We see him employing astrology in JSS 4, 6, though not in a professional or commercial way. In JS 148, the bodhisatta, when a jackal, nearly gets himself entombed in the corpse of a dead elephant because greed has made him negligent. These lapses are minor, however, and very infrequent. The norm is for the bodhisatta to be impeccably virtuous and a stalwart opponent of anything that smacks of false teaching or heresy.

We must now investigate the extent to which the Jātaka stories do actually impart specific Buddhist teaching of the type that is

summed up in the Four Noble Truths and the Three Marks of all
conditioned things, and epitomised in the life of the *arahant* and
the goal of *nibbāna*.

So far as the Four Truths are concerned, we are told in JS 87
that the bodhisatta, as a brahmin ascetic, repudiated the suggestion that something he had done was unlucky, saying "we have
no belief in superstitions about luck, which are not approved by
Buddhas, Pacceka Buddhas, or Bodhisattas". Having told the
story, "the Master" we are told, "proceeded further to preach the
Four Truths" (*cattāri saccāni pakāsesi*). It is not uncommon for the
Four Truths to be mentioned thus specifically, though it is also
quite commonly recorded that, having told the birth story, the
Master simply "declared the Truths" (*saccāni pakāsesi*).

So far as the content of the Truths is concerned, the element
which is most emphasised is that of craving (*taṇhā*) and the
need to break free of craving if one is to escape sorrow. We
shall now look at some of the stories which give prominence to this
theme.

JS 41 has, in its long introduction, introduced us to the elder,
Losaka Tissa, who, although he eventually attains to arahantship,
is dogged by the most atrocious luck. The Jātaka story informs us
that his troubles began when, in the time of the Buddha Kassapa,
he was a virtuous monk until a still more eminent monk, an
arahant in fact, took up residence with him and stole all his lime-
light. The squire who had formerly supported him very attentively
now pays more attention to the newcomer. The monk thinks, "I'm
losing my hold on the squire. . . . If this Elder stops, I shall count
for nothing with him". He decides, by practising deception, to
make the elder think the squire has rejected him and thus cause
him to leave. When he thinks he has succeeded, he is smitten with
remorse and moans, "Woe is me, . . . for my greed has made me to
sin". He then suffers in a succession of births until finally he is
born as Mittavindaka – the cycle of stories relating to whom we
reviewed in chapter one. The basic sin underlying all Mittavindaka's trouble is greed, his obsessive attachment to worldly
comforts, even as a monk. Underlying this attachment is *taṇhā*.
Other stories in the cycle emphasise this point. In JS 104, where
we have little more than the stanza, it is Mittavindaka's "insatiate greed" that is stressed. Again in JS 369, where also we have
little more than the stanzas (but five of them this time), the
"insatiate greed" is elaborated thus:

> . . . on and on thou, greedy soul, wert led
> Till doomed to wear this wheel upon thy head.
> So all, pursuing covetous desire,
> Insatiate still, yet more and more require.

JS 330 tells of an ascetic (the bodhisatta) who observes a hawk seizing some meat from a butcher's shop and then being set upon by other birds, which peck and claw both at the meat and the hawk until, in sheer self-defence, it drops the meat. The bird which captures the meat from the hawk suffers a similar fate, and so on. In each case, the captor bird knows no peace until it has let go the greatly coveted meat. The ascetic muses, "These desires of ours are like pieces of meat. To those that grasp at them is sorrow, and to let them go is peace". The same ascetic then overhears two lovers making an assignation to meet that night. He observes the girl, employed as a female slave, as soon as the day's duties are done, rushing to the threshold eagerly to await her lover. He does not come. The girl, torn by desire and disappointment, will not give up hope. She continues to wait there until dawn. Only then does she sleep. He then muses, "while hope in a sinful world brings sorrow, despair brings peace". In each case, it is *taṇhā*, the craving for food or the craving for love, that leads to sorrow. In the first case, the pain is physical, in the second, it is emotional, but in neither case is there any respite until the object of craving is abandoned. The ascetic then sees a hermit blissfully meditating, and concludes that, neither in this world nor in any other, can anything surpass the happiness of meditation. It will be obvious that his story, or series of stories, never strays far from the rubric laid down by the Four Truths.

JS 13 tells of a mountain stag who falls in love with a doe living near a village. Because the stag is unused to the wiles of the village hunters but, at the same time, cannot stay away from his beloved, he gets shot and killed. A tree-fairy (the bodhisatta) moralises: "Twas not father or mother, but passion alone that destroyed this foolish deer. The dawn of passion is bliss, but its end is sorrow and suffering".

In JS 421, the fortunate poor man (Ānanda) who gains the favour of King Udaya (the bodhisatta) and is allowed to share the kingdom with him, becomes known as king Half-penny. One day, Half-penny finds himself sitting with Udaya's head in his lap. Udaya is soundly asleep and the thought comes to Half-penny that, if he seizes this opportunity to chop off Udaya's head, he will then be sole king. He immediately rejects such a monstrous idea on the ground that he owes the half-kingdom he already enjoys solely to Udaya's friendliness; he could not be so ungrateful. Yet the idea recurs a second and a third time until finally Half-penny wakens his sleeping friend and confesses to him the evil idea that assails him. Udaya says that, if his friend desires the whole kingdom, he can have it with pleasure. Half-penny declines, saying, "I have no need of the kingdom, such a desire will cause me to be reborn in evil states: the kingdom is yours, take it: I will become an ascetic: I have seen the root of desire, it grows from a man's wish, from henceforth I will have no such wish". Here we see *taṇhā* manifesting itself as the lust for power and requiring, for its allaying, the usual radical treatment. In JS 258, a king goes to the heaven of the thirty-three and, because of his eminence, is allowed to share the rule of this heaven with Sakka. Greedy for power, he tries unsuccessfully to kill his rival and, because of his greed, drops to earth in human form and dies.

In almost all the stories in which a main character decides to renounce the world, the reason given (if asked) is that this act of renunciation is necessary in order to escape the doleful conse-quences of desire. Thus, in JS 488, when Sakka asks the bodhisatta why he does not seek the same things as other men, he gets the reply:

> Desires are deadly blows and chains to bind,
> In these both misery and fear we find:
> When tempted by desires imperial kings
> Infatuate do vile and sinful things.

The fabulous archer, Jotipāla (JS 522), (the bodhisatta), de-cides to renounce the post of commander-in-chief and become an ascetic, musing: "My skill . . . in the beginning is evidently death, in the middle it is the enjoyment of sin, and in the end it is rebirth in hell: for the destruction of life and excessive carelessness in sinful enjoyment causes rebirth in hell . . . great power will accrue to me, and I shall have a wife and many children; but if the objects of desire are multiplied, it will be hard to get rid of desire".

JS 46 (of which JS 228 is a simpler version) tells the fascinating story of an elder prince who, at his father's death, declines the throne in favour of his younger brother. He goes off to work in a merchant's family, but, as soon as his royal descent is known, the family "would not allow him to work, but waited upon him as a prince should be attended". When the king's officers come to the merchant to collect taxes, the merchant goes to the prince to request that, since he supports him, the prince should ask the king for the merchant's taxes to be remitted. When this request is granted, others come to the prince to say that, if he gets their taxes remitted too, they will pay them to him instead. These requests are also granted. "Then his receipts and honour were great; and with this greatness grew his covetousness also." Soon, the prince who had renounced the throne, has gone to his younger brother and demanded it back. Nor is this enough. His lust for power now knows no bounds and he starts craving to capture other kingdoms.

Sakka becomes aware of the king's avarice and decides to deal with it. He appears to the king as a young brahmin and tells him privately that he knows of a means whereby the king can acquire rule over three other cities. The king is highly delighted but when he sends for the young brahmin to learn more of his plans, nobody has any idea who he is or where he lives. The king is chided for not having given him hospitality (he was too greedy to do this) and thus kept him on hand. When the brahmin cannot be found, the king is consumed by frustration and soon becomes very ill with dysentery. A young doctor (the bodhisatta) comes to court and says that, if the king will tell him the origin of his illness, he will cure it for him. When the king finally explains about his thwarted desire for conquest, the young doctor says, "What, O King! . . . can you capture those cities by grieving". When the king admits that he can't, the lad continues, "Since that is so, why grieve, O great king? Every thing, animate or inanimate, must pass away, and leave all behind. . . . Even if you should obtain rule over four cities, you could not at one time eat from four plates of food, recline on four couches, wear four sets of robes. You ought not to be the slave of desire; for desire, when it increases, allows no release from the four states of suffering". Thus is the king cured, both of his dysentery and of his avarice.

Again, this story adheres remarkably closely to the Four Truths, teaching that *taṇhā* breeds suffering which can only be allayed by quenching *taṇhā*. The medical mould in which the Four Truths are cast is also exploited since, in this case, craving has led to actual illness – the psychosomatic nature of which is fully realised – and this is treated by a doctor who employs, not medicine, but Buddhist psychotherapy.

Another interesting feature of this story is that, underlying the doctor's "wisdom" is his profound awareness of *anicca* – the universal law which ensures that "every thing . . . must pass away". This reflects the canonical teaching that, in order to grasp the import of the Four Truths, one must clearly understand the Three Marks of all conditioned things, the first of which is *anicca*.

I have only located one place in the Jātakas where the three marks are specifically mentioned, though they are alluded to elsewhere.[164] This is in the introduction to JS 41, where we are told that the unlucky Losaka Tissa did eventually attain to arahantship by contemplating the three marks, *aniccam dukkham anantā*[165] Here, it is worth noting that, although the Pāli faithfully preserves the canonical order of the Marks, the English translation carelessly alters it, thus: "sorrow, transitoriness, and the absence of an abiding principle in things".

Although there is this one – and, so far as I am aware, only this one – mention of all three marks, we have already had occasion to note that the third of them, *anattā*, is consistently ignored in the Jātaka stories. The reason for this is, I am convinced, that mention of this doctrine of selflessness would have raised too many awkward questions relating to the basic premise of a Jātaka story, namely that the same basic personality transmigrates from life to life. Even here, in JS 41, the third mark is given as *anantā* rather than *anattā* (or the accusative, *anattānaṃ*, which we should have expected here). This could be a textual error, but Fausbøll records no variant readings at this point.[166]

Regarding the first two marks, there are many stories which lay great stress on the impermanence of things (*anicca*), especially the impermanence of human life itself, as a fruitful source of sorrow (*dukkha*). Most of these stories are concerned to show the futility of grieving for some loved one who has died, though, in the introduction to JS 25, the Buddha conjures up a lotus pond with a lotus that rapidly withers in order to provide a subject of meditation for a monk who, for his five hundred previous births, has been a goldsmith and is so used to the sight of gold that he is quite unable to grasp the idea of "impurity". When he sees the lotus wither, the monk thinks, "decay has come upon this beautiful lotus; what may not befall my body? Transitory are all compounded things!"

In JS 317, the bodhisatta (the son of a wealthy merchant) does not lament when his brother dies. To the accusation that he is hard-hearted and has welcomed this death, which brings him the whole of his father's estate, he replies that it is more appropriate to weep for oneself than for the dead because we all have to die: "All existing things are transient, and consequently no single compound is able to remain in its natural condition". The bodhisatta repeats almost exactly these words in JS 328 when a female ascetic, formerly his wife, dies. He adds the following observation: "While she was alive, she belonged to me in some sort. Nothing belongs to her that is gone to another world: she has passed into the power of others. Wherefore should I weep?" His stanzas end with the advice to

> Cherish all that are alive,
> Sorrow not shouldst thou survive.

In JS 458, the bodhisatta, having lived chastely with his saintly wife, returns to her when he has been re-born as Sakka, in accordance with a promise he had made during their life together. His wife wants him to stay, but he says this is impossible. In parting, he bids her remember that

> Youth passes soon: a moment – 'tis gone by;
> No standing-place is firm: all creatures die.

and also to

> Remember that this body food shall be
> For others; . . .

In JS 352, the bodhisatta's father is inconsolably grief-stricken by his own father's death. To cure him of his grief, the bodhisatta starts offering food and drink to a dead ox. When his father asks him why he indulges in such madness, the son replies that there is a better chance that the ox, whose corpse is still intact, will return to life than there is that the life of his cremated grandfather can be restored by tears. The father admits the wisdom of his son's words, adding, "it is known to me that existing things are impermanent". Somewhat similar devices are employed to cure the excessive grief of the bereaved in JSS 449 and 454.

JSS 372 and 410 both tell of a rebuke administered by Sakka to ascetics stricken with grief at the death of animals to which they have become attached. The stanzas are identical for both stories, and the last three are also found in JS 352. Sakka tells the holy men that

> To sorrow for the dead doth ill become
> The lone ascetic, freed from ties of home.

JS 354 furnishes another example of a family which shows perfect composure and absence of grief when their dearly-loved son dies. This time, Sakka comes to reward those who were bereaved with "the seven treasures in countless abundance" so that they never again need to labour with their hands. This is their reward for having "dwelt on the thought of death".

JSS 460, 476, 498 and 525 all, in various ways, stress the brevity and instability of human life: it is as transitory as dew (JS 460); its separate moments pass more rapidly than the swiftest bird in flight (JS 476); its duration is short and its end inevitable (JS 498); it slips through our fingers like water through a sieve (JS 525).

JS 388 is a story which has, one feels, got rather out of hand. It begins by being a simple tale about two pigs (one of them the bodhisatta) brought up by an old woman as if they were her own children. One day some "lewd fellows" get the old woman drunk and thus persuade her to let them have the bodhisatta's brother to kill and eat. The prospective victim realises what is afoot and runs in terror to his brother. He is told not to worry about what is inevitable, but then, "as he considered the Ten Perfections,[167] setting the Perfection of Love before him as his guide", the bodhisatta's voice, as he proclaims the law, reaches as far as Benares. From the king downwards, the people flock to hear the pig preach. The burden of his message is that one should be glad rather than sad at the prospect of death:

> Men that lose their life are glad,
> Men that keep it feel annoy:
> Men should die and not be sad . . .

The king is so delighted at this preaching that he adopts both pigs as his sons. The bodhisatta becomes the great spokesman for the law and, when the king dies, he performs his funeral ceremonies before retiring to the forest with his brother. We are told that his preaching "went on for sixty thousand years".

The story (JS 207) of the dead queen who, having become a dung worm, is callously indifferent to her grieving former husband illustrates the transiency of human ties of affection. For the believer in rebirth, grief for a departed loved one is misplaced since that one has passed to a new plane of existence where old ties are forgotten and new ones are being forged.

JS 447 sounds a rather different note. The bodhisatta is born the son of a very virtuous brahmin. He is sent to Takkasilā for his education. While he is there, the teacher's son dies. The bodhisatta is quite unmoved. He tells his teacher that one so young should not have died. The teacher says, "do you not know that such persons are but mortal?" The bodhisatta insists that in his family, nobody ever dies young. The teacher decides to put this to the test. He goes to visit the bodhisatta's father and tells him he brings sad news of his son's death in an accident. The father shakes with mirth and says the teacher is mistaken. Even when shown the supposed bones of his son, the father remains serenely confident that his boy is alive because "We walk in uprightness. . . . Therefore in youth not one among us dies".

The intention of this story is obviously to show that, in spite of the prevailing transiency of life, virtue has its reward in a long and happy life. This seems to leave out of account the possibility of demerit from some previous birth upsetting the calculations of the smugly complacent.

JS 97 has perhaps some bearing on the doctrine of *anattā* because it is saying that "a name only serves to mark who's who". One's name might be Rich, but one may still be poor. A name has a purely arbitrary and conventional function; it does nothing to alter the way things are. The story actually goes no further than this, but it is hovering on the brink of the important canonical truth that, though a name may continue unchanged, the thing denoted by the name is constantly changing. This idea is, in turn, closely linked to the idea that a "self" is a name and whilst the name of a given self might remain the same, the "self" it denotes is not an enduring entity but a constantly changing succession of moments of aggregates (*khandhas*) of "selfhood".

We have now reviewed the polemical element in the Jātaka stories and also the extent to which the Four Truths and the Three Marks are influential in the teaching imparted by the stories.

In concluding this chapter, we should examine what, if anything, the Jātakas have to say about *nibbāna*, the canonical goal of the holy life, and about the *arahant*, the man who personifies this goal.

Since the main character in the Jātaka tales is the bodhisatta, a being who, by definition, is destined to achieve birth eventually as Gotama the Buddha – and who can never therefore attain to arahantship or to *nibbāna* during his bodhisatta-career – it is intrinsically unlikely that the Jātakas will have very much to say about ultimate goals. Holy men abound and the bodhisatta regularly becomes a recluse destined for the heaven of Brahma, but arahantship is rarely mentioned.

We have already noted that, in the introduction to JS 41, we are told that Losaka Tissa, by contemplating the three marks, attains arahantship. This is an introduction, not a story, however. At the conclusion of JS 70, we are told that some of Gotama's hearers "attained to Arahatship", but again, this is in the epilogue, relating to present time, and not part of the story proper. Similar notes, relating to either introduction or epilogue, occur in JSS 522, 536, and 537. In JS 529, there is a paccekabuddha, Sonaka, who is described in one of the stanzas as "filled with the Arhat's holy calm".[168] At the end of the tale, we are told that, "At that time the paccekabuddha obtained Nirvāna".

Nibbāna (usually translated "Nirvāna") is similarly mentioned in the introductions or epilogues of JSS 156, 190, 248, 264, 459, 479. Passing references are made to *nibbāna* in the teaching of JSS 159, 196, 282, 487, 505, 520, 537. In two stories mention is made of people who attained to *nibbāna* in the time of the Buddha Kassapa – JSS 469 and 547 (see JS VI 248). In JS 536, beings attain to *nibbāna* as a result of the bodhisatta's teaching and, in JS 480, Sakka says that *nibbāna* is the aim of the bodhisatta's forest-dwelling.

This seems to be about the extent of the interest shown by the Jātaka collection in the canonical goals of holy living. What is very apparent, and will have become sufficiently clear in the foregoing chapters, is that the Jātakas very much accentuate the supernatural attainments of the holy man, especially his ability to fly through the air.

A very obvious manifestation of this supernatural emphasis is the emergence of the paccekabuddha. Apart from one passage in MLS III 110ff, where there is a recital of paccekabuddhas from a legendary five hundred said to have been "swallowed up" by the Isigili (*isi gilati*: "it swallows seers") mountain, the paccekabuddha plays no part whatever in the Four Nikāyas. So far as the latter are concerned, we are never in any doubt that the *arahant* represents the ideal of holiness. The difference between the *arahant* and the paccekabuddha is that, whilst the former attains *nibbāna* as a result of following the Path laid down by the Buddha, the paccekabuddha, like the Buddha himself, is self-enlightened. His difference from the Buddha is that, whereas the latter preaches the Truths relating to enlightenment to others, the paccekabuddha remains silent; he attains *nibbāna* himself, but does not attempt to assist others to the goal.

We may surmise that, at the time when the Jātakas were compiled in their present form (i.e. about a thousand years after Gotama's death), there were virtually no monks who claimed to have attained to arahantship. This being the case, the paccekabuddha served as a substitute for the ideal holy man. Since there was almost no mention of the paccekabuddha in the Four Nikāyas, it was easy to invest him with all kinds of supernatural power. If we look at the stories in which the figure of the paccekabuddha plays a prominent part – JSS 41 96/132 (one story), 221, 264, 378, 390, 408, 415, 418, 420, 421, 424, 442, 459, 490, 491, 495, 496, 514, 529, 531, 536, 539 – it is very noticeable that most of these stories occur in the later books; there are only three in the first book, and all but two of the others fall in book six or later. This means that the paccekabuddha is mentioned in stories which are, for the most part, accompanied by a substantial number of stanzas. It would seem to be a fair inference, therefore, that the semi-magical attributes of the paccekabuddha had become a favourite convention of popular Buddhist poetry by about the fifth century A.D. It would be hard to be certain about this, however, since there is still so much obscurity about the relationship between the stanzas themselves (which do not usually explicitly mention paccekabuddhas) and the accompanying prose commentary (which, in these later stories, often regards certain stanzas as referring to, or as being spoken by, a paccekabuddha).

In her valuable recent monograph on this subject, Ria Kloppenborg observes that "since the earliest times, ascetics who leave society" constitute "one of the most typical characteristics of Indian religiosity".[169] From the Rigvedic *muni*, who possessed supernatural powers enabling him to fly through the air and read the thoughts of others, this type of ascetic keeps reappearing amongst different groups and in different contexts. The dominant motive for withdrawal from the world was the desire to escape from the chain of *saṃsāric* existences, but "the acquisition of supernatural powers was another motive ... which is often mentioned".[170] Because they were believed to have such powers, ascetics were often accorded more respect, or even fear, than the brahmin sacrificial priests. In solitariness they had perfected skills which, by virtue of their own austerity, rendered them more powerful than those who relied on external mechanisms. Buddhism, with its emphasis on renunciation and individual effort, formed a natural link with the Indian ascetical tradition, although Gotama himself rejected the extremer practices of asceticism and, as we have seen, attached very little importance to the acquisition of supernatural powers.

Kloppenborg draws attention to Frauwallner's observation that, as early Buddhism developed, there was a growing rift between the dominant dogmatic and scholastic strains and the more individualistic mystical and yogic strains which grew up within the Order.[171] The scholastic monk is represented by the Four Nikāyas, with their emphasis upon *paññā* and the *arahant* ideal; the yogic monk is represented, in rather exaggerated form, by the Jātakas, with their emphasis upon *iddhi* and the *paccekabuddha* ideal. "The adaptation of the concept of the *paccekabuddha* in Buddhism ... presented the opportunity to include pre-buddhist recluses and seers in Buddhism".[172] In many ways the paccekabuddha, self-contained individualist that he was, was more consistent with the Indian ascetical tradition than was the *sammāsambuddha* (perfectly enlightened Buddha) who preached to others. "The fact that the Buddha actually proclaimed the Dhamma is difficult to explain against the background of the ascetic tradition of individualism, as this has found a place in the Theravāda scriptures. Most accounts invoke the divine interference of Brahma and Indra to make clear that this decision was a very special one indeed."[173]

The advent of the paccekabuddha seems to represent, then, both a development in the direction of popular yogic fantasy and in the direction of a return to the pre-buddhist ascetical tradition. With the virtual disappearance of claimants to arahantship and with the growth of a rather sterile scholasticism, cut off from the life of the lay community, within the Order, it is not surprising that the paccekabuddha, with all his marvellous attributes, makes a growing appeal to the popular imagination.

As presented in the Jātaka stories, the dominant characteristics of the paccekabuddha are: his yellow robes, of which even elephants are in awe (JS 221 cf JS 514); *paccekabodhi*, which is entered upon by coming to see "the principles of decay and death" and grasping "the three marks of things" (JS 378 cf JSS 408, 421, 491, 529; note that this is precisely the same route as leads to the canonical *paññā*); he flies through the air (JS 378 cf JSS 418, 421, 424, 459, 490, 491, 514) and, contrary to what we are led to expect, preaches *dhamma* to his friend (JS 378 cf JSS 421, 529), although he normally dwells in a Himalayan cave, the Nandamūla (JS 378 cf JSS 408, 415, 418, 420, 424, 459, 529); he may beg alms in a bowl in the same way as a monk (introduction to JS 390 cf JSS 420, 459, 531); on attaining his goal he utters almost the same cry of triumph as the canonical *arahant*: "The envelope of the womb is now fallen from me, re-birth in the three existences is ended, the filth of transmigration is cleansed, the ocean of tears dried up, the wall of bones broken down, there is no more re-birth for me". (JS 408 cf 418, 491, 529); he shaves hair and beard (JS 408) and has, in fact, precisely the same marks as those of a bhikkhu: "Three robes, bowl, razor, needles, strainer, zone" (JS 408 cf 420, 424, 459, 491, 539); he may, on occasion, preach to a large congregation (JS 408) or to one who invites him to his home for almsfood (JS 408 cf 424); he is destined for *nibbāna* (JS 418 cf 420, 424); he is a great source of merit to his benefactors (JS 420 cf 442, 514, 531); his attainment of the goal is described as gaining "perfect" or "supernatural" insight (JSS 421, 459 respectively – *vipassanaṃ* in both cases); his bowl and robes, may be made by supernatural power (JS 408 cf JSS 421, 459, 491, 529) and, echoing the passage in the *Majjhima Nikāya* (MLS III 111ff), there are sometimes said to be five hundred paccekabuddhas in the Nandamūla cave (JSS 424, 514); his "requisites" may also fly through the air (JS 424); he sometimes embraces the ascetic life in his youth and this is described as a "beautiful" thing to do (JS 459); a paccekabuddha may even preach to the bodhisatta to cure him of his pride (JS 490), although the bodhisattas "are omniscient, have a better knowledge and comprehension of ways and means than a Paccekabuddha" (JS 491); he can be described as an *arahant* (JS 539).

JS 529 is of especial interest because, as we saw in chapter five, it belongs to a cycle of six stories in which the chaplain's son and the prince are born on the same day and become great friends. JS 529 is the last story in the group in which the chaplain's son is not the bodhisatta. It is the only story in the group where the chaplain's son becomes a paccekabuddha rather than an ordinary ascetic. In this story the chaplain's son is not identified as either the bodhisatta or as Ānanda for the very good reason that, on this one occasion, he is destined for *nibbāna*, not the heaven of Brahma, as in the other versions. He has the conventional marks of the paccekabuddha – the marks of the layman disappear and the marks of the monk appear miraculously at the moment of enlightenment and he dwells in the cave of Nandamūla – yet these differences are purely conventional and superficial. They do not prevent his fulfilling his usual role of returning to preach to his friend – precisely the kind of activity the paccekabuddha is supposed not to engage in.

This strengthens the case for supposing that the paccekabuddha is a convention of the later stories in the Jātaka collection and a convention which, whilst it fantasizes the role of the ascetic *arahant* and endows it with more superhuman attributes, retains its subordination to the role of the bodhisatta and, in many important respects (e.g. dress, nature of enlightenment and goal), differs not at all from the canonical ideal. By this time, however, the realisation of the ideal is thought of as belonging to a largely fictional past rather than to the actual present.

8 *Mythological Elements*

It will be remembered that the aim of the present work is to investigate the ethical and doctrinal content of the Jātaka stories and to see how this compares with the teaching of the Four Nikāyas. Since mythology can hardly be said to be an intrinsic part of Buddhist doctrine, it can only be regarded as of peripheral importance for the present study.

It should also be borne in mind that mythology is a vast and complex field in itself. A detailed study of the mythology of the Four Nikāyas and of the Jātakas, set in the context of Indian mythology as a whole, and relating this to the mythologies of other countries, would require a separate and, one suspects, a rather large volume of its own.

On the other hand, it would be a serious omission in the present work if nothing was said about the mythological content of its sources. One of the main reasons for studying the Jātaka stories (apart from their intrinsic charm) is to discover the content of popular Buddhist thinking in Theravāda countries. Since the Jātaka stories, through vernacular translations and village dramas, through paintings and sculptures, through their influence on other popular literature in the countries concerned, and in many other ways, have been the major single written influence in shaping this popular thinking, it is important that no substantial element be left out. Nobody who reads the Jātaka stories could deny that its mythological colouring does constitute a substantial element. It is intrinsically likely, therefore, that the thinking of the average Theravāda layman will reflect this mythological colouring. Everything we learn about him from such studies as those of R. Gombrich in Sri Lanka,[174] M. E. Spiro in Burma[175] and S. Tambiah in Thailand[176] confirms that this is in fact the case.

For the purposes of this chapter, myth is defined as "that which employs categories or concepts which, whilst they might purport to be factual or historical, go beyond anything which has been scientifically verified and may therefore be regarded as the product of fantasy or creative imagining".

(a) THE FOUR NIKĀYAS

The only element in what could be regarded as the central teaching of the Nikāyas which could fairly be classified as mythological is that which relates to the doctrine of rebirth. As we have noted in chapter three, there is strictly no basis in the intellectual content of Gotama's teaching for retention of this doctrine. Gotama clearly had ethical reasons for wishing to retain it and would doubtless maintain that the doctrine was validated in the experience of the monk, who, by becoming adept in concentrative meditation, was allegedly able to recall his previous births. Nevertheless, it cannot be claimed that the phenomenon of rebirth has been scientifically verified. It would, moreover, be exceedingly difficult to see how such a "phenomenon" could be conclusively validated to the satisfaction of a scientific investigator. Since the concept of rebirth cannot be included in the categories of the factual or the historical, therefore, it falls within our definition of mythology.

The capacity to recall previous births is, in fact, one of the "supernormal powers" (*iddhi*) which the monk was supposed to be able to develop through meditation. There are six of these powers, termed the "six superknowledges", listed in DB III 257f, etc. They include: (1) the power to multiply one's bodies, then make them one again, to become invisible, pass through solid objects, walk on water, travel through the air, touch the sun and moon and reach the heaven of Brahma, (2) the "heavenly ear" which can hear all sounds, (3) the power to read the thoughts in other people's minds, (4) the power to recall one's previous births, (5) the "heavenly eye" which sees other beings pass from one birth to another, (6) the "mirror of truth" which assures one that arahantship will be attained and that there will be no more woeful rebirth.

Jayatilleke observes that "these six came to be known as the 'six (kinds of) higher knowledge' (chaḷabhiññā), but since the first is a case of 'knowing how' and not of 'knowing that' . . . the latter were known as the 'five (kinds of) higher knowledge' (pañcābhiññā)".[177] Later in the same work, after observing that all six "higher knowledges" were supposed to be attained by entry into the fourth *jhāna* (trance), he says, "Of the six, only three are necessary for the saving knowledge". These are the last three since, between them, they establish pre-existence (4), karma (5) and salvation (6). He goes on, "not everyone . . . was capable of verifying the doctrine in this manner. . . . only sixty out of five hundred were capable of attaining the 'higher knowledge' ", the rest being "emancipated by knowledge alone (S I.191)". The difference depends on a "difference in their faculties". The latter group would need faith (*saddhā*) since they would lack means of personal verification.[178]

What Jayatilleke says in the above quotation is borne out by a passage in MLS II 159 where Gotama refutes the idea that he is all-knowing and all-seeing and makes no claim, even for himself, beyond that of being a "three knowledge man" (the three knowledges in question being those which Jayatilleke has classed as "saving knowledge"). KS II 84–92 explicitly denies that becoming an *arahant* involves *any* of the six mystic powers listed.

It is thus clear that, although the "superknowledges" are mentioned quite frequently in the Nikāyas, they are not held to be essential for the attainment of arahantship and can thus not be regarded as central to Buddhist teaching. A *belief* in rebirth is central; *knowledge* of rebirth in one's own mystical experiences may or may not be achieved.

It is not proposed to go into any detail regarding the various gods and other supernatural beings alluded to in the Four Nikāyas since this ground has been covered by Joseph Masson in *La Religion Populaire dans le Canon Bouddique Pāli*, (Louvain, 1942). Unfortunately, Masson's work is not available in English. A summary of the contents of his book will, however, give a good idea of the range of material to be found in the Nikāyas.

Masson deals first with the gods as listed in the three planes of existence, that of sense (*kāmadhātu*), that of form (*rupadhātu*) and that of the formless (*arupadhātu*) and notes some of the cosmological features of these planes of existence and some of the ways in which the Buddhist literature (as opposed to Indian literature in general) has developed these themes. He then deals in turn with the three "heavens of desire" (the heavens of the Four Great Kings, the Great Gods and of the Thirty Three). The last of these, being under the domain of Sakka, includes a note about the derivation of Sakka from the Hindu god, Indra, and a further note about the evolution of the concept of Sakka within Buddhism itself. Next comes the Brahma world, with Brahma himself distinguished by several different epithets – Baka, Sanamkumāra, Sahampati, "certain Paccekabrahmā" and Tissa. He notes that, whilst Hinduism seems eventually to have lost interest in Brahma, preferring to worship either Vishnu or Shiva (the other two gods of the Hindu *trimūrti*), Buddhism, because of its canonical anchorage, retained its emphasis on Brahma.

Masson next deals with Yama and the various hells over which he presides, tracing his antecedents in Hindu literature as well as his place in the Canon. The following sections deal in similar fashion with Māra (treated at two levels as a popular deity and as a monastic deity),[179] the Asura, the semi-divine beneficent deities (the Gandhabbhā, Accharā and Garuḍā), the Yakkhā (and their development as malignant powers), the semi-divine malignant deities (the Nāgas, Kumbhaṇḍā, Rakkhasā and Pisacā) and, finally the various nature-spirits associated with vegetation, clouds, thunderbolts and rain.

(b) THE JĀTAKAS

I propose to divide this section into three main sub-sections: (i) gods and anti-gods dwelling in the heavens, (ii) various other mythological beings dwelling on the earth and (iii) magical phenomena. A fourth section will deal with one or two miscellaneous items.

(i) *Sakka*

The bodhisatta himself appears twenty-one times in the form of Sakka. In the collection as a whole, Sakka makes well over fifty appearances. In the references which follow, stories in which the bodhisatta appears as Sakka will be referred to in italic numbers. *JS 31* depicts Sakka as virtuous, but not above getting the Asuras drunk in order to evict them from his "heaven of the thirty-three". Sakka eventually marries an Asura of great beauty and makes her "chief of twenty-five millions of dancing girls". There is another reference to his "twenty-five millions of heavenly nymphs" in *JS 535* and another reference to the battle against the Asuras in JS 380. In *JS 386*, Sakka copulates with an Asura when they are in the form of he-goat and she-goat respectively. In the introduction to JS 40, Sakka advises a heretical fairy about the best way of becoming reconciled to the faith she has opposed, and is thus instrumental in converting her. Sakka is called Indra in JS 70,[180] a tale which furnishes the first example of two features which frequently recur in the collection. These are: (1) his throne becomes hot, or is made to tremble, as a result of somebody's phenomenal virtue. This heating of the throne may, as here, be produced without any special intention of the virtuous person or, alternatively, it may result from an urgent prayer for help made by somebody of exceptional merit.[181] When his throne becomes hot, Sakka either (as here) responds sympathetically and helpfully (see also JSS 75 (intro), 194, 220, 243, 347, 354, 440, 472 (intro), 485, 489, 519, 531, 538, 539, 540.) – JS 542 is very similar, except that here Sakka apparently hears the cry of virtue without his throne being affected – or, alternatively, he interprets the heating of his throne as a sign that some other person's merit has made that person a formidable rival for his throne; Sakka's response in these cases is to attempt to seduce his rival from the path of virtue. Examples of this rather immoral reaction occur in JSS 281, 340, 433, 480, 523, 526. There are one or two instances where the heating of the throne is caused by somebody's pious resolution, which Sakka then regards it as his duty to test; see JSS 316, 429. In JS 488, Sakka rather amusingly has to apologise to an ascetic (the bodhisatta) for having resorted to theft in order to test the virtue of the ascetic and his brother-ascetics. In JS 546[182] Sakka is again rebuked by the bodhisatta for resorting to theft in order to give the latter a chance to display his wisdom. It is noticeable that there are no stories in which the bodhisatta is Sakka in this group; (2) Sakka orders Vissakamma, "the architect of the devas" to build a hermitage for a recluse or, more often, a large number of recluses who have just renounced the world – see also JSS 522, 538, 540, 547. Sakka returns to earth in JS 78 to teach his miserly son the error of his ways and to demonstrate, by his own magnificence, the rich rewards awaiting the open-handed. This is also the theme of *JS 535*, though in this case it is the sixth in line from the bodhisatta (now Sakka) who has become the miser. In JS 186, he has, in his previous life, been the eldest of four brothers who became recluses. He returns to each of his brothers to "lend them a helping hand". He does this by giving each a magical means of meeting his needs but, in each case, the magic has disastrous consequences since it falls into the wrong hands and results in the murder of all three hermits. Sakka sometimes decides to intervene in human affairs because the non-arrival of new gods in his heaven has indicated a fall from virtue amongst humankind. Such instances occur in *JSS 202, 391, 469*. In these situations, Sakka acts like the Hindu *āvatar* of Vishnu, overcoming evil and restoring the proper moral balance. There is the same concern to save

India from ruin in *JS 512*. In JS 537, however, when India is threatened by its fearsome, man-eating king, Sakka has to admit that he is unable to help; he refers the tree-nymph who has implored his aid to the virtuous prince of Kuru (the bodhisatta). It seems that Sakka can only fulfil this particular role when he is himself the manifestation of the bodhisatta. In JS 483, we have the reverse situation where Sakka feels impelled to discover "whence came all the new sons and daughters of the gods, whom he beheld so numerous about him". He discovers that the reason is the great virtue of the king which is causing "multitudes" in his kingdom to do "good deeds" with the result that "heaven was being filled". A somewhat similar situation occurs in JS 494. In JSS *228* and 467, Sakka comes to earth to cure a king of greed so that India can be restored to the path of righteousness. In the stanza of *JS 264*, there is the odd note that "I (the bodhisatta), Sakka, was your slave, at beck and call". This is addressed to King Panada who became a paccekabuddha, breaking the rule that the latter is subordinate to the bodhisatta. JS 258 tells us that Mandhāvā survives as co-ruler of the heaven of the thirty-three throughout the co-reign of thirty-six Sakkas, each of them ruling for thirty million, six hundred thousand years. In JS 276, Sakka comes disguised as a young brahmin to test the integrity of a courtesan. In JS 301, he comes to "pay his respects" to the bodhisatta and, in response to the latter's inquiry, predicts the outcome of an impending battle. When the outcome is contrary to the prediction, Sakka says in effect that courage and resolution can reverse a course of events which would otherwise have been inevitable. After testing the hare's virtue in JS 316, Sakka daubs the sign of the hare on the moon. In JSS 340, 480, after showing jealousy at the merit produced by the bodhisatta's generosity, Sakka becomes reassured when he learns that the bodhisatta is seeking "neither Sakkahood" (and is thus not his rival), "nor Brahmaship, but . . . omniscience". Sakka visits the earth in *JS 344* in order to end the deceptions of a false ascetic or, in *JS 393*, to put to shame ascetics who are not diligent and, in *JS 372*, to prevent an ascetic from being grief-stricken at the death of his pet animal. In JS 545, Sakka actually decides to perform the duties of an ascetic himself, but, finding "that there were obstacles in the world of the gods", he descends to the world of men for this purpose. In *JS 374*, he, with two other gods, enacts a little morality play to teach a lustful and treacherous woman the folly of her ways. In *JS 386*, he prevents a king from sacrificing his life by imparting a charm to his wife. A wronged mother-in-law is restored by Sakka to her son's family in *JS 417* and the virtue of a chaste former wife is confirmed in *JS 458*. JS 523 presents Sakka as the servant of ascetics, building a hermitage for them, sitting a respectful distance from them (though protesting that this is not because he dislikes the "odour of the saints"!), asking them questions and delighting in their answers. In JS 541, Sakka sends his charioteer, Mātali, to collect the virtuous king Nimi (the bodhisatta) so that the gods may see the king whose fame has spread to heaven. In JS 546, as in a number of other stories, Sakka takes action because "he looked over the world of mankind" and observed that something needed to be done. In these cases, he acts because of his own vigilance and not because his throne has become heated or shaken. In the last birth story (JS 547), Sakka gives Prince Vessantara the opportunity "to attain the supreme height of perfection" by coming in the form of a brahmin to beg for his wife.

Other gods and goddesses
There are three introductions to stories in which reference is made to gods: JS 469, where the bodhisatta is said to have "taught full comprehension of the law to eight hundred millions of deities" in the heaven of the thirty-three; JS 481, where Kokālika's "spiritual teacher", the Brahmā angel, Tudu, tries in vain to get Kokālika to repent for having made false accusations against Sāriputta and Moggallāna; JS 531, where allusion is made to the five signs which herald the end of an "angel's" sojourn in heaven: 1. withering garlands, 2. soiled robes, 3. body growing ugly, 4. perspiration and 5. loss of pleasure in its heavenly abode.

In the stories themselves, we learn, in JS 41, of Mittavindaka's dalliance with three, eight, sixteen and thirty-two "daughters of the gods" in turn. In each case he only stays a week because these "palace-ghosts enjoy happiness only for seven days at a time" and then have to depart for a period of punishment (presumably because their karma is mixed). There seems to be no problem attached to a human being's cohabiting with this order of deity. Similarly, in JS 167, a "daughter of the gods" (also called a "nymph") falls in love with the bodhisatta and tries in vain to seduce him from his ascetical vows. As the fabulous musician, Guttila, the bodhisatta is (in JS 243) able, with Sakka's help, to employ nine hundred nymphs to dance for him in order to win the contest with his presumptuous pupil (Devadatta). It is seeing "the exceedingly delightful splendour of (Sakka's) court with its heavenly nymphs" that makes the bodhisatta resolve (in JS 543) to throw off his "frog-eating snake-nature" and, by fasting, himself become a god.

In the two stories in which the bodhisatta is an archer of miraculous skill (JSS 181 and 522), we learn in one (JS 181) that he can shoot one arrow as high as the heaven of the Four Great Kings and a second "as far as the heaven of the Thirty-three Arch-angels" which "the deities caught and kept". This reflects the idea of a tiered series of heavens in ascending order of splendour.[183] In the other (JS 522), the bodhisatta renounces his skill and becomes an ascetic, entering a hermitage built for him by Vissakamma, on Sakka's instructions. As we have already noticed, the main function of Vissakamma, the heavenly architect, in the Jātaka stories, is to provide accommodation for illustrious ascetics. The other of Sakka's adjutants about whom we hear a good deal is Mātali, the charioteer, whose usual function is to go, at Sakka's bidding, to collect a mortal whose virtue or skill has achieved fame in heaven and who is therefore taken in Mātali's chariot to visit the heaven of the thirty-three. The person so collected is always, in fact, the bodhisatta – see JSS 243, 494, 541. In JS 535, we are told that Sakka's chariot, which Mātali drives, is called Vejayanta (chariot of victory, cf JS 31).

Mātali is, in JS 535, one of four gods who have been reborn in heaven because they have, in their preceding lives, followed in the footsteps of their virtuous ancestor, a generous Treasurer (the bodhisatta), who has now become Sakka. Together with Sakka, these four embark on an amusing exercise designed to convert the miserly sixth-in-line from his miserliness. JS 494 tells us a little more about the way in which Sakka's entourage was envisaged. There is reference to "the princes of heaven, sitting in full conclave in Sakka's justice hall" and reaching a decision very much in the manner of a comparable human assembly. In JS 522, unspecified "gods", outraged at the way in which a king has abused a holy ascetic (the bodhisatta), send a flood followed by a shower of "blazing weapons", then "blistering embers" then, finally, "fine sand" to kill, burn and bury the people of the land.

There are two references to a "parasol deity" (JSS 538 and 546) who dwells in the white umbrella signifying royalty. On one occasion, she gives advice to the bodhisatta (JS 538) and, on another (JS 546), she asks the king four questions which only the bodhisatta can answer.

JSS 539 and 540 refer to the protective functions of certain goddesses. In JS 539, the goddess in question has been appointed "guardian of the sea". She had been negligent of her duties during the seven days after the bodhisatta's shipwreck "for they say that her memory had become bewildered in her enjoyment of her divine happiness, and others say that she had gone to be present at a divine assembly". The deity in JS 540 "had been a mother to the Great Being in his seventh existence before this one" and "was continually thinking of him with a mother's affection". Yet she too has been negligent in the hour of the bodhisatta's need. On the day that he was shot by a poisoned arrow, "in the enjoyment of her divine bliss she did not remember him as usual; and her friends only said that she had gone to the assembly of the gods". The gods, it seems, are too fickle (or, if one wishes to be kind, have too many other duties) to be relied upon in an hour of crisis, though their help, even if tardy, can be a great boon.

JS 405 makes it clear that even a god in the Brahma heaven is capable of falling into heresy and stands in as great a need of the bodhisatta's teaching as anybody else. On another occasion (JS 392), however, a goddess rebukes an ascetic (the bodhisatta) for "stealing" the scent of a lotus. The ascetic protests that his "sin" is as nothing compared with that of the man who was, just at that time, breaking off and carrying away whole lotus flowers, yet the goddess says nothing to him. The goddess replies that this other man disgusts her:

I have no speech with men like him, but I deign to speak to thee.
When a man is free from evil stains and seeks for purity,
A sin like a hair-tip shows on him like a dark cloud in the sky.

The bodhisatta is so impressed by this that he begs the goddess to let him know if he offends again in future – only to be told:

I am not here to serve you, no hireling folk are we:
Find, Brother, for yourself the path to reach felicity.

Here again, popular Buddhism has found a "middle way".

Divine assistance is sometimes accorded to the virtuous, but the wise place their confidence in their own efforts, not in some external source of salvation.

Māra: Although a good deal in evidence in the Nikāyas, the evil genius of Buddhism makes surprisingly few appearances in the Jātakas. In JS 40, where he is referred to as "lord of the Realm of Lusts" (intro.), "the Wicked", "the Enthraller", Māra conjures up a pit of red-hot embers between the Treasurer (the bodhisatta) and a paccekabuddha. The intention is to prevent the former from offering food to the latter and thus to deprive the former of merit and the latter of life. The plot is foiled by the miraculous appearance of a huge lotus flower over which the bodhisatta is able to pass with ease to make his offering. In JS 389, Māra is the serpent which (not from spite, but to do a favour for a friend) bites the bodhisatta. Apart from a few quite incidental references (mainly in the introductions or epilogues rather than in the tales themselves), Māra is conspicuous by his absence. His place is taken by the other malevolent beings described below.

Asuras: Reference has already been made to the war between Sakka's gods of the heaven of the thirty-three and the Asuras whom Sakka had made drunk and then evicted from his heaven, where they had formerly dwelt (JS 31) as also to the Asura who became a she-goat in JS 386 in order to provide a mate for Sakka (in the form of a he-goat). Sakka again consorts with an Asura nymph in JS 429. The war between Sakka and the Asuras (here translated "Titans") is again alluded to in JS 267. The "Titans" are here said to have made a drum out of the claw of a monstrous crab but to have abandoned it when fleeing from Sakka. Sakka now uses it himself to make the sound men call thunder. The Asura who keeps a captive maiden imprisoned in a box in his belly (JS 436) has, prior to this episode, been described as a "demon" and shown just the same man-devouring propensities as a yakkha. His falling in love with, rather than eating, his prey exactly parallels (with a reversal of sex roles) the behaviour of the bodhisatta's yakkha-mother in JS 432.

When the Asuras are evicted from heaven by Sakka in JS 31, they land on Mount Sineru, a mountain which is mentioned a few times in the stories, though not usually in connection with the Asuras. In the introduction to JS 512, Gotama himself is reputed to have stood on this mountain. A footnote in the introduction to JS 483 conveys the information that "Mount Meru or Sineru, the Indian Olympus, is surrounded by seven concentric circles of hills, the innermost of which is Yugandhara". In this introduction, the Buddha is said to have been standing with one foot on Sineru and the other on Yugandhara. The mountain is sometimes called Neru as well as Meru (see JS 380). The seven hills ringing Sineru occur in JS 541. Mātali progresses from there to the heaven of the Four Great Kings and from there to the heaven of the Thirty-three.

In the introduction to JS 94, a "heretic" named Kora is said to have been reborn as an Asura.

(ii) *Yakkhas, Rakkhasas, Ogres and Goblins*
The Pāli word, *yakkha*, is variously translated in the Jātaka stories by simple transliteration or by the words "ogre" or "goblin". The yakkha is characterised by bloodthirstiness and a taste for flesh (often human). JS 537 is the story alluded to in chapter four in which a king, having been a yakkha in a former birth, acquires a taste for human flesh – with dreadful consequences. At one stage in the story,[184] the man-eater is assisted by a spell taught him by a yakkha who had been his friend in his former (yakkha) existence. The bodhisatta manages to convert the king and restore him to the path of virtue. In JS 1, "goblins" trick and devour all the men and oxen travelling with the foolish caravan-leader; the wise leader (the bodhisatta) is not deceived, for he sees in the red eyes, aggressive bearing and the absence of a shadow of the would-be deceiver the marks of a goblin (*yakkho*). In JS 398, a yakkha (also called a "goblin") is empowered by Vessavaṇa, the yakkha king,[185] to devour all living beings who take shelter beneath a certain banyan tree. One day, the king takes shelter beneath this tree and is about to be eaten when he persuades the yakkha to eat a deer the king has just caught instead. The king is made to promise that, in exchange for his own life, he will send the yakkha a man bearing rice every day. The king does this so long as there are prisoners in the jails (the yakkha devouring both rice and bearer) but then, in desperation, offers a thousand pieces to anybody who will take rice to the yakkha. The bodhisatta claims the money and gives it to his poverty-stricken mother, then takes the rice (having also taken a number of wise precautions which put him beyond the power of the yakkha). He manages to convert the

yakkha by pointing out that, if he continues to kill the bearers of rice, soon there will be nobody left who dares to bring it. The yakkha is persuaded that it will be in his interest to have a daily rice meal brought to him and to forgo the human part of his diet. The bodhisatta also points out that the yakkha is as he is because of his cruelty in past times but that, if he now practises virtue and abstains from murder, he will reap blessing in the future.

It is a feature of the yakkhas that, in spite of their terrifying forms and gruesome appetites, they seem to be basically well disposed. They are in the grip of their past karma but seem very amenable to the bodhisatta's efforts to convert them. Even when not converted, they often show an innate respect for goodness, as in JS 51, where two "ogres" (*yakkho*), having had a dispute about a corpse settled for them by King Goodness (the bodhisatta), use their power to reinstate the king and oust a usurper. The latter, when he learns what has happened, is very abashed and says to the bodhisatta, "I, though blessed with human nature, knew not your goodness; but knowledge thereof was given to the fierce and cruel ogres, whose food is flesh and blood". In JS 55, there is the lovely story of the bodhisatta, who, though locked in mortal combat with an "ogre" (*yakkho*), and though all his weapons and physical strength are of no avail, yet wins a moral victory. The ogre is so overwhelmed by his victim's courage and fearlessness and by his eventual preaching on karma and its consequences, that he is converted and made "fairy of that forest" instead. JS 513 tells the curious and convoluted story of a prince carried off by an ogress, reared by her, acting like an ogre by devouring human beings until he encounters his nephew (the bodhisatta). When the latter reveals to the "ogre" that he is really a human being, and when this fact has been confirmed by "an ascetic gifted with supernatural vision", the "ogre" abandons his cannibalistic practices and himself becomes an ascetic. In JS 432, the bodhisatta himself is born of a flesh-eating yakkha (who has also been allotted a certain territory by Vessavaṇa), but his father is a brahmin and the son seems to have escaped contamination by any yakkha-qualities. In JS 155, we read of a "goblin" (*yakkho*) who has been authorized by Vessavaṇa to eat any who stray on to his territory unless they sneeze and repeat a life-preserving formula. Again the bodhisatta manages to convert the goblin from his man-eating ways and, by establishing him in the five precepts, makes him "as obedient as an errand-boy". Very similar is the "water-sprite" (*yakkho*) in JS 6 who has been permitted by Vessavaṇa to devour all who entered a certain pool except for those who knew "what is truly god-like". The bodhisatta is able to give a satisfactory answer, thereby gaining the release of two brothers who had fallen into the yakkha's hands and, once again, working the conversion of the yakkha. In JS 347, the yakkhas are said to be "enraged against the Bodhisatta" (the virtuous king who had ended animal sacrifice) "at losing their offerings, and calling together an assembly of their kind in the Himalayas, they sent forth a certain savage Yakkha to slay the Bodhisatta". Their plan is thwarted by the intervention of Sakka. In JS 459, the people in a village of Kāsi beg to be allowed to make their customary sacrifice of animals for an "offering to the Goblins" (*yakkhānam balikammaṃ*). JS 204 mentions that, during a famine in Kāsi, men were unable to make "offering to goblins and snakes" (*yakkhanāgabalikammaṃ*).

The "she-goblins" (*yakkhiniyo*) of JS 196 entice shipwrecked sailors to be their husbands, making them think them human. They then kill and eat them during the night. In JS 96, the "ogres" and "ogresses" (*yakkhiniyo*) "make villages and houses arise by the wayside" in which "their magic sets a costly couch shut in by fair curtains of wondrous dye. Arranged in celestial splendour the ogresses sit within their abodes, seducing wayfarers with honeyed words. 'Weary you seem', they say; 'come hither, and eat and drink before you journey further on your way.' Those that come at their bidding are given seats and fired to lust by the charm of their wanton beauty. But scarce have they sinned, before the ogresses slay and eat them while the warm blood is still flowing". The paccekabuddhas warn the bodhisatta that he can only safely take the short cut which runs through their territory if he subdues his senses and resolutely refuses to look at the ogresses. The "middle mango tree" in JS 281 is in the domain of King Vessavaṇa and is guarded by "thousands of millions of kumbhaṇḍa goblins" (*koṭisa hassa kumbaṇḍarakkhasā*),[186] who kill and eat intruders. In JS 510, a queen has all her babies devoured by a "she-goblin" (*yakkhini*) who had been a jealous co-wife in her previous existence.[187] Only by building an iron house is the queen able eventually to protect a child (the bodhisatta) from the goblin's spite. The she-goblin is killed, we are told, because, being thirsty, she "had been destroyed in trying to fetch some of the water of Vessavaṇa".[188]

The term "yakkha" may, however, be used in a good sense. The prose story of JS 547 tells us that the "gods", out of pity for the outlawed family of King Vessantara, had shortened their journey. The stanza says: "the Yakkhas made the journey short". In this instance, the term "yakkha" is simply a synonym for "god".[189] In JS 497, the "deities of the city" (*nagaradevatā*) are incensed at the way in which a king has reviled his saintly father (the bodhisatta); "the eldest goblin (*jeṭṭhakayakkho*) among them" seizes the king and, sparing the king's life only for his father's sake, twists his head on his shoulders so that it faces backwards. In the introduction to JS 40, a repentant "fairy who was a heretic" (*micchādiṭṭhikā devatā*) who has formerly been trying to dissuade Anātha-piṇḍaka from giving so generously to the Order, is advised by Sakka to use her "goblin power" (*yakkhānubhāvaṃ*) to restore the pious merchant's dwindling fortune. In JS 439, the bodhisatta is addressed as a "goblin" (*yakkho*) and, in JS 458, Sakka describes himself as a "Goblin" (*yakkho*). In JS 513, the moon is said to be addressed as "Yakkha". There is a mysterious reference in JS 546[190] to a man's being taken possession of by a goblin (*yakkho*) who causes him to "bark like a mad dog". The "ogress" (*yakkhinī*) in JS 41 was, we are told, "ranging about in the shape of a goat".

Nature Deities

The bodhisatta himself is born in this category thirty-nine times.[191] The deities in this group differ from the gods considered in section (i) because they are located, not in one of the heavens, but in some aspect of the natural world. They are designated "gods" (*devatā*) – though often rendered in the English translation as "sprites" or "fairies" – and usually with a prefix such as "wood-" (*rukkha-*; JSS 72, 74, 257, 307, 402, 537; or *vanaṃ-*: JS 48), "river-" (*nadī-*: JSS 288, 511), "ocean-" (*samudda-*: JS 146), "air-" (*ākāsaṭṭha-*: JS 147). These beings are usually passive witnesses of the action of the stories, their sole function being to applaud the hero or moralise about the story at the end. A good example of this last function is provided by JS 13, where the bodhisatta is described in the epilogue as "the fairy who preached the Truth showing the sin of passion" (*kāmesu dosaṃ dassetvā dhammaṃ desitadevatā*). The "truth" preached on this occasion is the familiar Jātaka theme: "infamous . . . is the land which owns a woman's sway and rule; and infamous are the men who yield themselves to women's dominion". An interesting footnote to this would be the observation that the same culture which produced this adage also produced one of the world's few women premiers – evidence perhaps of the contra-suggestive influence of written rules! In JS 146, a crow and his wife get drunk and the hen-crow drowns in the sea. Hearing the wails of the stricken mate, other crows gathered and attempted a rescue operation by emptying the sea, a beakful at a time. When "their mouths and jaws were dry and inflamed and their eyes bloodshot" from the salt water, they realised the hopelessness of their task and fell to praising the beauty of the dead bird, comforting the mate with the thought that "it was her excellencies that had provoked the sea to steal her from them. But as they talked this nonsense, the sea-sprite (the bodhisatta) made a bogey appear from the sea and so put them all to flight". According to JS 74, the "tree-fairies" dwelling in "trees and shrubs and bushes and plants" come under the sway of King Vessavana, as do the yakkhas. We further learn that when one Vessavana dies, his replacement is appointed by Sakka and the change-over affords an opportunity for the various *devatā* to re-locate themselves if they so choose. If a tree chosen by a deity is destroyed, that deity becomes a homeless refugee. In JS 412, a tree-spirit fears that the droppings from a bird will implant the seed of a fig or banyan which "will arise and go spreading all over my tree: so my home will be destroyed". JS 147 is exceptional in that here the bodhisatta is a "Spirit of the Air" who does not appear until the epilogue and has the sole function of making the story known. A human being is capable of falling in love with these deities (JS 234), but is unlikely to be able to consummate his love. The nature deities exercise a protective role and, according to JS 257, it is in return for the protection they offer that men make offerings to them. In JS 307, a "tree-spirit" (the bodhisatta) is so pleased with the faithful devotion of a certain brahmin that he appears before him "disguised as an aged brahmin". The sprite wants to "find out why he thus worships (him), and grants him his desire". He learns that the brahmin worships this tree-spirit because he believes the spirit guards some "sacred treasure". The bodhisatta is so delighted by this answer that he not only grants his devotee the treasure but, to save him the trouble of digging it up, miraculously delivers it to his house.[192] JS 442 presents us with a paccekabuddha who, foreseeing that a certain merchant is going to be shipwrecked and need help, appears to the merchant so that the latter can offer him his shoes and thereby earn the

merit which makes it imperative for a deity charged with pro-
tecting virtuous men in peril at sea to rescue him when he actually
is shipwrecked. In JS 402, a warning given to a brahmin by a
tree-spirit (called a yakkha in the second stanza) enables the wise
Senaka (the bodhisatta), "by his knowledge of expedients"
(*upāyakosallañānena* – another indication of Mahāyānist influence!),
to locate a poisonous snake hiding in a sack. In JS 511, a "river-
goddess" provides an ascetic with a constant supply of ripe
mangoes since, being "the slave of his appetite", the ascetic
would otherwise have refused all other food and fasted to death.
Surprisingly, although there is no hint of the "slavery" being
overcome, we are told that the ascetic "was destined to the
Brahma-world". In JS 537,[193] a tree-nymph is embarrassed by the
promise made by a banished man-eating king that he will bathe
the trunk of her tree with the blood of one hundred and one
princes if she restores his wounded leg within seven days. The
wound heals of its own accord, but the king is determined to make
the sacrifice as he is convinced that the nymph has cured him.
The nymph, in desperation, enlists the bodhisatta's help in converting the man-eater and averting the bloody sacrifice.

Nāgas and Garuḍas (Garuḷas):   The snakes (*nāgā*) and huge birds
(*garuḍā*) are mentioned together because they are so often linked
within the mythology itself. The nāgas are rarely presented simply
as snakes but are embellished with many mythical attributes. Thus
they can produce smoke and flames (JSS 81, 133); they have a
king (JSS 253, 256, 472, 506, 524, 543), who dwells in great
splendour; they can cause a lake to boil (JS 133); they can trans-
form themselves into various other forms – a jewel (JS 154), a
great ship (JS 190), a man (JS 253) or Sakka (JS 506); they can
display great magnanimity and generosity (having much wealth
in their possession), especially toward the bodhisatta (JSS 256,
506); if they fight with each other, they turn clear water turbid
(JS 257); they may be fierce and passionate or loving and for-
giving (JS 304). In JS 472, the serpent king saves the bodhisatta
when he is hurled over a precipice and shares his kingdom with
him for a year. In JS 506, a snake (the bodhisatta) becomes an
ascetic and is able to practise *ahiṃsā*, even under stress. In JS 524,
a king who has become an ascetic (the father of the bodhisatta)
instructed the Nāga king and a "numerous company of snakes"
in the Law. The bodhisatta visited his father and saw the snake

king and "by reason of the great magnificence of the Nāga conceived a longing for the Nāga world" which caused him to be
reborn as the next Nāga king. He soon "grew sick of this magnificence" and longed to be a man again (cf JS 506). JS 543 is a long
story which, except for the final section, is set mainly in the Nāga
world. Nāgas assume human forms and one of them marries a
human queen, thus becoming the father of the bodhisatta (who is
consequently of mixed Nāga-human parentage). Again the bodhisatta is dissatisfied with his "frog-eating snake-nature" and longs
to become a god as he has already visited Sakka "with the Nāga
assembly" and been impressed by his splendour – and his nymphs.
In JSS 154, 412, 518, 543, 545, there are references to the traditional enmity between the Garuḍas, whose chief food is the snake,
and their nāga prey. Yet, in a number of these stories, the enmity
is at least temporarily resolved in a bond of trust and friendship.
Even in JS 518, where an ascetic (Devadatta) betrays the Nāga's
secret enabling them to escape capture by the Garuḍas, a snake,
when caught, is set free again and an uneasy truce is established:
"Inspire a trust in all, but put thy trust in none". In JS 545, the
Nāga and Supaṇṇa (equals Garuḍa) kings each claim great virtue
because whilst the former regards the latter as "a destructive
enemy of our race" he yet bears him no malice and whilst the
latter regards the former as his "chief food", he yet restrains his
hunger and does not eat him. In JS 154, a Garuḍa is prevented
from getting its prey by the preaching of a recluse (the bodhisatta)
which causes it to renounce its predatory habits and live in peace
and harmony with the nāgas. JSS 412 and 543 (**IV**) both have
as their theme a roc-bird (JS 412) or a Garuḍa (JS 543) which
seizes a snake coiled round a tree and, in carrying off the snake,
uproots the tree as well. JSS 327 and 360 are the tales alluded to
in chapter five where the Garuḍa king comes in human form to
gamble with the king of Benares, falls in love with the latter's wife
and abducts her – later to complain of her infidelity! JS 203 is,
in effect, a charm against snake bite devised by ascetics, too many
of whom had been bitten whilst "lost in the rapture of
meditation".

There are, then, a number of allusions in the Jātaka stories
to the enmity between the Garuḍas and the Nāgas – even though
this traditional enmity is often overcome and mutual friendship
established. Heinrich Zimmer gives a fascinating account of this
theme in Hindu literature:

The bird is addressed as "He who kills nāgas or serpents" (*nāgāntaka, bhujagāntaka*), "He who devours serpents" (*panna-gāśana, nāgāśana*). His proper name is Garuḍa, from the root *gṛi*, "to swallow". As the relentless annihilator of serpents, he is possessed of a mystic power against the effects of poison; hence is popular in folklore and daily worship. At Puri, in the Indian province of Orissa, persons suffering from snakebite are taken to the main hall of the Great Temple, where they embrace a Garuḍa pillar filled with the magic of the celestial bird.[194]

Garuḍa was the vehicle of the Hindu god, Vishnu, and was described by Krishna as the "arch enemy of all serpents". (*Ibid* p. 86) Clearly, both Hindu and Buddhist mythology is drawing on the same common stock of ancient Indian folklore.

It is interesting to observe, however, that, whilst the Hindu tendency is to regard the serpent as the enemy to be vanquished or banished, the Buddhist tendency is to regard the serpent as a friendly, protective semi-divinity. As Zimmer reminds us, the legend of the great cobra, Muchalinda (who, by spreading his hood over the head of the newly enlightened Gotama, made an umbrella to protect him from an unseasonal storm), forms the basis of much Buddhist art. According to Mahāyānist tradition, it was only the nāgas who were able to receive the full import of the Buddha's teaching about the Void; it was they who eventually imparted this teaching to Nāgārjuna, the "Arjuna of the Nāgas". (*Ibid* pp. 66–8) The Jātakas certainly reflect a pro-nāga bias in their account of the conflict between the Garuḍas and the nāgas. This could perhaps be construed as a Buddhist predilection for keeping its feet (or its belly) on the ground as opposed to the Hindu preference for taking to the air in great flights of speculative fancy.

(iii)   There is space here to do little more than list the various kinds of magical or mythological phenomena which occur in the Jātaka stories and to note at least some of the stories in which they occur.

The talking animal: Much the most common magical phenomenon in the Jātaka stories is that of animals – or insects – which think, feel and speak exactly like human beings. This occurs frequently and is a widespread convention in folklore generally. The talking animal in an Indian context has the added significance that, granted belief in rebirth, all men (including the bodhisatta) will actually have lived in a multiplicity of animal bodies in the past and may well do so again in the future. If, as an animal, one is to gain promotion in a future birth, there has to be the possibility of gaining merit as an animal. One therefore has a vested interest in believing, as an existential possibility, not merely a mythological convention, that an animal is capable of moral choice and virtuous conduct.

Multiplication of bodies and Metamorphoses: We noted in the previous section that both Nāgas and Garuḍas are capable of appearing in forms other than the serpent and the giant bird with which they are, respectively, normally associated. We have also seen that Sakka and other divinities as well as the yakkhā and other "goblins" are capable of assuming different bodies at will. Stories in which this phenomenon occurs include JSS 96, 121, 190, 253, 374, 386, 393, 429, 467, 469, 543, 546, 547. The multiplication of bodies occurs in JS 4. In JS 190, the "other body" assumed is not that of an animal, but of a ship, and, in JS 154, it is a jewel.

Walking, Sitting/flying cross-legged or being suspended in mid-air: This phenomenon is alluded to so often and so matter-of-factly that belief in its possibility has obviously become part and parcel of popular Buddhist faith. Stories in which it occurs include JSS 7, 18, 40, 66, 70, 77, 78 (intro.), 99, 122, 207, 234, 251, 263, 303, 314, 351, 408, 423, 426, 433, 459, 465 (intro.), 467, 479 (intro.), 498, 507, 509, 514, 522, 530, 532, 536 (intro.), 538, 544 (intro.), 545, 547 (intro.). JS 122 is particularly noteworthy in that here, even in the form of an elephant, the bodhisatta, "with the marvellous powers which flow from Merit", can, "Dumbo-like", fly. There are a number of instances (e.g. JSS 251, 263) where an ascetic assailed by sensual passion either loses his power to fly altogether or, having become airborne, has to make a rather unseemly crash landing.

I would be inclined to account for the tradition that ascetics can fly, by locating its basis in the very convincing illusion-experienced-as-fact which may occur in certain stages of trance. This is closely analogous to the very vivid "experience" of "walking on air" (which I myself have frequently had) whilst in a hypnogogic state.

Great longevity: JS 422 relates to the "first age", when a king lived for an "*assaṅkheyya*". According to the footnote, this denotes a period of years numbering 1 followed by 140 ciphers. JS 9 tells of a king named Makhadeva (the bodhisatta), in "Mithilā in the realm of Videha" who "for successive periods of eighty-four thousand years had respectively amused himself as prince, ruled as viceroy and reigned as king". He spent yet another eighty-four thousand years as an ascetic, bringing his total lifespan to a phenomenal 336,000 years. The story ends with the note that he was reborn in the realm of Brahmā and "passing thence, he became a king again in Mithilā, under the name of Nimi". The story is taken up again in JS 541, where again we start with Makhadeva. He is succeeded by 84,000 princes less two, who each reign for 84,000 years before renouncing the world for their final 84,000 year period. He is then reborn as the 83,999th prince, to "round off the family" and is thus given the name Nimi (or Nemi) – "Hoop". My calculator informs me that this would involve a dynasty in ancient Mithilā which lasted for no fewer than seven thousand and fifty six million years (i.e. 7,056,000,000)! A good deal less remarkable is the assertion in JS 458, repeated in JS 539, that "in that age they say that the length of man's life was ten thousand years". In JS 489, King Suruci (again in Mithilā) is said to have been childless for fifty thousand years. In JS 491, the golden peacock (the bodhisatta) has, by reciting his charm, been able to resist the snares of lust for seven thousand years.

Underlying the very common mythology of a golden age in the remote past when man's lifespan was incredibly long (a myth which is particularly in evidence in the Indian and Chinese traditions, but is found almost universally) there may well be the fact that man only became acutely, traumatically aware of his finiteness with the relatively recent emergence of individualism as opposed to a more primitive "corporate personality" or "herd consciousness". In this primitive phase (depicted in the myth as a golden age in the remote past) the continuity of the herd would have overshadowed the fact that individuals were constantly being born into it or dying out of it; only the corporate continuity would have registered and this would have fostered the dimly remembered illusion of agelessness.[195]

Magical Practices: These include the power to interpret dreams (JS 77 plus intro.); the belching of smoke (JS 78); inducing rainfall (JS 75 intro.); the power to raise the dead (JS 150); Sakka's gift of a magical axe, drum and milk bowl (JS 186) and the magical gem and magical mango, which occur in the same story; the capacity to walk on water (JS 190); a spell to "subdue the world" (JS 241); a foal with magical powers (JS 254); the conjuring up of a palace from the bottom of a lake by a prince who had formerly inhabited it (JS 264 intro.); a cock which brings good luck (JS 284); recovery of stolen property by magical means (JSS 288, 336); the magical causing of a storm (JS 360); a voice that carries for twelve leagues (JS 388); the magical turning of a palace into gold (JS 406 intro.); the slippers which rule a kingdom by beating on each other if a decision is wrongly made (JS 461); the magical location of treasure at sea (JS 463); the miraculous, instantly-growing mango tree, and the staircases made of gems by Vissa-kamma, the heavenly architect (JS 483 intro.); the half-body dance of the "divine dancer" (JS 489); the wonder-producing banyan tree (JS 493 intro.); the divinely built hermitages (see previous chapter); the Elder whose supernatural powers, which enable him to travel to the heavens, are hindered by his bad karma (JS 522 intro.); restoration of sight and miraculous causing of dawn (JS 540); the magically-made home, wish-granting jewel, ālambāyana spell, miracle powers of Datta, etc. (JS 543); a miracle horse and miracle jewel (JS 545); the miraculous medicinal herb, the magical play-hall, etc. (JS 545) and rain which falls selectively (JS 547 intro.). There are also many signs and wonders at various points in the actual story of JS 547.

Supernatural powers are also used to conjure up a lotus pond with a lotus that rapidly decays (JS 25 intro.), a begging bowl (JS 40), a staircase forty five leagues in compass (JS 78 intro.), six-coloured rays emanating from the Buddha and reaching as far as heaven (JS 148 intro. cf 320 intro., 512 intro., 514), the requisites of the paccekabuddha (JS 378). Supernatural power can also protect from a yakkha (JS 55), a poisonous snake (JS 81 intro.), from the hazards of journey (JS 532) and from fire (JSS 40, 316). A charm can, at the right conjuncture of the planets, cause it to rain the "Seven Things of Price" (gold, silver, pearl, coral, catseye, ruby, diamond) – though this may be the source of great misfortune because of the covetousness it engenders (JS 48), or it may enable its owner to trace footsteps even after twelve years (JS 432). In JS 453, however, the bodhisatta, when asked to say which are the truly auspicious omens, replies that these are the omens of a pure and virtuous character. In JS 289, on the other hand, the bodhisatta (as king) richly rewards a brahmin astrologer whose readings are more accurate than those of the court astrologers. In the "first age", a king was supposed to have four magical powers – to walk through the air, to command four defending "angels", to have a body smelling of sandalwood and breath smelling of a lotus (JS 422).

Hardly less than magical are the prodigious skills exhibited by the bodhisatta in some of his incarnations – the archer, whose skills are not elaborated in JS 80, but scale the heights of fantasy in JS 181; the chaplain's son who can master the three Vedas and the elephant lore in a single night (JS 163); the marvellous needles – "how he made them is not to be told, for such work prospers through the greatness of Bodhisattas' knowledge" (JS 387); the uncanny wisdom, and skill at untangling problems, even whilst still a boy (JS 546).

(iv) *Aetiology:* Quite frequently one finds that various mythological events recorded in the Jātaka stories are used to account for facts or customs which are still extant. When the bodhisatta, in the form of a monkey, cheats a water monster by drinking from his lake using a bamboo cane as a drinking straw, he hollows out the canes. Now all canes are hollow, because the bodhisatta, while he was fashioning his straws, "calling to mind the Ten Perfections displayed by him", performed a truth-act which hollowed the canes. He then issued the command, "Let all canes growing here become hollow throughout" (JS 20). A note forming part of this same story informs us that this is the fourth "Era-miracle" (i.e. a miracle whose effects last throughout the whole Era). The first is Sakka's daubing of the moon with the mark of the hare (JS 316), the second is the dousing of a fire by another act of truth when the bodhisatta, in the form of a quail, was threatened by a forest fire; that area was said to have been immune to fire for a whole era (JS 35). The third era miracle, concerning a house on which no rain ever falls, is not recorded in the Jātakas.

In the introduction to JS 78, we are told that "to this day a spot called 'The Crock-Cake'" is found at a certain cave. This is because the surplus crock-cakes, which refused to diminish after a miracle-feast were, according to the Buddha's instruction, thrown away there. JS 270 purports to tell why it is that crows and owls are for ever quarrelling; the incident in question took place "in the first cycle of the world". JS 283 claims to explain why, "when people make a king now-a-days, he is placed on a fine chair of fig-wood, and sprinkled out of three shells", whilst JS 309 gives the alleged derivation of "the custom for the lords of the city to wear a wreath of red flowers on their neck". Similarly, we find claims to know the origin of the name "Sirisayana" in JS 382, of the post "judgeship of all the merchant guilds" in JS 445, of the naming of liquor after Sura and Varuna in JS 512, of the fact that deer do not devour crops in JS 482, of the naming of a certain town as "Kammāsadamma" in JS 537, and of the practice adopted by royal advisers of wearing skullcaps in JS 546.[196]

Links with Hindu Mythology: Apart from the links already mentioned, we also find a considerably abbreviated and substantially altered Buddhist version of the Hindu Epic, the Rāmāyana, in JS 461, and a reference to the five great Pāṇḍava princes who, especially Ajjuna (sanskrit: Arjuna), are heroes of the great Hindu epic, the Mahābhārata, in JS 536.[197]

Appendix

JĀTAKA STORY 273: KACCHAPA-JĀTAKA

[In the English translation edited by Cowell, this story (good humoured but somewhat bawdy) was translated into Latin rather than English! It is here offered for the first time in English. The *samodhāna* can be found in English in JS.]

When Brahmadatta was reigning in Benares, the bodhisatta came to birth as a brahmin in the kingdom of Kāsi. When he came of age, he went to Takkasilā to devote himself to study. Soon, his passions subdued, he went to live as a hermit in Himavant. With twigs and leaves he built a forest hermitage on the banks of the Ganges where he fostered the supernormal powers and lived in rapturous meditation. In this birth, the bodhisatta perfected the virtue of equanimity.

When he was sitting on the threshold of his hermitage, a cheeky, unprincipled monkey would come and copulate, having put its penis in his ear. The bodhisatta, quite unhindered, would sit there in perfect indifference.

One day a tortoise came out from the Ganges and, as it basked in the sun, fell asleep with its mouth wide open. The lascivious monkey, when it saw this, promptly copulated in its mouth. The tortoise, however, having woken up, bit on his penis, enclosing it as if in a box. An acute pain arose and, being unable to bear it, the monkey cried out: "To whom can I go for release from this agony?" Thinking, "there is not another ascetic able to set me free from pain; I must go to him for peace", he took up the tortoise in both hands and went to the bodhisatta for peace.

The bodhisatta made fun of the unprincipled monkey in the first verse:

> Which brahmin comes for food, or monk seeks alms,
> With hand outstretched and proffered bowl?

When he heard this, the unprincipled monkey spoke the second verse:

> I am a fool, a mindless idiot,
> Release me, reverend sir, that I may go free.

The bodhisatta, now talking to the tortoise, spoke the third verse:

> The tortoise is of the clan of Kassapa, the monkey
>   of Koṇḍañña;
> Kassapa and Koṇḍañña having been conjugally joined,
>   you can now release him.

The tortoise, being highly amused by the bodhisatta's words, released the monkey's penis. The monkey, having been set free, respectfully took leave of the bodhisatta and ran away, never again visiting that place – or even looking at it. The tortoise went on its way with salutations. The bodhisatta, never lapsing from his contemplation, went at last to the heaven of Brahma.

Notes

1a e.g. R. Gombrich, *Precept and Practice*; M. E. Spiro, *Buddhism and Society*.
1b – King, 1964, pp. 42ff.
2 Indological Book House, Varanasi & Delhi.
3 Malalasekera, 1960, vol I, p. 951.
4 see GS II 6, 110, 193f; III 71, 133, 257; IV 75.
5 see Cunningham, 1879; Malalasekera, 1937, vol I, p. 951; Malalasekera, 1928, pp. 118f; Geiger, (2ed.) 1968, pp. 131f; Rhys Davids T.W., (2ed.) 1903, pp. 189ff.
6 Malalasekera, 1928, p. 119, quoting Giles.
7 see Wickramasinghe, 1964, pp. 90f, 96, 101, 112, 122, 178, 182, 198–200; cf comment by Mrs C. A. F. Rhys Davids in KS IIIx.
8 Spiro, for instance, quotes Professor G. Luce as saying: 'it would scarcely be an exaggeration to say that they (the Jātaka) have formed the basis of half our art and Literature'. Spiro, 1971, p. 19; see also Khaing, M. M., 1962, pp. 151ff.
9 Malalasekera, 1928, pp. 120f.
10 DB II 199ff cf JS 95; MLS II 268ff cf JSS 9 and 541. In the following instances, the Four Nikāyas present 'similes' or allusions which, though themselves not in the form of Jātakas, are closely related to the Jātaka story noted: DB II 364–6; cf JS I; DB II 368 cf JS 91; DB III 21f cf JS 335; DB III 60 and KS V 125f cf JS 168; MLS I 388ff and KS I 179ff cf JS 405. Other Jātaka material is found in the Vinaya – see Rhys Davids, 1903, pp. 195f.
11 see DB I 175–181, II 259ff; MLS II 243–250; KS I 194–6; GS I 95–7, II 262–5. In the last case, there is a reference to the "Velāmaka Sutta" in the Introduction to JS 40 where, in JS vol I, p. 101, a footnote observes that "This Sutta is referred to at p. 234 of the *Sumaṅgala-Vilāsini*, but is otherwise unknown as yet to European scholars". The "Velāmaka Sutta" is, in fact, this passage in GS II 262–5.
12 Almost all the Jātaka stories noted in the two preceding footnotes as occurring in the Four Nikāyas could be regarded as improbable and far-fetched.
13 see, e.g. Woodward, 1935, p.v.: "As to the *Jātaka* verses, which progress in number like the Aṅguttara or *Gradual Sayings*, it is doubtful whether they are genuine utterances, with the exception of the very brief ones, while the stories applied to them, with their commentary, are romances, and in some cases folk-lore, common to most nations."
14 see DB I 131; II 14ff; III 137ff; MLS II 318ff.
15 Jayatilleke, 1975, p. 33 cf Jayatilleke, 1963, pp. 331, 431f, 437ff.
16 see DB I 278ff; III 106f; KS II 84–92, but note that, in MLS II 159, the Buddha, whilst denying that he is all-knowing and all-seeing, does claim to know his previous births and the destinies of others. Note also that French, 1977 has drawn attention to the ambiguity of the canonical evidence and has observed that "perhaps legends came to be written teaching that the *iddhi* (supernormal powers) were of dubious value, because, in fact, they were not being performed" (p. 51). This last possibility seems unlikely in view of the fact that false boasting of supernatural powers is one of the four unforgivable sins in the Vinaya; any monk violating this prohibition automatically expelled himself from the Order.
17 Geiger, (2ed.) 1968, p. 31.
18 Malalasekera, 1928, pp. 122–7; see also Burlinghame, 1921, p. 60.
19 Burlinghame, 1921, p. 1 f.n.1 dates the Jātaka in the *early* fifth century A.D.

On p. 49 he says, "Nothing is more certain than that the Jātaka Book is earlier than the Dhammapada Commentary. The Dhammapada Commentary refers frequently to the Jātaka and contains from forty to fifty stories derived from it, nearly one half of them being verbally identical with Jātaka stories." He goes on to say that, since the Jātaka refers to Buddhaghosa's undisputed commentaries, the latter are earlier than the Jātaka.

20 see Gehman, 1974, pp. 15f, 24, 38ff.

21 Feer, 1875, ET 1963, p. 5.

22 In the Department of Oriental Manuscripts at the British Library, Dr Marrison kindly showed me a delightful nineteenth century Burmese illuminated leaf-book depicting this incident. In the centre of the picture, the becalmed boat was modelled on the Irrawaddy Paddle Steamer. This affords a good example of the way in which the Jātaka tales are kept alive in their host cultures.

23 JS VI p. 127.

24 The translator's footnote simply observes, after the reference to the Punnaka Birth: "No such title occurs in the collection, nor in Westergaard's Catalogue." This simply means that the Pāli editor has misremembered the title of the Jātaka intended – or was using a collection with different titles – a not infrequent occurrence, as we have already had occasion to notice.

25 Feer, 1875: ET 1963, pp. 12ff.

26 JS 101, though it omits the story, does in fact give the verse. Since this occurs immediately after the title – the only occasion on which this happens – a quotation would be redundant in this case.

27 see Bollée, 1970.

28 This story is one of those very well illustrated at the stūpa of Bhārhut – see Cunningham, 1879, Plate xlv, 5.

29 Malalasekera, 1928, p. 121.

30 An interesting indication of the extent to which the introduction has become an integral part of the Jātaka collection in the modern Theravāda world is the fact that, when Htin Aung came to edit the *Burmese Monk's Tales* of the nineteenth century Thingazar Sayadaw – and these function as modern Jātakas except that they do not purport to relate previous lives of the Buddha – he prefaced each tale with an Introduction placing each of the stories in its context in the actual ministry of the Thingazar Sayadaw and showing the relevance of the story in this context.

31. This was when the bodhisatta was incarnate as the ascetic Sumedha, as we are informed in the Nidāna Kathā, the introduction to the Pāli Jātaka collection. See Rhys Davids, 1880, pp. 95ff.

32 see Rhys Davids, 1880, p. lxxii.

33 That is to say, not in a main incarnation in a given story, though JS 538 makes it clear that the bodhisatta had, prior to his present birth, spent eighty thousand years in hell.

34 The *asuras* were a kind of anti-god, though usually classed with gods and humans as belonging to the higher planes of existence. In the Four Nikāyas, although *asuras* are quite often mentioned as being at war with the gods – see KS I 283–6, IV 133f, V 377f; GS IV 290 – the *asuras* are not usually classed as a separate order of existence, as they frequently are at a later stage (see e.g. Gehman, 1974, p. 105).

35 *Yakkhas* are treated in full in chapter eight.

36 The work of Sen, 1974, explores the Jātakas from an historical standpoint, though his findings are often (and necessarily) sketchy and tentative. He gathers material gleaned from the Jātakas relating to Indian kings other than Brahmadatta in his final chapter; see Sen, 1974, pp. 187ff.

37 Geiger, 1968, p. 17.

38   *ibid*, p. 19.
39   *ibid*, p. 11.
40   *ibid*, p. 12.
41   *ibid*, p. 12.
42   *ibid*, p. 18.
43   *ibid*, p. 19.
44   see DB II 28, III 224, 255; MLS III 82; KS III *passim*, V 48f.
45   Jayatilleke, 1963, pp. 371ff. cf Jayatilleke, 1975, p. 75.
46   Jayatilleke, 1975, p. 82 cf pp. 128ff, 152ff.
47   see DB I 254–7, 257ff, III 128ff; MLS II 97ff, 164ff, 230, 237; KS II 150f, III 101, 138, 157, 160, 302, V 354, 370, 378; GS IV 39f, V 127ff.
48   see GS I 175.
49   The passage at M III 19, referred to by Jayatilleke and quoted above, is a case in point; another example occurs at MLS II 70ff, where the heresy that there is no world beyond is vehemently refuted, though no argument is advanced in support of the refutation.
50   Jayatilleke, 1975, p. 35.
51   Shaftel, 1974, p. 47.
52   see GS I 107f, 199, 201, 208ff, 210, 215, 219, 223f, II 84f, 141, 143, IV 69, V 207; MLS I 360ff.
53   This theory exists in two forms, one involving ten factors and the other, probably later, involving twelve. It maintains that from cognition/name-and-form (in the ten link chain) or ignorance (in the twelve link chain) to all manner of suffering, there is a series of linked causes and effects which, in sum, constitute the whole karmic fabric of *saṃsāra*; see Shaftel, 1974, pp. 28f, 13; Jayatilleke, 1963, p. 451.
54   see DB III 102f, 219, 227; GS I 102, 212ff, IV 193.
55   see chapter eight.
56   e.g. MLS III 224ff; KS II 169ff; GS I 124f, III 250.
57   see especially GS V 82.
58   JS IV 282.
59   see chapter one.
60   This word is very variously transliterated. The form here is that adopted by Rhys Davids in vol. I of DB. In vol. 2 and subsequently, an "n" was inserted hence "*arahant*", which is closer to the Pāli root than "*arahat*". The Sanskrit form of the word is transliterated "*arhat*".
61   JS V 141–4.
62   JS V 149f.
63   JS VI 1f.
64   JS VI 3, 13.
65   JS VI 87.
66   see the introduction to JS 472.
67   We are not told how it is possible for Devadatta to spend such long periods in hell so often, and yet appear repeatedly in human form "in the reign of Brahmadatta"!
68   see JS VI 53f.
69   JS VI 57–61.
70   see JS VI 123–5.
71   There are a number of studies of Buddhist ethics based mainly on the Pāli Canon. Two of the most helpful are those by Saddhatissa, 1970 and by Tachibana, 1926.
72   I have followed the English translation of Saddhatissa, 1970, p. 87.
73   see Tachibana, 1926, p. 58.
74   Tachibana, 1926, pp. 249ff.

75 see DB III 43f, 125; KS V 307–11, 338f; GS II 221f.

76 see e.g. MLS III 85ff.

77 GS I 191, II 107, 231, 240, III 26, 129, 150f, 153ff, 199, 303, IV 4 149, 169, 179, 190, 245, 273, 299, 304, IV 170f, 260, VI 59ff, 124f. By splitting the seventh precept into two separate ones and adding one more, forbidding the handling of silver or gold, we arrive at the Ten Precepts binding on the monk.

78 Tachibana finds eloquent testimony to the central importance attached to the harmful states associated with *taṇhā* in the list of words he discovered in the Pāli scriptures to describe this cluster of states. He lists no fewer than seventy-two synonyms. Tachibana, 1926, pp. 73–5.

79 see DB III 210f, 253; MLS II 168; KS & GS – passim.

80 DB III 97, 101, 235, 258f; MLS III 129, 327; KS III 81, IV 259ff, V 51ff, 277, 291ff; GS I 11, 48, II 16, 242, III 278, IV 14, 82f, 101, V 117, 148.

81 DB III 238f, 261; GS IV 216.

82 DB III 227, 255; MLS II 282f, 310; GS III 53, 117f, V 10ff.

83 DB III 228, 256, 259; MLS II 154; KS V 169ff, 194f, 195–7, 197ff, 202ff; GS I 35, II 154ff, III 7, 8, 200, IV 82f, V 117.

84 DB III 236; GS IV 2f, 14, 22, 99, 233ff.

85 see p. 53 above.

86 GS I 107f, 199, 201, 208ff, 210, 215, 219, 223f; II 243, III 84f, 141, 143, IV 69, V 207; MLS I 36off.

87 DB III 207f; GS I 88ff, 95, 97, 99, 105, 121f, 135, 139, 249, II 139, 163f, 234, 238, 242, III 2, 99, 102, 115, 195, 208, 250, 254, 274f, 311, IV 24ff, 48, 72, 119f, 126, 131, 241, V 176ff, 187.

88 see chapter seven.

89 see DB III 173ff.

90 e.g. DB III 227, 255; MLS II 282f, 310; GS III 53, 117f, 182, V 10ff.

91 JS 423, on the other hand, tells of a handsome young brahmin who lives in the forest by hunting and eating deer and as a result grows old and ugly and wretched. This is a reminder that even the Jātakas are unwilling to give outright approval to the eating of meat.

92 see JS II p. 254. The five precepts are enumerated immediately after this incident; see p. 255.

93 see Speyer, 1895, pp. 291–314.

94 KS I 113, cf V 2f, 29ff, 84f; GS I 10–12, V 217.

95 Rhys Davids C. A. F., 1931, pp. 339f.

96 GS II 163ff, cf KS II 175, IV 28of.

97 DB III 107f.

98 MLS III 78ff.

99 DB III 225, 247, 255, MLS II 17, 106f, 138–40, III 294; KS V 48f, 52, 70f, 78f, 124, 102ff; GS I 2ff, II 224 – etc.

100 DB III 210f, MLS II 168, KS III 26, IV 120, V 5; GS I 176f, II 18f, III 339, IV 23, V 23 etc.

101 DB I 232, III 209, KS IV 171ff, GS II 225, III 80, IV 123 etc.

102 Horner, 1938, I p. 48.

103 KS V 249, GS III 228, V 75.

104 GS IV 257f, cf GS V 75f; MLS II 179.

105 Spiro, 1971, p. 330, observes that many monks in Burma seem to spend an inordinate amount of their time asleep. They would perhaps cite this passage in their defence!

106 The *Gandhabbā* were semi-divine beings inhabiting the lowliest of the heavens. It was considered to be a disgrace for a monk to be born amongst them. See Malalasekera, 1931, vol. I, p. 746.

107a GS IV 184f.

107b I am indebted to Miss I. B. Horner for drawing my attention to two passages which modify my text at this point. In GS II 69f and GS III 211–14, Nakula's parents are held up as models of lay discipleship. Prominent among their virtues is the fact that they "use loving words one to the other". Though married in childhood, they have been perfectly faithful to each other and they desire "to behold each other not only in this very life but also in the life to come".

108 see DB III 59, 74.

109 Along with this group should be noted JS 408 where four separate stories are told to admonish five hundred brethren who had "had lustful thoughts at midnight". The fourth story tells of a king who observes two bulls fighting to mate with the same cow. One of the bulls is killed in the fight and the king reflects, "this bull through lust has reached death: other beings are also disturbed by lust".

110 The *Garuḍa* is a huge mythical bird which preys on *nāgas* (serpents); more will be said about them in chapter eight. It is only in these two Jātaka stories and in JS 543 that we read of a *Garuḍa* appearing in human form.

111 Bollée, 1970, p. 117.

112 see JS IV, p. 237.

113 JS IV 296.

114 This is almost certainly an allusion to JS 436 where, as we noticed earlier in this chapter, an Asura tries unsuccessfully to retain sole rights to the woman he has captured by keeping her in a box in his belly.

115 see the following chapter.

116 In fairness it should be pointed out that this is in sharp contrast to JSS 282, 303, 351, 355, where courtiers guilty of similar conduct in the king's harem are forced to flee to neighbouring countries where they foment trouble for their former sovereign.

117 see JS II, p. 259.

118 see JSS 9, 541. The same theme occurs in MLS II 267, so there is canonical precedent for it.

119 The prince in this case is a former incarnation of Ajātasattu, the prince who in Gotama's lifetime and (according to Buddhist tradition) at the instigation of Devadatta, murdered his father King Bimbisāra.

120 Had Darimukha been identified as Ānanda, one feels that JS 378 would have ended in the same way.

121 It ought to be noted here that there is one story, JS 303, where the bodhisatta as king of Benares is actually bound and held upside down by Ānanda as the rebel prince Dabbasena. The story implies that Dabbasena has been misled by his wicked councillor (Devadatta, according to JS 51, to which JS 303 claims to be the sequel); he later craves and begs forgiveness from the bodhisatta.

122 see JS V 194ff.

123 Again, we are not told how it is possible for Ānanda (like the bodhisatta) to spend such huge periods in prayer, spend repeated, incalculably long periods in the world of Brahma between incarnations, and yet keep turning up so often in various life forms on this planet within a relatively short space of time.

124 see Ling, 1973, pp. 89f.

125 These are the two centres about which we hear most, since it was in these two cities that Gotama apparently did most of his teaching; Ling, 1973, pp. 99ff.

126 see GS II 84f, where it is said that the goodness or evil of the king filters right down through the state; it even affects the gods, and through them, the weather; cf GS III 22f, 178, 281; IV 91, 225.

127 Ling, 1973, pp. 154ff.

128 see GS IV 68.
129 It is the marked tendency of Ling, 1973, to underplay Gotama's renunciation of the throne and all that this renunciation implies.
130 It is interesting to note that no infringement of the fifth precept is included in this list – a further indication of its subordinate status.
131 see DB III 65–76.
132 see supra pp. 55f.
133 MLS II 310ff, 340ff, 366ff, 379ff.
134 see chapter eight.
135 e.g. JSS 396, 482, 483, 520, 521, 530.
136 see p. 16f.
137 JS 345 tells how the king's minister (the bodhisatta) is able to cure a king of his laziness.
138 see note 126.
139 In JS 540, Vissakamma is commanded to make a similar provision for a hunter and his wife who have decided to become ascetics. Sakka describes them as "great beings" because although born into a hunter's family, the husband has never harmed a living being, and though forced into marriage by their respective parents, husband and wife "lived apart like the archangel Brahman, without descending into the ocean of carnal passion". They thus seemed to have merited royal treatment.
140 see JSS IV, 251; VI, 251.
141 I recall a number of Hindu poems studied when I was learning Tamil, particularly those by Avaiyar, which rhapsodised on the theme that the truly great-hearted man, however hard-pressed himself, would never draw back from giving, just as the moon, in spite of its own blemishes, never ceases to bestow light on others, etc.
142 see p. 26.
143 Again and again in the Jātaka stories we read of hermits venturing into the civilised world, *loṇambilasevanatthāya* translated as "for salt and vinegar" or "for salt and seasoning".
144 JS V 252f.
145 see pp. 59f.
146 see p. 89.
147 see pp. 25, 46f.
148 see chapter eight.
149 JS VI 51.
150 JS VI 121.
151 JS V 275.
152 JS VI 78f.
153 JS VI 109ff.
154 cf DB III 249, 265; MLS II 117ff, 222ff; KS V 18; GS II 233, IV 149.
155 These three marks are *always* given in this order in the Nikāyas, since this is the order which expresses the logic of the Buddhist *paññā*. Many writers on Buddhism have failed to see this and have misguidedly tampered with the canonical order. See Jones, 1976, pp. 190ff.
156 Watson, 1963, chapter two.
157a or some "Hindus", though the term "Hindu" has to be used even more loosely of this period than it does of later Indian religion, since the ideas which later became characteristic of "normative Hinduism" were only now evolving.
157b The nearest thing to a Pāli equivalent is the concept of the *gandhabba*, the ghost-like presence which along with parental coitus and the mother's period, constitutes one of the three conditions which must obtain, it is held, before a being can be conceived. Kalupahana, 1975, pp. 116ff argues on the basis of

such passages as M I 265–66 and D II 63 that the *gandhabba* is identified with *viññāṇa*, but in an "eschatological" rather than a "psychological" sense (in which latter sense it occurs as one of the five *khandhas*). He goes on to say that this "eschatological" consciousness "stands for the connecting link between two lives, a form of consciousness that later came to be designated "rebirth consciousness' (*paṭisandhi viññāṇa*)". I can see no way, however, of reconciling the belief in a surviving *gandhabba* with the much more rigorous doctrine of the *khandhas*. The claim that this *gandhabba* can leap, independently of any physical basis or support, from a dead body to a spatially distant womb is a metaphysical not an empirical claim. Even if the alleged power to recall previous births be allowed to count as empirical evidence – and as we have seen, there are grave objections to such a concession – there is still a big gap between the memory of one's previous lives and the claim that it is the *gandhabba* which constitutes the link between them.

158 see MLS I 176ff.

159 KS IV 113–15, V 32f, 38, 42f, 63, 116, 118, 266.

160 see KS II 95ff, V 384ff, 396ff.

161 It is interesting that, while Jayatilleke, 1963, pp. 475f, does adopt a transcendentalist view of *nibbāna*, his former pupil Kalupahana, 1976, pp. 87f, rebukes him for this and reasserts the more commonly (in Theravāda circles) held cessationist view.

162 Except in the puzzling and ill-defined sense of a "pseudo-self" which *does*, in some unexplained way, survive death. As we have seen, the Jātakas consistently evade the problems to which this doctrine gives rise by simply ignoring the doctrine of *anattā*.

163 see pp. 66–8.

164 see JSS 378, 408, 421, 491.

165 J I 236.

166 I consulted Miss I. B. Horner on this point and she, in turn, conferred with Dr W. Rāhula. They both agree that the Fausbøll reading, *anantā*, must be a misprint for *anattā*; Miss Horner assures me that this latter is the reading in the Thai version of the story.

167 I. B. Horner has introduced and translated, together with the Pāli original, ten Jātakas each illustrating one of the ten *Pāramitā* (Perfections). These, with the stories Miss Horner has chosen to illustrate them, are (1) Giving – 316, (2) Virtue – 86, 362, 330, (3) Renunciation – 9, (4) Wisdom – 463, (5) Energy – 2, (6) Forbearance – 313, (7) Truth – 73, (8) Resolute Determination – 538, (9) Friendliness – 385, and (10) Even-mindedness – 94. See Horner, 1974. See also JS 490, where a paccekabuddha informs the Bodhisatta that he is destined to be a Buddha named Siddhattha when he has "fulfilled the Perfect Virtues".

168 JS V 130.

169 Kloppenborg, 1974, p. 3.

170 *ibid* p. 4.

171 *ibid* pp. 5f.

172 *ibid* p. 6.

173 *ibid* p. 7.

174 Gombrich, 1971.

175 Spiro, 1971.

176 Tambiah, 1970.

177 Jayatilleke, 1963, p. 423.

178 *ibid* pp. 466ff.

179 Another study of Māra is found in Ling, 1962 and a comparison between the Buddhist Māra and the Christian Satan in Boyd, 1975.

180   see also JSS 78, 347, 513, 545.

181   A note in JS 440 informs us that "This throne, they say, grows hot when Sakka's life draws towards its end, or when his merit is exhausted and worked out, or when some mighty Being prays, or through the efficacy of virtue in priests or brahmins full of potency".

182   JS VI 165f.

183   JS 258 also makes it clear that the Heaven of the Four Great Kings is inferior to that of the Thirty-Three.

184   JS V 257f.

185   In JS 545, Puṇṇaka, described as "the yakkha general", is "nephew of the great king Vessavaṇa", and is hastening "to a gathering of yakkhas". He captures the bodhisatta with a view to cutting out his heart and taking it to his Nāga bride-to-be, but is eventually converted by the bodhisatta's teachings and does him no injury.

186   Note here the word "goblins" translates *rakkhasā* rather than the more familiar *yakkhā*. They are still under the rule of King Vessavaṇa however. The word *rakkhaso* also occurs in JSS 20, 58 and 519. In JS 519, the word *dānavo* is also used for a goblin.

187   cf JS VI 163 (story 546) and JS 513.

188   A similar fate befalls the ogress in JS 513.

189   Dhammapala, 1975, pp. 190ff, has an interesting note on the meaning of the word *yakkha*. He points out that in JS 442, the term indicates "one who has mysterious power" and is "adorable" and not "a fearful demonic character". He notes that (as for instance, in M I 386) the term is occasionally used in the Nikāyas as an epithet for the Buddha himself and is also applied to various deities (e.g. D II 204). This use of the word derives from the old meaning of the root *yaks*: "to move or to appear quickly" combined with the root *yaj*: "to sacrifice". In Pāli the female form *yakkhi* or *yakkhiṇī* usually denotes a more fearful and evil-natured being than the masculine form *yakkha*.

190   JS VI 194.

191   see table on p. 18.

192   see also JS 288.

193   JS V 527f.

194   Zimmer, 1946, p. 75.

195   see Zaehner, 1963, pp. 44–67.

196   JS VI 187.

197   JS V 226.

Bibliography

Only books or articles referred to in the text are listed here. Textual references simply give author's name and date of publication. Full details are given below. The major primary sources have been listed separately.

Bollée W. B. (ed. and tr.), *Kuṇāla Jātaka* (*Sacred Books of the Buddhists*, vol 26), London, 1970.

Boyd J. W., *Satan and Māra: Christian & Buddhist Symbols of Evil*, Leiden, 1975.

Burlinghame E. W. (tr. and ed.), *Buddhist Legends* (Dhammapada Commentary) 3 vols (Harvard Oriental Series, vols 28–30), Harvard, 1921.

Cunningham Sir A., *The Stupa of Bharhut:* a Buddhist monument ornamented with numerous sculptures illustrative of Buddhist legend and history in the third century B.C., London, 1879.

Dhammapala Rev Y., First draft of thesis to be submitted for degree of Ph.D. (Sri Lanka) entitled: A Study of Verse Narrative in the Pāli Jātaka with especial reference to sections x–xi, Unpublished, 1975.

Feer M. L., A Study of the Jātakas (tr. of, "Études Bouddhiques; Les Jātakas" in *Journal Asiatique*, May–Sep 1875), Calcutta, 1963.

French H. W., article, "The Concept of Iddhi in Early Buddhist Thought" in *Pali Buddhist Review*, vol 2, no. 1, pp. 44–54, Ilford, 1977.

Gehman H. S., Stories of the Departed (ET of *Petavatthu*, with its commentary) (*Minor Anthologies of the Pāli Canon*, part IV), London, 1974.

Geiger W., *Pāli Literature and Language* (tr. 1937), 2 ed., Delhi, 1968.

Gombrich R. F., *Precept and Practice*. Traditional Buddhism in the rural highlands of Ceylon, London, 1971.

Horner I. B. (tr.), *Ten Jātaka Stories* (re-issue), Bangkok, 1974.

Horner I. B. (tr.), *The Book of the Discipline* (ET of *Vinaya Pitaka*), vol 1, London, 1938.

Htin Aung M., *Burmese Monk's Tales*, New York, 1966.

Humphries C., *The Wisdom of Buddhism*, London, 1960.

Jayatilleke K. N., *The Early Buddhist Theory of Knowledge*, London, 1963.

Jayatilleke K. N., *The Message of the Buddha*, London, 1975.

Jones J, G., article, "The Four Truths and the Three Marks" in *RELIGION*, vol 6/2, pp. 190–195, London, 1976.

Kalupahana D. J., *Buddhist Philosophy: a historical analysis*, Honolulu, 1976.

Kalupahana D. J., *Causality: the Central Philosophy of Buddhism*, Honolulu, 1975.

Khaing M. M., *Burmese Family*, Indiana (USA), 1962.

King W. L., *A Thousand Lives Away: Buddhism in Contemporary Burma*, Oxford, 1964.

Kloppenborg R., *The Paccekabuddha: a Buddhist Ascetic:* a study of the concept of the paccekabuddha in Pāli canonical and commentarial literature, Leiden, 1974.

Ling T., *The Buddha: Buddhist civilization in India and Ceylon*, London, 1973.

Ling T., *Buddhism and the Mythology of Evil: a study in Theravāda Buddhism*, London, 1962.

Malalasekera G. P., *Dictionary of Pāli Proper Names*, vol 1, London, 1937; vol 2, London, 1960.

Malalasekera G. P., *The Pāli Literature of Ceylon*, Colombo, 1928.

Masson J., *La religion populaire dans le Canon Bouddhique Pāli*, Louvain, 1942.

Matics M. L. (tr.), *Entering the Path of Enlightenment* (ET of Santi-Deva's *Bodhicaryāvatāra*), London, 1971.

Rhys Davids C. A. F., *Sakya, or Buddhist Origins*, London, 1931.

Rhys Davids T. W., *Buddhist Birth-Stories:* the commentarial introduction entitled *Nidāna-Kathā*, the story of the Lineage. Tr. and introductory essay, 1880 (re-issue), Varanasi, 1973.

Rhys Davids T. W., *Buddhist India*, 2 ed., London, 1903.

Saddhatissa H., *Buddhist Ethics: essence of Buddhism*, London, 1970.

Sen B. C., *Studies in the Buddhist Jātakas*, 2 ed., Calcutta, 1974.

Shaftel O., *An Understanding of the Buddha*, New York, 1974.

Speyer J. S. (tr. and ed.), *Jātakamālā:* garland of birth stories of Aryaśūra, London, 1895 (re-issue), Delhi, 1971.

Spiro M. E., *Buddhism and Society: a great tradition and its Burmese vicissitudes*, London, 1971.

Tachibana S., *The Ethics of Buddhism*, London/New York, 1926.

Tambiah S., *Buddhism and the Spirit Cults in North-East Thailand*, Cambridge, 1970.

Watson B. (tr.), *The Complete Works of Chuang Tzu*, London/New York, 1968.

Wickramasinghe M., *Buddhism and Culture*, Dehiwala, 1964.

Woodward F. L. (tr.), *Verses of Uplift* (ET of *Udana*); translator's preface, London, 1935.

Zaehner R. C., *The Convergent Spirit*, London, 1963.

Zimmer H., *Myths and Symbols in Indian Art and Civilization* (ed. J. Campbell), New York, 1946.

General Index

Eight bases of slackness 54
Eightfold Path 52f., 55, 73f., 146f.,
149
Energy (*viriya*) 54f.
Enlightenment 75
Era-miracles 192

Fa Hsien 3f.
Family 51, 74ff., 96f., 99, 102, 160
Fausbøll V. 11, 202
Feer M. L. 8, 11f., 204
Fetter (*āsava*) 75, 99
Five Hindrances 54
Five Precepts (*pañca sīla*) 49ff., 57ff., 84,
98, 109, 113, 117f., 120f., 125, 127f.,
136f., 182
Four Nikāyas 3f, 22, 24, 27ff., 33ff.,
49ff., 72ff., 116, 117ff., 146ff., 157,
166ff., 171ff.
Four Noble Truths 73, 122, 147ff.,
158ff., 162, 165
Frauwallner E. 168
French H. W. 196, 204
Freud S. 114
Friendship 72ff., 105ff.

Gambling 93f., 134
Gandhabba 77, 174, 199
Gandhāra, King of 108f.
Garuḍa 83, 91, 140, 174, 186ff., 200
Gehman H. S. 197, 204
Geiger W. 6, 27ff., 196, 204
Gluttony 53
Goblin 102, 128, 143, 181ff.
Goddess 44f., 104, 142, 177f.
Gods (*devas*) 14, 77f., 95f., 173f., 177ff.,
200, 203
Gombrich R. F. 171, 196, 204
Goodness, King 182
Gotama, *see* Buddha
Gopikā 77
Gradual Sayings 196
Guṇa 155
Guttila 40, 177f.

Half-penny, King 159f.
Hate/anger (*dosa*) 54f., 120
Heaven 22, 37ff., 40ff., 91, 124, 154ff.,
173, 178ff., 203
Hell (purgatory) 9f., 22, 25, 37f., 42ff.,
67ff., 86, 126, 129, 139f., 154f., 174,
197

Heresy 153ff., 174, 179, 184
Hinduism 22f., 33, 37, 44f., 49ff., 56f.,
92f., 96, 103f., 122f., 129, 133f., 144f.,
149ff., 153ff., 167f., 173ff., 187f., 193,
201
Homosexual love 78ff., 107f., 110f.,
112ff., 124
Horner I. B. 79, 199, 200, 202, 204
Htin Aung M. 197, 204
Humphries C. 72, 204
Hypnogogic state 189

Iddhi, see Supernormal powers
Ignorance 75
Illusion (*moha*) 54f.
Impermanence (*anicca*) 106f., 111, 119f.,
148ff., 162ff.
Incest 76, 121
Indapatta, King of 127
Intoxicants 50f., 59f., 117, 119, 136ff.,
180, 185, 201
Intuitive wisdom (*paññā*) 35f., 53, 124,
146ff., 169

Jains 56, 155
Jātaka Stories, *see* Index to the Jātaka
Stories; Form of 7ff.; Groups of 21;
Identification in (*samodhāna*) 24ff., 39;
Introduction to (*nidāna kathā*) 197; In-
troductory story of (*paccuppannavatthu*)
13ff.; Origin of 3ff.; Quotation in 12f.;
Story proper (of the past – *atītavatthu*)
15ff., 23; Title of 12; Verses of
(*gāthas*) 3, 7, 23f., 167
Jātakaṭṭhavaṇṇā 6
Jātakamālā 70f.
Jayatilleke K. N. 5, 33ff., 172f., 198,
202, 204
Jealousy 53f.
Jhāna (trance) 75, 172f., 189
Jones J. G. 201, 204
Jotipāla 160
Justice 68, 70

Kalābu, King 129
Kālinga 127f.
Kalupahana D. J. 201f., 204
Kammāsadamma 193
Kapilavatthu 143
Kappa 114f., 124
Karma 7, 10, 21f., 25f., 33ff., 39ff., 51,
70, 118, 123, 134, 136, 141ff., 149ff.,
172, 177, 182

Index to the Jātaka Stories

(*N.B.* Numbers in bold type refer to the number of the Jātaka Story)